CALLED FROM THE FIELDS

Called From The Fields

The Life of a Missionary in Papua New Guinea

Fr. Michael Donovan, SVD

Copyright © 2021 Michael Donovan

ISBN: 9781731194510

CONTENTS

Introduction — *1*

Part I: Timbunke, 1981-1994 — *7*

Part II: Ambunti, 1995-2005 — *135*

Part III: Port Moresby, 2005-2010 — *207*

Images — *255*

Part IV: Goroka, 2011-2018 , Port Moresby, 2011-2021 — *269*

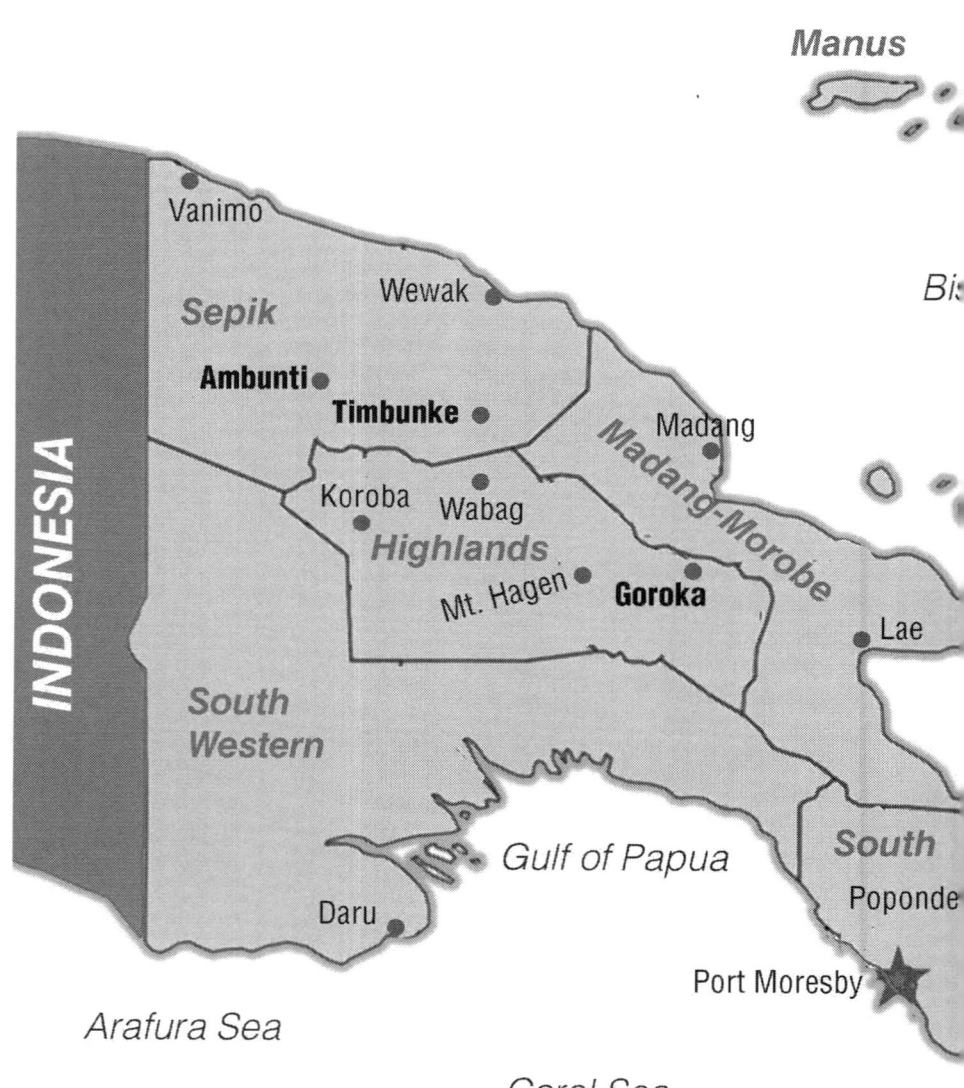

PAPUA NEW GUINEA

Taskul

Pacific Ocean

...ck Sea

New Ireland

Kimbe

New Britain

Buka

Bougainville

Arawa

Solomon Sea

Tufi

Alotau

200 km

INTRODUCTION

"You must be crazy." "God help you." "You will have it tough." These are just some of the opinions expressed to me when my friends heard I was going to study for the priesthood. Others wondered if I knew what I was letting myself in for—"But sure there's no harm in trying it for three months and getting it out of your system."

At this stage I had left school eight years without completing my formal education and I was approaching 24 and didn't look like a candidate for the priesthood. I was a farmer, as they say, from my mother's womb. I loved farming and when I left school after breaking my ankle playing football, I thought I would be a farmer for the rest of my life. At that stage I had no notion of becoming a priest. I was just a routine Catholic who went to Mass on Sundays like everybody else. However, the Rosary was said some nights in our home and there was a holy picture in every room, so religion and faith in God were always present, or at least not too far away.

The turning point came in my life on July 27, 1967, when I had a wonderful religious experience and life was never the same again. How to explain it in human terms is beyond me. To this day I am still trying to understand what took place. It was evening time and I was walking home through the fields when something happened to me like a fright, and I was pushed backwards to the ground. I tried with all my strength to straighten up, but I was unable to. There was nothing to be seen and when I stood up and looked back there was the image of Christ carrying his cross. He looked at me with a face of love, compassion, pain and…sorry, I just cannot describe his face in any other terms. While he looked at me his two fingers moved, indicating I should follow him. Then he disappeared like you would have turned off a light. At that moment I was filled with joy and I felt so happy that I cried and cried, and I said, "I will follow you and I don't care how hard it will be or how long it will take, and I will go anywhere in the world that you need me." It was like a moment in heaven but still being alive to tell the story. That level of emotion lasted about three days, and then I began trying to figure out what had happened. I kept asking myself, "How can I become a priest?" I had left school at this stage for four years, and I was looking forward to the day I would finish school. If I were to follow this call I would have to start all over again. But as scripture says, I chose you, you didn't choose me.

With this in mind, I told my mother I wanted to become a priest. She had no hesitation in telling me to forget it and to put it out of my mind. That was it, it was all over—or so I thought. In the meantime, life kept moving on but I could not forget the experience and the memory of that face kept looking at me saying, "Just trust in me, and I will do it." It was thus with complete faith and trust in the Lord that I had the courage to write to the Divine Word Missionaries in Donamon, Co. Roscommon who were starting a new programme in Ireland for late vocations in 1971. This time I told nobody I had written the letter and to my surprise I got a reply within three days saying that Vocation Director would call to interview me on the following day. I asked myself what I should do: dress up for the interview and wait for his arrival or let him find me as I am out in the fields? I opted for the latter. It was late in the afternoon when word came out to the fields that a strange priest had called to the house. My father nearly died when he heard it, saying nothing good could bring a strange priest to the house. I told him there and then that he had come to see me. I dropped everything and went to meet this strange priest, who turned out to be Fr Hugo McClure SVD.

Fr. McClure went straight to the point. "Come and see and you will soon find out whether the priesthood is for you or not." When I arrived in Donamon Castle there were eighteen young men all like myself, all starting off to complete their formal education and with the same fears, concerns, and expectations. The first year passed by and a few students moved off quietly throughout the year and during the summer break. It was during the summer holidays that two lay workers in the seminary, Seamus O'Connell and Maurice Canty, called to see me in West Cork. Both had worked many years with clerical students and had helped many young men through the seminary as well as helping others who had left to find a job. Both Seamus and Maurice have gone to their final reward now. In their young days both had a great desire to be ordained but they could never make the final commitment and felt they were making a greater contribution to the Church by helping young men through their formation for the priesthood.

During their visit to West Cork they invited me out for a meal and it was during this meal that Seamus started asking me some serious questions. He asked me how I felt about my first year. I told him it had passed by and I had survived. Then Seamus continued, "You know we are worried about you. We have observed you for one year now and we think it is not God's will for you to be a priest. If God wanted you to be a priest, you would have finished school, but not to worry we can get a job for you. A sister in Galway is looking for an ambulance driver and you are the right man for the job."

It all sounded so rational and it would have been so easy to give up. Instead I looked at both of them and said, "I am going back in September." Then came the vital question, "Why do you want it so much and what is the driving force behind your motivations to be a priest?" In this situation I was challenged to share my religious experience there and then and told them what had happened to me on July 27, 1967. That was followed by a long pause, as if both men had been taken by surprise. Then Seamus asked me if I had shared this with anyone before. I told them they were the first. After a long discussion on the matter, they advised me to repeat the first year and that would give me a good head start. That I did and I never looked back. After two years some friends asked me, "Do you think you can make it?" My reply was simply, "So far so good." Four years passed, and the same people said, "Do you know if you will make it now?" Six years passed, and the question changed to "How many years have you left?"

After three years in the seminary Fr John McCarthy, then a student, and I applied to get a summer job in London working as auxiliary nurses. We got the job and it was a great experience. When I returned home after three months my father gave me a great welcome as if I had been away for ten years. It turned out a few days later through casual conversation that he thought I might not return at all and that I had given up studying for the priesthood. The following years I worked in the Sacred Heart Hospital in Castlebar, the Simon Community in London, on a building site near

Heathrow airport, and in the Cumberland Hotel in London. The following two years a large number of us students worked in the Daimler-Benz car factory in Germany. All these summer jobs gave us great exposure to the real world. It was a great experience to work with all kinds of people from the down-and-outs in London to the millionaires in the Cumberland Hotel.

Back in the seminary it wasn't all study and prayer either, as there was a lighter side to it too. We played soccer and hurling and we played with local teams, Athleague and Ballintuber. In Maynooth, where I spent three years studying theology, it was the same. I played with the intermediate hurling team and was elected captain one year. That same year I was a sub on the senior team. There were also athletics, cross-country running and road racing. There was never a dull moment, and the nine years in the seminary went by quickly. Then it was ordination and another chapter in my life came to an end and another just as challenging was about to begin in Papua New Guinea.

After one year's introduction in Papua New Guinea to the language, culture, and pastoral work I was appointed to Timbunke, a large mission station in the middle of the Sepik region, where I stayed for thirteen years. My next appointment was to Ambunti in the upper Sepik for a further ten years. The Sepik region is a large flat plane, which gets flooded during the wet season. The people live in villages which are long distances from each other. There are no roads, except to Timbunke station, and therefore water transport, light aircraft and walking are the only ways to reach these villages. Pastoral patrols must be well planned and these bush trips could take two or three weeks. Usually, "Safe trip" and "When will you be back?" were the departing words from those on the shore. When I arrive in a village it is the church leader who is the contact man. He is the one who provides accommodation and arranges time for Mass, Confession, religious instruction and a meeting with the village leaders.

Timbunke parish also has a large cattle farm to teach young men in cattle management. After two years the trainees are given four or five calves to take home with them and start their own cattle farms. Having spent some time on the land, I was able to make a contribution to this training centre. It's easy to look back now to see what God had in mind when I left school at an early age.

INTRODUCTION

Ambunti was my second parish on the Sepik River. This was one of the most remote and least developed provinces in the diocese. A Sepik missionary may have many homes and yet has no home he can call his own because he is always on the move from one community to another. It is the same process week after week, taking down the mosquito net and rolling up the mattress and moving on to the next village.

During my time on the Sepik I had seminarians and newly ordained priests to introduce to the culture and pastoral work. After a few months these extra hands were a great help preparing people for the sacraments and also encouraging the youth to get involved in playing sport.

In 2005 I moved on from the Sepik. Saying goodbye was not easy. It was a privilege and a honour for me to be a missionary on the Sepik River for twenty-two years. I must thank God, the SVD and the SSpS community and the local people for making it a worthwhile experience. I must also thank my people back home for their prayers and financial support. After all those years, their generosity and interest in the missions never seem to wane.

In that same year 2005 my superiors asked me to join the formation staff in the major seminary at Bormana Port Moresby and take up the full-time role as spiritual director. This was another new chapter in my life. Heading back to the seminary after twenty-five years was not what I had in mind, but I took up the challenge and it turned out to be a very fulfilling ministry. I thought my role would be confined to the seminarians only but as the years went by I had over thirty junior sisters in formation. There was also prison visitation, helping out in Kuriva, an SVD parish, and airport ministry when necessary. During that first year I was appointed Spiritual Animator. That meant I was the one to co-ordinate all the other spiritual directors and call a meeting with them every few months.

The next appointment in 2010 was to the House of Prayer in Goroka. This is my eighth year in this ministry as a spiritual companion to the future priests and sisters of Papua New Guinea and also as a spiritual director to priests and sisters in religious vows for years. I have heard some beautiful vocation stories over the course of these years. I must confess these have been the best-kept secrets in religious life. Pope Francis encourages us to share our faith with others, and it is indeed uplifting to hear why young people want to commit their lives to following Christ, even when you are told you are wasting your life, or crazy. The nine years in the seminary were quite a challenge for me, but I knew down deep in my heart, the Lord would do it for me.

The letters in this book were written by me from the missions in Papua New Guinea (PNG) over the past forty years. I am grateful to the following people who assisted me with collecting and typing them. They are: Fr. John McCarthy, Fr. James Perry, Fr. Garrett Roche, Kitty O'Donovan and her daughters Anna and Verona, Nan Murphy and her daughters Maura and Una, Cecilia O'Donovan and her daughter Cecilia, and Rosemary O'Donovan. I would also like to acknowledge all those who arranged to send *The Southern Star* to me in PNG for twenty-seven years. Finally, a special thanks to all those who contributed in any way to the missionary work in PNG.

Fr. Michael Donovan, SVD
Papua New Guinea, 2021

PART I

TIMBUNKE: 1981-1994

WEWAK, EAST SEPIK PROVINCE (ESP), PNG

August 31, 1981 I arrived in Papua New Guinea (PNG) after a delightful trip across the globe. Fr. George Miller and Fr. Larry Finnigan drove me to Dublin airport. At 2.30pm on Wednesday, August 19, I was on my way to the other side of the world. The flight from Dublin to Amsterdam was by Air Lingus. Then I was transferred to a KLM Boeing 747 carrying 400 passengers. By 10.10 pm, we were on our way. Within five minutes we had climbed into the night sky, and soon we were full steam ahead at 600 miles per hour. This was a six-and-a-half-hour flight to Dubai. Dawn had already come as we touched down. After a one-hour delay we were on our way across the Equator and the great Indian Ocean, a nine-and-a-half-hour flight. As I sat back in my seat I said to myself, this does not happen every day, so I might as well enjoy myself. Brilliant sunshine streamed into the cabin, but it did not last long as we were leaving the daylight behind and flying into the night sky.

After experiencing some strong head winds, we were forced to land in Perth, Australia, where it was winter. From Perth we continued our journey right across to Melbourne. It was morning time again. After a short delay we flew over the east coast of Australia and after one hour of flying time I was to make my final touch-down that day in Sydney. Once down, it was through immigration and, to my surprise, I met an Inspector White from Dublin. He called me to one side and asked me how things were back home. It was now 10.10 am, Friday, August 21, local time. I still thought I was in the Boeing 747.

Next morning, I was back in Sydney airport again to catch my plane to Port Moresby. Fr. Vincent Twomey and other SVD members were at the airport to meet me. Fr. Twomey gave me a grand tour of Port Moresby and later that evening we had lunch out together. The following day I was back in the airport again to complete my journey to Mount Hagen. The Provincial, Fr. Arnold Steffen, and Fr. John McCarthy were there to meet me. Our stay was short as we rushed away to say Sunday Mass in the bush. We drove along the highway for fifteen miles and then turned off towards the out-station. We drove right into the bush, up and down some dozen hills or more. We crossed some homemade bridges and I was wondering would they be still there on my way back.

Finally, we came to a stop. "This is it," John said, and out we went. I thought after driving all this far we would have no one for Mass. Then the catechist struck an empty gas container with a stone to make a bell like sound. It must have been heard right across the valley for out of nowhere people began to appear. Some were young, some were old, some were too young to walk and others too old to walk came by car. The women carried *bilums*[1] on their heads, and children on their shoulders. Some of the men had paint on their faces and feathers in their hair; some were scantily dressed in leaves or greenery from the jungle. The men carried no heavy loads; instead, they brought their knives and hatchets. These were their working tools.

As Mass started they all gathered under the shade of the bamboo trees. The dogs came and sat under the shade too. When they started to sing, I knew then I was in a foreign land. After Mass I received a warm welcome from the locals, and it was there I learned my first two words of Pidgin: *apinum*, which means afternoon, and *gut apinum*, which means good afternoon. Then it was back to the car again to make our way down the mountain and back to Fr. John's parish house where I stayed for two weeks. I could write you many more pages of my first impressions, but I will keep them for another time. God Bless for now.

October 4, 1981 On Wednesday September 2 I left Mount Hagen and flew down to Wewak to learn Pidgin English. I was met by Fr. Edward Baur at the airport, and he, like Fr. Vincent Twomey, showed me around the town of Wewak.

Wewak is not like a European town with roads called South Circular

---

1 A hand-made string bag made in Papua New Guinea.

Road or Victory Road; instead, their roads are known as Banana Road, Sun Road, Star Road, etc. Most of the housing estates are hidden in coconut plantations, and the one main street is no longer than 500 metres. At the end of this street and across the main road is the Pacific Ocean. Its sandy beaches stretch for miles along the coast. The water is blue, and clear and you can see the ocean floor for a half a mile out to sea.

After three hot days in Wewak I went on a boat trip to Kairiru Island and there I met some of our future priests of PNG at St John's seminary. On my first day there I went by foot across the island to see the hot springs on the east side. When I got there, I was looking forward to having my first swim in the Pacific Ocean.

Now that the honeymoon was over, it was back to Wewak to study the language. I stayed in Tangugo pastoral centre for three weeks and I did nothing else except learn Pidgin English. To my surprise, in that short time I felt confident to speak to the local people, with the result that I left Tangugo and went out for one week to Timbunke, which is on the Sepik River

At this stage I am beginning to understand a little of the culture and the people. I have discovered I knew very little about PNG before I arrived. Now I know it is not only a beautiful country, but it is also interesting and challenging to be a missionary here.

What I find most interesting is the part the sun and moon plays in their lives. They rise with the sun and retire with the sun. When the sun is straight over head, half the day is left. This means in a land where time is so flexible that the church bell is used pretty often. The moon, on the other hand, is their means of counting the months. This tradition is changing fast, but only for those with access to education. The traditional dress is also going out of fashion. However, in the highlands the grass skirt is very much part of life.

Our missionary work is concentrated mainly in the highland provinces, Madang Province and East Sepik Province. There are only 500 priests here in PNG and nearly half of them are SVD. The population of PNG is 3.5 million, so there is plenty of work to be done. We have no television or newspapers at the out-stations. We have our own radio transmitter and we can contact each other during breakfast time. We have two seasons, wet season and dry season. Every day is very hot; just some days are hotter than others. I will sign off now by wishing you well and take care.

November 16, 1981 Now that I am here almost three months I want to write and thank you and all the staff for making those years at Maynooth pleasant ones. Those years are behind me now, but they are very much part of our SVD society here in PNG. This I saw very clearly when we priests and brothers met in Wewak to elect a new Provincial. Those who failed to come were either on home leave, sick, or stranded due to flooded rivers. While we were congregated in Wewak, the other provinces in PNG were also coming together for the election, and we were all linked up by telephone to the central station in Mount Hagen.

The voting began at 3 pm, and after the first count we received word from Mount Hagen that Fr. Bernard Kuhnert was our new Provincial for PNG. Then we proceeded to elect the consultors, and this went on until 11 pm. The priest I am staying with, Fr. Cornelius van der Geest, was elected assistant Provincial. The following day was a family feast, and, like what we did in Ireland, we took part in playing volleyball and other less strenuous games. That night we had our family feast dinner, followed by a singsong. Now we are back in our various mission stations again. You may be wondering where in PNG I am stationed. My postal address is in Wewak and from there my mail will come either by plane or by missionaries coming through to their own stations. I am actually half way between Maprik town and the Sepik River. The name of the parish is Kunjingini, and I am here for my introductory year to pastoral work with Fr. Cornelius.

To fly over PNG, it looks like one massive jungle with little brown dots planted in the valleys. These brown dots are the precious homes of the PNG people. A few weeks ago, I was called out to anoint a sick boy, and when I arrived in the village the men were sitting around a big fire with the sick boy lying on a mat in the middle. The women were praying, as I thought, and the children were all asleep on sleeping mats. The little ones were also asleep in their mothers' arms. I said the usual prayers and blessed them all with Holy Water. Everyone present then joined in for a decade of the Rosary, and I gave them the final blessing and left them in peace. I heard a few days later that the boy recovered and is out and about again.

When one dies in this area of PNG, the people make a grave close to the village, and after closing the grave they but the person's belongings on top of the grave—which is usually a bush knife along with the person's everyday clothes.

The Church is challenged here by the presence of other religions. There are at least eight other religions in the town and in the thickly populated areas. In this parish of Kunjingini, there are nineteen villages, and eleven of these have their own bush church. Some of these villages are isolated, and the people love to see you coming to pray with them and to say Mass. I have been to most of these out-stations now; most can be reached by car in the dry season and a few others by foot.

Last Sunday week I drove fifteen miles to say Mass in the bush. Everything went as planned until I started for home. I filled the Suzuki car with people and at the first wooden bridge one of the wheels went down through the plank. The people got out to push me clear, but in the process I damaged the petrol tank and ran out of petrol. I abandoned the car and four hours later arrived back at the mission station. There was no need to go for a jog that day.

Pidgin English is not too difficult; it suits me as it is a language of associations and easy to remember, but after one year when I go to a new parish I will have to learn a new language, Tokples, which is not easy. I have a lot to live up to here as our Irish SVDs are settled in well and thought highly of by the local people. Fr. Liam Dunne is doing a good job in Wewak. Fr. John McCarthy, Fr. John Ryan and Fr. Garrett Roche are well known in the Highlands. Fr. Vincent Twomey will soon be going home, and he will be missed by all of us. I will sign off now, so happy Christmas and every blessing for the New Year.

February 28, 1982 I was delighted to get your Christmas greeting and good wishes. My post was here in my room when I returned after my first Christmas in the bush. I arrived home really tired but happy after spending ten days constantly on the move. I had arranged beforehand to go to an out-station and stay one day at each village, making it a day of prayer followed by Confession and finally Mass in the evening, and the next day

I would walk to the next village two or three miles away. Some days we had Mass in the bush church and other evenings we said Mass outside as lots of people came to fulfil their Christmas duties. It was interesting to stay in the village at night. During this time the longest day of the year was approaching. However, night fell at 7pm, and once darkness fell we would sit outside and tell stories about each-other's country. Later, we would retire to the bush house with one room and sleep the night through, the men going to the house for men and the women going to the women's house with their children. The boys and the girls also had their separate departments.

Each clan has its own customs as regards family rules depending mainly on the size of the clan or tribe and from what district and province they come from. Another interesting feature about the houses is that they have no chimneys, so the smoke goes through the roof and keeps the termites from eating the house away, and it also keeps out the insects and mosquitoes. The houses are built close together, with a large space in the middle of the village. At night the village people come together to play cards or tell stories in this area near their homes.

The food is mainly yams, sago, and various types of fruits. There is no poverty as regards food. The bush and gardens produce a vast amount of tropical fruit during the wet and dry season, and each family has three or four gardens to make sure the supply chain won`t run out.

Before the white man came to PNG, the children were schooled by word of mouth or by performance rather than by writing. The form of teaching was mainly through legends, myths, and fairy tales. Some are passed on through action, dance, crafts and games. At night, the jungle in the tropics is alive with all kinds of creatures and insects. The most obvious of the insects is the fire-fly. At night its tail-lights up and shines in the dark. The crickets chirp from sunset and go well into the night. The wild birds calling at night are hard to distinguish from the animal cries. Among the animals, the flying foxes are the ones we dislike the most. They live in colonies along the Pacific. During the day they sleep in caves or hang from trees, usually the same tree, and at night they fly in large flocks to their feeding grounds. They are pests in many parts in PNG, because they destroy the people's fruit gardens, and they know exactly when the fruit is ripe.

The roads in PNG are not the best. We don't complain, because we missionaries have our own light aircraft which gets us over many a mountain. We also have our own radio. Two mornings ago, a local man came on the radio to tell his daughter not to come home because there was no road to the place. The river had flooded, leaving the area completely cut off. When it rains, parts of the roads are like river–beds, which explains why it's so difficult to travel by car or truck. I will sign off for the time being. Wishing you good luck and God's blessing.

May 25, 1982 It gives me great pleasure to be able to write to you from the frontiers of PNG. I did promise to write, and being one of your ex-pupils[2] how could I forget? One year has almost gone since I set foot on mission territory, and I must admit it was a very interesting one. I came here with a desire to learn and listen and observe and I have discovered that one never stops wanting to learn the rich culture of the people. It may be simple or old fashioned, but it is full of wisdom.

The newness of the Gospel is very effective; nevertheless, you can lose your parishioners just as fast as you win them. Some see the Church as "*sios bilong*[3] Fr. Michael", other see it as rich, foreign, a business, while others see the Church as "We are the Church". In our own small way, we SVDs are laying a few stones to bridge this gap of what the Church should be and how best to understand its role in the community.

I am getting very good now at giving the weather forecast, as the pilot contacts us by radio every morning before he takes off, and if he thinks the weather is too bad he will not come. Sometime ago, I was asked to help the locals with the transport of a pig, which would involve the mission truck here at the main station. The locals had the pig tied on a stretcher and were prepared to take it all the way to their village if I would not help. After loading the pig in the truck, we started out along the trail that leads to the village. Behind followed an army of men and children who chanted a song to their ancestors for giving them such a fine pig.

I had a very busy Easter here at the main station. Fr. Richard Seward came to help us out during Easter week, and he went to an out-station. On

---

2 The letter is addressed to Seamus O'Connell, a teacher in Donamon.
3 Tok Pisin for church.

the Friday after Easter, Fr. Kees and I went to see Fr. Seward on a social trip to discover he was very ill. The following day we brought him to the main station and arranged with the pilot to take him to Wewak hospital the following Monday. On Sunday night Fr. Richard got very sick so the sisters and I stayed up with him, and at 3am I gave him the last blessing just before he died. It was nice to be present at his death, and I was fully in charge, as the parish priest had gone to a meeting in Mount Hagen. I contacted all stations by radio at 7am, and the plane came to collect his body for its final resting place in Wewak. Before the plane set up directions for Wewak, it flew over the out-stations and villages, and the people were able to wave their last goodbye to the priest who was part of their lives for thirteen years.

Since I came to PNG, I have walked many a mile and I have enjoyed every moment of it. It is hard at times but very rewarding. PNG may sound remote and far away from Ireland, but it is another spot in the palm of God's hand, and, looking at it from that angle, we are indeed very close to one another. Would you believe it, a few months ago I walked eight miles to an out-station to say Mass? I thought it was the most isolated place in the world, but as Mass progressed I discovered the people were singing the same hymns that we sang in Donamon and Maynooth—only they were singing them in Pidgin.

Next month I am being transferred to Timbunke Parish on the Sepik River. There is a Holy Spirit Convent there, which means the food will be good and the plane will bring our mail from Wewak every week. The Sepik rises in the Western Ranges and loop its way over 600 miles to its mouth in the Bismarck Sea. Along the river and its surrounding hilly country live some 150,000 people belonging to a number of different clans and tribes. Two weeks ago, I stood by the bank of the river, and the day-flies came up. After one hour you would think it was snowing, they were so plentiful. Then the local people began to appear from everywhere in their canoes to catch the day-flies to cook them. The locals tell me the day-fly emerges from the river about every two months, and it lives only one day and hence its name.

All our Irish missionaries are keeping well here. As regards myself, I must thank the Lord for his goodness to me and I think he wants me right here in the frontiers of PNG. Keep up the good work at home, with best wishes take care and God bless you.

August 2, 1982 I hope you are all keeping well and enjoying the summer days in Ireland. Now that my introductory year is complete, I thought it a good time to write to you again. I received a royal send-off from my former parishioners. The young children gave me flowers and some elderly people gave me shrubs to plant on the Sepik as a sign of their appreciation for my time spent there. Now that I have left it all behind, I will miss the people and those long mountain trails that became so familiar to me. My main task there was to tell the people about the Risen Lord, and I always tried to let Christ be the Pastor. I think the greatest moment I had in that parish was when I sat beside Fr. Richard Seward's bedside and gave him the last blessing before he passed away to his eternal reward.

I have moved into a new parish now. However, my address stays the same—"Cathedral Parish". The name of this parish is Maranatha Parish, which is made up of four parishes: Timbunke, Kanengara, Amboin, and Kapamari. The parish has four married deacons, several catechists and prayer leaders. Fr. Ben Jansen is the parish priest and Br. Mathew is involved in health care; there are also three SSpS[4]. sisters involved in pastoral work and in mother-and-child healthcare.

As I am writing this letter to you I am looking out at the Sepik River flowing gently by, like a conveyor belt carrying logs and many tropical plants to its mouth in the Bismarck Sea. It is only ten metres from my window. This has its disadvantages too, because at night when I have my lights on it attracts millions of flies and moths to my room. To overcome this problem, we have put our lights outside the windows. We have a diesel generator here at Timbunke, and we run it for three and a half hours every night starting at 6.30pm.

I arrived here in this parish on June 18 to discover that vast amounts of the area is made up of swamps and thick sago jungle, and in between the grass lands are many lakes and lagoons. It is the home of the crocodiles, wild pigs, and mosquitoes. I have also seen a heard of wild cows numbering over 500 grazing on the river bank and in the swamps. These were once

[4] Holy Spirit Missionary Sisters

village cows which were badly managed and eventually went wild.

It is the dry season now, and this has its own blessings, and hardships. For the many people who live mainly on fish, this is a time when their catch is above average, for the lakes and ponds are drying up, leaving many fish stranded in pools of water. The wild pigs and the crocodiles also take advantage of this situation.

The wet season too has its advantages for the huntsman; many wild pigs are left stranded by water and take to the high ground. This time, the crocodile will have pork instead of fish. By the way, the wild pig can swim but it has to put a lot of effort into it, and they are quite helpless in the water. You may be wondering why I am telling you all this, but to understand the work I am doing, it is necessary to understand the people`s way of life. The Sepik people are mainly hunters or gatherers, and not sowers like the people from the inland areas.

When I arrived here at the main station, I gave the first week going around to the villages and meeting the people and at the same time getting to know my way around.

Last Monday week, Br. Mathew and I prepared for a bush trip to Kanengara, which is thirty miles upstream. The preparations began on Sunday after Mass and we were still loading some important items on Monday morning. It was well over a ton of cargo, which consisted of tinned meat, tinned fish, biscuits, salt, sugar, soap, rice, two drums of petrol for the outboard motor, and two drums of diesel for the generator. Then there were the medical supplies and our own supplies for the week. Br. Mathew and I left Timbunke at 10am, and we arrived at Kanengara at 4.45 pm. It was a long, hot trip under the blazing sun. We drove up the Sepik River, and then we went left up the Karawari River. As we approached the out-station there were men, women, and children there to greet us. They had seen us and heard us battle against the river with our fifty-horsepower motor from the hill-top. The rest of the day was taken up unloading the cargo for the store. Br. Mathew looked after the medical supplies, and I set up "Father's house" Kanengara, where we stayed for the week. One of our married deacons is stationed here, so in the following days we went around to the villages, and the deacon introduced me as their new priest. On Wednesday, it was back to the water again, and this time we used the deacon's boat as it was a light aluminium speed boat, and it was easy to pull it through the grass. We drove upriver from Kanengara station, and the scenery was beautiful. Tall trees towered over us, and then the river came to a stream and our luck ran out as the river was blocked by floating grass islands. We had to get out of the boat and pull it over the grass until we came back to the water again. Eventually we came out into a lake called Lake Governmas. I thought it was the most beautiful place in the world. Finally, we arrived at the village where there was a bush church, and this time there was no one there to meet us. Why? They thought we could not come because the river was blocked, and all those that were able had gone off hunting in the bush. Those who were left behind were three old ladies, two old men, and a young mother with a sick child. We stayed about four hours in the village, and I said Mass for the few people that were there. The next day I said Mass in a village called Krimbit and over 200 people attended. Then it was on to another village called Taragai, and then Governmas, and on Saturday it was down to Kambraman. On Sunday I had Mass at the main station in Kanengara and the church was full. At this stage everyone knew what the new priest looked like. There was a lot of handshaking from the local people, and some gave me gifts of pineapples and bananas. After all that we headed home to Timbunke, and it was much easier going down stream.

Since I came here, *The Southern Star*[5] is making a regular trip across the Equator, so I am up to date with all the news from home. With that I will sign off. God Bless for now.

December 12, 1982 Many thanks for your letters and papers, they are all arriving in good time. I am keeping well, and I am trying to write a few Christmas letters before I head out to the bush. I am just after returning from a bush trip in a place called Yambi-Yambi. The people there very seldom see white people, with the result the children ran away when they saw me. When they realized I was staying for three days, they gradually came back in twos and threes to have a good look at me. In these areas the people make you feel very welcome once they know who you are. A night in the village can vary from one extreme to another. Sometimes we

5 A West Cork newspaper published in Skibbereen

would arrive in the village like tired soldiers, so we would sleep the night through. Another night we would stay up late and give the whole night telling stories from times past.

Rats were always a big problem when staying in bush houses, and for that very reason we store our food in iron boxes. Ants can also be a problem if any sugar or jam is not kept in sealed containers. It's all a learning experience. During the same trip last week, I arrived in a village called Mamari with the deacon, and we baptised eighteen children, married four couples, and thirty children made their first Confession. The catechist was preparing them for three years, so they were well prepared. They even had a number of roosters for the occasion. That night we retired to the bush house but there was no sleep, because underneath the house were eleven roosters crowing all night. The following day they were killed to mark the celebration of the eleven families who had their children baptised. The night of celebrating was followed by a *singsing*[6] dance, which went on until the next morning. The people in the bush very seldom travel out at night, the main reason being that they are afraid of poisonous snakes and bad spirits.

During the wet season, bush trips can be very difficult as our clothes get wet, and there is no way to dry them. If this happens, we usually call off the trip. The wet season is here now, and we are already getting in the supplies to see us through it. This year we have twenty forty-four-gallon drums of petrol for the outboard motors. One drum gets us to the furthest out-station and back. I am getting a new twenty-five-horsepower motor from a parish in England where I gave a mission appeal in 1980. It costs eight hundred pounds.

When the priest arrives in the village or passes through, the people usually beat the *garamut*, which is a huge log drum used to send out a message to the people working in the gardens or to those in their homes. This drum can be heard about five miles away in the early morning. Each clan has its own drum beat, and so has the Father.

The local people have many different kinds of ceremonies and festivities. The best known is the Initiation Ceremony. This ceremony entails the young men having a crocodile pattern cut into their skin and all along

---

6 Singsing is the Tok Pisin term for the festivals held all over Papua New Guinea featuring dancing and singing.

their back, shoulder, and arms. They are then regarded as mature men, which means they have a say in the affairs of the village.

There are eight different clans in this area. A clan lives in a common territorial area and may share a common ancestor with myths and folklore. Each clan has a Spirit House or House Man where the images of spirits and carved figures of ancestors are kept. Women are not allowed into these Spirit Houses.

When a man wants to make a canoe, he must go into the jungle and chop down a tree. If it's a heavy tree, he will shape it roughly and partly hollow it out with an axe. He then will get some village people to pull it to the water. From there he can paddle it home and complete the job in the village underneath a shade tree. The most important part of the canoe is the clan pattern, which is carved into the head of the canoe.

For the people on the Sepik, the canoe is their main mode of transport, and canoe-making is vital for their survival. They make all shapes and sizes—single canoes, family canoes, and motor canoes. The local women paddle a canoe to their favourite fishing place every day to check their nets and reset them again. There are plenty of lagoons and streams near the villages, and fish is part of their diet every day.

I was in Mount Hagen some time ago to meet Fr. Phelim Jordan, SVD, a new Irish priest for PNG. The Queen was in Hagen town the same day, so we decided to go and see her. Over 30,000 people waited for three hours under the boiling sun to see her. She had just arrived when the skies opened, and the rains poured down. The local people saw it coming and fled for shelter in the town. The Queen was left standing in the stand with a few dignitaries and police men. Fr. Phelim and I were so wet that we decided to stay on, so we had the Queen to ourselves in PNG.

One Sunday I was saying Mass in the bush, and in walked a white man. I had no idea how he happened to be there. When Mass was over he came up to me and said, "What part of Cork do you come from?" He was Noel Kennedy from Dublin. He is an engineer working with the government, and during the weekends a government plane takes him around to different parts of PNG. Before he returned to Ireland we had a get-together on St. Patrick's, night this time in the main station. That is all for now. happy Christmas and good luck for 1983.

February 25, 1983 Another Christmas has come and gone, and I hope you had a happy and peaceful one. I had a very busy Christmas, and now that it is all over I am happy that all went well. I started saying my Christmas Masses at the out-stations on the tenth of December. I said three masses some days, going from one village to another, and finally I arrived back to Timbunke to say Mass on Christmas night. The following morning, I was on the move again, this time into the grass country to say Mass for the people living along the Timbunke highway. It was a good time to meet people, especially the ones who had returned to their villages to be with their families for Christmas.

The parish priest, Fr. Ben Jansen, took the most difficult part of the parish at the far end, and he did not return until December 28. He was very sick when he returned to the main station, and he is now recovering in hospital in Australia. I was on my own up to last week, and a new priest, Fr. Don Grant, is assigned to the upper half of the parish. It is high-water time or wet season at present, which means the river has risen nine feet with the last two months, and most of the houses in the area are standing in water. The river will rise another three feet or more, and then the whole area will be flooded. The people don't seem to mind as they have adapted well to their surroundings. They go around the village in the canoe, and they make cat-walks from one house to another. Some village people move out and stay with relatives in the town. The children take a canoe and go to the higher ground to play games. Many other creatures also take to the high ground, including millions of ants. The ants also climb the trees and go into the people's houses.

The people here live hand in hand with nature. You could say nature is very good to them, and other times of the year nature is very cruel to them. At this time, the sago swamps are full up with water, so the people paddle into the swamps with their canoes and cut down sago trees and bring them back to the village to be processed. It is the job for the men to cut open the bark of the sago tree. Then the women make pulp of the fibre inside the bark. After this the women wash the pulp with water inside a trough. And then the women squeeze the pulp to wash the pure sago out of it. The water and the sago flow through a strainer into a canoe. After some time, the sago settles in the bottom of the canoe, and the water runs off. The fibre or pulp is thrown away at this stage of the process. It is important to have water to process sago so in the dry season it is made near a stream or by the river. It sounds complicated to make it, but the people are making it for hundreds of years. One good tree of sago would do a family for a month. Fish and sago make a good meal, and it is the staple diet for the Sepik people. The people here have a saying: a man can travel one hour after a meal of sago, but after a meal of sago and fish he can walk for a full day.

At this time many people get sick, and I help out in the transport side of things. This I cannot avoid, because when I am in the bush and sick people want to go to hospital I must take them along. The people's needs are many, and there is a struggle for a fuller life in all its social, technical, economical, and religious aspects. They want to find out more than they now know and to find their way in this part of the world. I am just back at the main station after giving two weeks in the mountain villages showing films. I have a film projector and a portable generator for this purpose. I got two good films from our film library in Wewak. One is called, "The Redeemer" a film on the life of Christ, and another called "Laurel and Hardy". It's good to have a bit of entertainments at times with Laurel and Hardy. If the projector breaks down it is a terrible disappointment for the people. But so far, I have been lucky. I also know quite a lot about the projector now, which means I can repair it on the spot if the fault is only a minor one such as the bulb blowing or the speed belt slipping. It is very impressive to see the local people taking the film equipment across the swamps and through the rainforest. Any type of visual aid is very helpful for teaching the people, as they have developed tremendous eyesight over many years. Some interesting questions arise from the films, like was that the real Christ in the film? Or why we don't build houses in PNG like the ones we saw in the picture?

Next morning after the movies, I said Mass and had a meeting with the prayer leaders, church leaders, and catechist. I listened to their worries, gave them some work to do, and told them I would be back before Easter. While the meeting was going on, other men were taking the film equipment out to the river. The children and several young people all gave a hand, each one willing to help Father to take his Mass kit, oil stove, water flask, mattress, etc., out to the river edge, and the show goes on to the next village.

I went to Wewak on the second of January, and I was on my way to Goroka for a one-month course at the Melanesian Institute, when the bishop asked me to put it off until next year as the parish priest was sick, so I returned to the parish to keep the show going. Before I returned, I met Fr. Liam Dunne, and he told me his mother was flying into Wewak that evening, and it would be nice of me to be at the airport to meet her. I went along with four other priests, and about one hundred of Liam's parishioners were there to see his mother walk off the Air Niugini plane. She was handed a wreath of flowers from the parish chairman as she stepped off the plane, and just then another hundred people came to see who was the important lady that had just arrived. Outside the door of the parish house was written, "Welcome to Boram Mama Bilong Father Liam" I will sign off by wishing you a happy St Patrick's Day and all the best for Easter.

March 1, 1983 One of my bush trips in February was very difficult because the river was blocked in several places. The River Sepik never gets blocked, but the tributaries that flow into it do. It's when the Sepik is in flood, the back waters have less clearance and the water backs up causing the tributaries to jamb with debris, and floating grass islands. This day the Sepik and the Krosamari rivers were carrying a large volume of water from the mountains, and when I turned on to the black water river it was running back instead of coming out. Then, further up the river, the water was at a standstill and it was here the rubbish had gathered. I had a helper with me and after one hour we got through the first blockage. The second blockage was worse. It took twenty minutes to go the full length of the boat. It was harder than any tug-of-war. The third, and final blockage on the river was a different experience. By this time, it was evening, and the air was getting cool and down came the rain. We got so wet we just didn't care anymore. It was night when we arrived at the out-station that day. As it turned out, I stayed ten days, and the rubbish and the grass were already floating down the Sepik River, and going out to sea. For the journey home, I left at 7am, and before 9am I was already on the main river and going full-steam ahead.

I always look forward to the journey home, and it can be a pleasant trip too. However, it`s not all sunshine because once on the river you are exposed to either wind, rain or sun, all three make the journey difficult, but it's the wind I fear the most. To avoid all three, it is best to set out at sunrise.

Here is a bit of cheerful news, the bishop is buying a hover-craft, and I dare say it is coming to Gods people that I am looking after. It can ride over those whirlpools and those waves and all that jungle rubbish that I had to pull myself through. I don't want to build my hopes too high in case it may not come to the parish. I will end on a happy note by wishing you the joys of Easter. Take care and God bless you.

March 27, 1983 We are just after experiencing a big flood on the Sepik. For three months the river was rising. This occurs every year during the wet season. It rained for several weeks and the river got higher and higher and instead of taking its normal course, a mile further up from the main station it went straight through, cutting us off completely by road. The air-strip was also watered logged, so no plane could land. The water came right through the local village Timbunke and filled up the swamps behind the station and found its way back to the Sepik some four miles downstream. Lucky for us the first missionaries had built the station on the highest piece of ground available next to the river, but we still had less than one foot to spare above water level. It is in times like this that we hear all about the fathers, brothers, and sisters who were stationed on the Sepik, and how they managed to survive.

The whole Sepik area was covered with water. And, at one stage, the government and relief workers were quite concerned as how best to cope with the rising waters. It was a hectic time, and we were up to our eyes in water and work. Now that the water is receding, we are up to our knees in muck. There was nothing we could do with rising waters, only takes all precautions necessary, and I don't think the mission suffered any great loss. Many people took to the higher ground, and others made for the town of Wewak and stayed with relatives. The government brought food, and a helicopter made a daily round to check up on stranded families. I was glad to be part of it all.

On the March 15 I was taken out by boat and a government truck took me to Wewak to bring back supplies. I stayed two days in Wewak, and I stayed for St Patrick's night, fifty miles from the Sepik and in spirit I was many more. Fr. Liam Dunne had arranged "An Irish night" and we celebrated St. Patrick`s night in his house along with mother and four Irish sisters. If you happened to pass by, you would think we were back home in Ireland having a party.

The following day I was back at the main station again. I got a truck from the Wewak mission and collected a full load of rice, sugar, tinned fish, biscuits, and salt. There was a canoe to meet us at the river to pick up the cargo. The following day the food was distributed to those who needed it most.

Now the sun is shining again, and the government officials are going up and down the river assessing the damage and measuring the water level. It is not known how much damage is done, but from my own observation many houses are not standing in their normal position. Some houses have collapsed altogether, and I was told one village down-river has only three houses left standing at this time.

The people who live in the Sepik area have their houses built on stilts five or six feet off the ground to cope with the floodwaters. When the house is standing a long time in the water, the ground gets soft and it easily give way to the weight of the house and falls over. The biggest fear the people have at this time is an earthquake—one shake and the whole lot collapses. The people make cat-walks from one house to another, and it is here the locals have a good laugh at me. I cannot walk on a cat-walk, which is a single post held up by bamboos. It shakes a lot but for the natives it is second nature. I told one of the fathers in Wewak my problem. He said, when you will be there ten years you will be just as good as the local`s themselves. The locals have a saying: whatever day God made PNG, he certainly had plenty of water.

And so life goes on and so does the Sepik river, and some things go on the same such as my prayers for you and yours for me. I will sign off here, God bless you.

August 12, 1983 I hope you are all keeping well. I received your letters some time ago, and I receive the *Star* every week; it keeps me up to date with what is happening around West Cork. I hear too you had a real good summer. Right now, we are experiencing a long dry season. The floods have disappeared, and the ground is hard and dry again. You would think we had no rain for months, but the local people think differently because they are busy rebuilding their houses. It will be another year before they will be back to normal. The bishop received aid from overseas to help the Sepik people. He also made an appeal to the mountain people to collect banana seedlings, coconuts and taro bulbs to help the flood victims to restart their gardens.

During the flood, millions of eels made their way down to the sea to spawn. They floated down river because they were full of eggs and the village people were out all day catching them. Since the high waters, a new type of fish has come to the Sepik area. Some time ago I went out fishing at night with the Deacon Tina and his family, each one of us holding a spear. With the light we could see the fish resting in the waters, and we picked them up with the spear. I caught four that night.

I am now at one of our out-stations overlooking the Chambri Lakes. The lake is drying up now, leaving hundreds of fish trapped in pools of water. Many die, and when that happens it is impossible to stay here because of the smell coming from the lake. The birds eat a lot of them, and the people too catch baskets of them before they die. There is also a large variety of birds attracted by the mud and the dead fish once the lake starts to dry up.

There is an island in the middle of the lake, and there are over one hundred cattle grazing on it. Ten years ago, the Australian administration put twelve cows on the island. Although the cattle are gone wild, if the people want something to eat they can shoot one, but fish and sago are what they are eating at the moment. Near the Chambri Lakes are the Chambri mountains. This week I will visit the six villages in the area. Like most isolated areas, the people are moving out of here and heading for the towns. Out of 2,000 people who lived here, half of them have moved out for a better life in the modern world.

A few months ago, I was attacked by a flock of vultures. I saw what appeared to be a body coming down stream, and I went towards it. Then about twenty vultures flew off and into the air, so I went closer to discover the vultures were flying in to attack me. I drove off at full speed and left them to eat what turned out to be a dead cow. The people in the area told me a man was missing from their village and his body may be floating down river, so I was on the look-out for such a thing as a floating corpse.

Some people in the bush ask me how I found my way to PNG and if I could find my way back again. I told them I buy a ticket, get on the right plane, and the pilot knows the way. The pilot has all the necessary instruments to fly his plane to whatever country he wants to go to. Before, the sailors used the stars as a guide for their destination. Well, ever before the missionaries came to PNG the people had only to look up to the sky and they could see the great Southern Cross formed by a combination of stars. Maybe that's why God put it at this side of the globe. That is all from this side of the world. God bless and take care,

November 23, 1983 It is time once again to bring you up to date with events over the last four months, and quite a lot has happened since. On October 16 we celebrated the golden jubilee of the Church in this parish. To mark the occasion, the local people carved a statue of St. Paul from a trunk of a tree. It is St Paul's Parish and that is why he is held in such high esteem here. The statue was made on the church grounds by one of the clans who invited the first missionaries to settle here and Fr. Cherubim, a local priest from Timbunke, was the main carver. As St Paul reached its final stage, more and more people were coming to make a daily inspection of his progress, and he is now standing in front of the church. Fr. Kirschbaum, a German priest, was the first missionary to set foot here, and after some difficulty with the people, he bought a piece of ground where the mission is today. It was a piece of ground where no native people would live, because it had been a battlefield in tribal fighting in days gone by.

One of the high points of the jubilee was the drama of the first contact, which was acted out by the elderly people in the village who had heard their fathers relate the story about the first missionaries in the Middle Sepik. September had just begun when a television team from the BBC came to make a film, "Great River Journeys". They stayed in the mission house for one night. It should be on television next June or July. The Sepik may not be the biggest river in the world, but it certainly is one that has mystery and traditional culture. You may see me popping up somewhere on a TV screen sooner than expected.

We have given a number of courses for prayer leaders this year to most of the fifty-eight villages that have prayer leaders. We try to give them some new ideas to conduct prayer meetings and Sunday services, and we teach them new hymns so that they don't have the same ones every Sunday. A follow-up of the course is very difficult and sometimes an impossible task as we may not see the prayer leader for four to six months again. It's a slow-moving church here in PNG, and most of the Christians are first-generation Catholics. There is no place for people in a hurry in this part of the world, so you must march with the band if you want to be part of it. One thing that is changing village life is the radio; it may not be always working, but when it is, it is on full volume.

The government has set up a radio station in Wewak, and we get free service when we want to use it. For example, when we want to go to a village or have a parish board meeting, I write a note to Radio Wewak, and they will announce it for two nights in a row, and someone in the village is bound to hear it and pass on the information. There is one village I visit about very four months, and the first thing the prayer leader asks me is, "Did you bring along the batteries?" He wants them for his radio to listen to the news, and maybe a message for himself. When the missionaries arrived in PNG, it was the garden tools that made the greatest impact. The hatchet and the bush knife were a vast change from the stone-age tools.

This year quite a number of village people got sick. Some blame the dirty water from the river. When a person dies here on the Sepik, his or her canoe is used for the coffin. After the burial, one can see on the river women covered with clay or ashes during mourning time. When a man is in mourning, he lets his beard grow, and some won't comb their hair for several months.

Before I came to the Sepik, there was a retreat given to one of the villages. Most of the big men attended; however, one man thought it was a good day for hunting. That evening his two dogs returned to the village, but there was no sign of the hunter. The village people set out to look for him and after a short time they discovered his body, which had been mutilated by a wild pig. There was no question asked because the people knew that if he had attended the retreat he would still be alive. Now, when there is something important happening in the village which has to do with Church matters there is always a good attendance. Events like this the people will never forget, and they have a mental picture of these happenings which they often refer to when speaking about the past. It is not surprising to find most village people have no idea when they were born. Instead, they refer to an event which occurs around the time there were born—for example, "I was born before the war" or "Father so-and-so baptised me when I was a child". Then you find out the name of the father and the child and go to the parish Baptism book and find the date of birth or as near as possible to the correct date. I find the people have a good memory for what is necessary in their lives. Even the children who are seven or eight years of age can tell you the names of trees and plants, which ones they can eat, and which plants they can use for local medicine. They know their own ground and places of danger where poisonous snakes hide out and where wild pigs dwell.

Some local news: a group of rascals from the upper Sepik took an out-board motor from the station one night. They took it back to their village and buried it underneath their house. One old man in the village woke up when he heard the digging and he asked them what they were doing. They told him the roof was leaking and they were making a drain for the water to run out. The next evening the news reached the village that the motor was stolen, so the old man went to investigate what was in the drain. When he discovered it was the motor he came to the station next day to tell the owner where the motor was, but he wanted a case of beer and twenty *kina*[7] for his troubles. He got what he asked for, but the man who brought back the motor was lucky to get back alive as the village people were very angry with the whole affair. I will sign off now by wishing you a happy Christmas, and I wish you every blessing for 1984.

May 13, 1984 (after first home leave) I am back with the people, the heat and the rain, and it seems I am getting familiar with this journey to the East. There was something about this round trip that made me feel glad to be an SVD. A half-hour after receiving word on the radio that my mother was very ill and that she was not expected to hold on for too

---
7 The Papua New Guinean currency.

TIMBUNKE: 1981-1994

long more, I was beginning the first stage of my journey home. Two days later, I arrived home and Mother was still with us, but only for another five days. She passed away while I was saying Mass at her bedside. I think a mother's wish had come true, that I was present during her last moments.

My journey back was at a much slower pace. I called to Donamon Castle and Maynooth, and a week later I left for London where I spent four days. I stopped at Hong-Kong to see my *wantoks*[8], Fr. Brian Lawless, Fr. Paddy O Regan, and Fr. Pat Canavan. I stayed at Kowloon, Floor nine, so I was in cloud nine for three days before hitting the ground in PNG.

I stayed almost four months in Ireland, making the best of the good food and observing life in the western world. Some said the faith was dying, others said it was changing, but if I were to judge by the people's generosity and their requests for prayers I would say the faith is still very much alive.

There were some changes in Timbunke when I arrived. Two new fathers were assigned to the Marenatha Team Parish, and one, Fr. Stephan, is assigned to me for his introductory year. This means my role as a bush missionary will change somewhat for the next twelve months. Fr. Ben Jansen, a lifelong father on the Sepik River, has decided not to return to PNG.

Happily, everyone was in good form, and I arrived in time to share the Easter Liturgy and the joy of the risen Lord with them. About now too, thirteen missionaries from the Wewak Diocese are preparing for home leave. Most take their holidays during the summer months and avoid the winter if at all possible.

The river was well behaved this year, no floods and very few mosquitoes. Some were complaining because the river was too low for logging and they had great difficulty in pulling the logs to the water. Indeed, it may be said, these people seem much happier than the people in the western world. Their only worries are those in the village, and they show very little interest in problems outside their world.

Going back to Ireland brings home the reality that things are not the same as when one left. The nieces and nephews have grown up, older faces have got a little older, some have gone to their eternal reward, and familiar faces which one would half expect to bump into in Donamon or

---

8 Pisin for close friends—from "one talk".

Maynooth are scattered over the globe.

The Pope has come and gone, and like his journey throughout the world, it was just as colourful and as successful in PNG. Over 300,000 people gathered to see him in Mount Hagen. It was the biggest crowd of people ever to assemble in this country. Several groups of people from the bush walked for three or four days before reaching the town. A group of 1,000 people walked from Enga with Michael Gibson, an Irish SVD student, and they congregated for two days in the town before finally appearing in their traditional dress. Fr. John Ryan SVD was conducting the choir, while the rest of the missionaries were bringing in car loads of people. The police were lenient on the truck drivers that day, so it was a question how many people could fit into the trucks and buses. It was a day of achievement and joy for our catechists and missionaries. This was the "harvest" of fifty years work in the highlands. The Pope's visit shows how much work is already done and it was a time to recall the ups and downs of missionary life. The Pope also gave a special mention to the Divine Word Society. His message was one of love, and that was the atmosphere in Hagen town as he flew out of Kagamuga airport.

For many, the long march back to the bush had begun at that stage, but they were happy they had seen the Pope. Now it's back to life as usual and to continue the Lord`s work. The Pope`s visit has given us new courage to carry out that task, and please God his presence will be felt here in PNG for a long time. I will sign off for the present, and I hope this finds you in good form and good health. God Bless and take care.

July 1, 1984 Three months have passed since I have returned PNG, and it seems I have never been away, but once I came ashore at the out-stations, the local people soon reminded me my visit was overdue. Then I must explain how I went home to Ireland as my mother was very ill and had since died. Once that was done, I introduced Fr. Stephan as the new priest, and they felt assured we had not forgotten them all together. I still have not completed visiting all the villages since I returned. However, once Fr. Stephan knows his way around this will all change. We both went on a bush patrol two weeks ago, and after talking to the people for some time they showed us the house we were to sleep in. I walked in first, followed by Fr. Stephan. Then the old lady of the house moved along the floor on her hands and knees and crawled under our feet. This was her way to show us how pleased she was at having us stay in her house. Once before I had a similar experience—a time when Mass was over, and all the women folk sat down on the ground, and I had to walk over their feet. This is the traditional way of welcoming a big man to the village.

Just now the Sepik people are experiencing some of the effects of western civilisation. The more educated ones have moved to the towns, taking their families with them. This was the trend in the last five years or more. Now all those who have no work are ordered back by the government because of the law-and-order problems they are creating in the towns. The government claims the Sepik way of life has a future for all, and that is true if only they would appreciate it. It seems the newer lifestyle has robbed them of their culture and the education system has opened a new world to them. Now there is a loss of traditional values and a lack of understanding for many new ones.

This was the situation that led to cargo-cult thinking twenty years ago, and this type of thinking has not changed much since. Cargo-cult is a new type of religion where people feel that if they believe and pray, God will give them the cargo. The cargo could be anything from store goods to money, but it is usually what comes in ships and planes, and it is the missions that get it, because they believe in God and pray to him. God said, "Ask anything in my name and you will get it." This does not mean the people sit down all day and do nothing; it simply expresses their way of thinking. To be fair, some work very hard, and if I were to go by the cracks and blisters on their hands when they present them for the blessed sacrament, one could only think they were signs of their hard work.

One Easter Sunday, I was returning from an out-station when I saw the King of the Sepik. He was having a rest on a log by the river when I disturbed him. He dived into the river, and I continued my journey. These creatures look horrifying, but it seems the less one knows about them the more afraid one is of them. The people call the crocodile the King of the Sepik because he is the most feared creature on land and in water. Each year one or two people are nabbed by crocodiles. Last April a student from the teachers' training college went missing off the coast of Wewak, and it is thought he was taken by a crocodile as the body has never been recovered.

I was just gone on home leave when a parcel arrived for me, and some Fathers in Wewak thought it was a cake and decided to eat it as it would be gone off before I returned. When they opened the parcel, it was a flash lamp that was inside. They must have been disappointed, because no one knew what happened to it, until one day I phoned Seamus Casey, and Fr. Liam was in the room at the time, and just then the incident of the cake occurred to him. The lamp was in Fr. Liam`s room. Well, this is it for another while. Take care and God bless you,

August 10, 1984 Just now it is the dry season, and my fourth in PNG. It is difficult to say which is the most pleasant as both bring their blessings and hardships. For sure, the wet season makes boating easier, and some villages can be reached only in this time. The wet season is also mosquito time, and they can make life unbearable if one is not prepared with mosquito net and mosquito repellent. Mosquitoes are most active around sunset, and if you happened to be in the village it is best to be under your mosquito net. I told Fr. Stephan one evening, when we arrived in a village known for the worst type of mosquitoes, to set up his net because once dusk comes, they will eat you. He was in no great hurry, as he did not know the situation and as night fell he was surrounded by millions of mosquitoes. There was no point in killing them as there was a million more waiting to land on him. It was his worst experience so far on the Sepik, and that night he told me that once his introduction year was over, he would not stay on the river.

Up to now we have plenty of drinking water. One good thunder shower would keep us going for a month, and we got that last week, to the delight of everyone. We see a lot of grass fires during the dry season. The people burn the dry kunai grass and wait along the edges of the fire with spears and kill any wild animal that may come out. Many wild pigs are killed this way. The people also believe that if there is a long drought they must light the fires to bring the rain.

This is the tourist season on the Sepik. I met several Europeans on my pastoral rounds. Some buy a canoe and paddle it down to the Middle Sepik or further. Others hire out a motor canoe at enormous prices. Five tourists came to me recently and complained that the canoe owner charged them too much. After hearing what the complaints were, I told the tourists it was a reasonable price, because it costs the owner more money to go back upriver than to bring them down.

Other tourists think I should keep them free in the parish house. To avoid any trouble, I refer them to the school board. Four middled-age ladies studying Sepik art arrived one day and told me they knew Fr. Ben Jansen, the priest I took over from, so I had to keep them for three nights. They were interesting to talk to, and they told me Sepik art was famous all over the world. I knew there was a ship-load of carvings along the Sepik River, ranging from a baby crocodile to a life-sized man.

Some carvings represent the spirits of the ancestors or wild animals in the bush. Every house has carvings tucked under the roof or over the smoking grill. The carving buyers like old carvings, so the local people have a cheap way of making a new carving look old. When the buyer arrives, he looks for old carvings, and the village people have got wise to this, so they present the carving, saying "We have it from our grandfather's time"—and it would have all the look of it too. It did not take them long to learn the salesman's skills. Only two weeks ago, a buyer from the Gold Coast bought two hundred pounds worth of carvings from one man. The village man was so delighted that he went to Wewak to see his friends, and they had a drinking session. I met him last week in Timbunke hospital, and he told me the drink had nearly killed him.

This man has died since from a heart-attack, and I thought it a real pity as he was going back to his village to tell his people that too much drink could kill you. Now the local village people say he should not have sold the carvings of his ancestors, and that was the cause of death. The ancestors have punished him.

Just now the Olympic Games are in full progress in Los Angeles. I get the results on my radio, which is quite good, and I find BBC world news very good. All I need is the batteries. Prince Charles was in Wewak recently, and I was there to see him, along with 40,000 local people. I will sign off now by wishing you well. Take care.

November 10, 1984 Well, November is the month to say where did the year go? I have already wished a few people, happy Christmas, which is a reminder the New Year is not far away. Anyway, 1984 did not pass by without leaving some important events to be remembered both at home and in PNG. I would say without doubt that the Pope's visit was the most important single event, n*umba wan samting*[9], to occur during 1984. There was one other event which was overlooked and that was the opening of the new House of Parliament in Port Moresby. The House of Parliament was opened by Prince Charles. The building is an expression of PNG culture from the four corners of the country, and it cost thirty-two million US dollars to design such a building. Its design is in the form of a spirit house, where all power rests. Most of the woodwork is carved out by Sepik artists to express the importance of several different cultures united in one beautiful national monument. You may be surprised to hear the chandeliers which are displayed from the ceiling of the main chamber came all the way from Ireland. It would have slipped my attention, only for the container which brought the precious ware to PNG fell off the fork-lift after been discharged from the ship. The dockers feared the worst, but later complimented the Irish for their professional packing which saved the Waterford glass.

The most pleasant event of the year for myself was the morning I celebrated Mass in a bush church to mark the fourth anniversary of my ordination. I had a congregation of twenty children and ten adults; none of them were baptised and none of them knew it was my ordination anniversary until I told them, but I was glad to be among them and to share Christ`s love with them on that particular day.

I had a call from the civil aviation inspector last week. He came to inspect the air-strip, and it did not meet his requirements because I had no markers, so he closed it down. I told him the schoolchildren used to take away the markers on a wet day to put over their heads and keep themselves dry while walking home from school. You don't have to guess what I was doing this week—I was hammering into shape and painting copper until I had forty-two markers completed.

Our new pilot, Br. Bill, SVD, is making good progress now at the flying. I have not flown with him yet, which means I am staying for longer

9 The best of whatever is there.

periods in the bush. Fr. Tom Russel is getting an ultra-light plane to visit his out-stations. An organisation in England called "Survive" is providing the cash, and we missionaries are hoping Fr. Tom will survive, that he doesn't crash. Fr. Tom has a large swampy area which is not suitable for boats, and he has to walk on fallen logs all lined up one after another during the dry season to reach his parishioners. For the natives, this is no trouble as they are doing it all their lives. Well, it is not all bush and swamp in the Sepik District, at least not for the moment, because the government has five D7 bulldozers working on the Sepik highway for the last two months. The road is going right along the top of the mountain ranges where possible. To get up and down the valleys that connect the mountains, the dozers must cut into the side of the mountain, and you can see the fresh soil slipping down the valley one hundred feet below. The locals stare all day at these yellow giants tearing down what was once their sacred jungle. The money for this road is coming from the World Development Bank, and the engineers that are constructing the road are from overseas.

As I am writing this letter, sounds of axes can be heard chopping down two large rain trees from the garden of my neighbour, Philip Luki. There are about fifteen men there with two axes, and each one takes it in turn to chop his share of the tree. By now the operation is almost complete, and it would surprise you what they can do with these tools when they put their minds to it. Philip Luki is our member of parliament, and he is building a bulk store to help his people in his area. I will sign off by wishing you a happy Christmas and good luck for 1985. Take care.

January 1, 1985 As usual, Christmas is one of the busiest times on the river, and now that the festivities are over, I can give you an update account on some of the activities which occurred during the renewal of Christs coming.

It was early on December 8 when Deacon Tino and I began our Christmas rounds. One last check and we were on our way to Yambi-Yambi. As we pulled out from the river bank, the Deacon's family waved us goodbye, and his two small children hit the ground and were screaming their heads off as they wanted to come along with their dad. But we were soon out of sight with our new Mariner outboard motor. The Deacon took over the steering, and I sat back reading the September *Furrow,* which had arrived a few days before. The river was calm, and the reflection of a few water birds flying overhead could be seen on its glassy surface.

Radio Wewak had already announced our itinerary, so each village knew exactly when we were coming. Yes! It was Christmas again, even though the signs had not yet come to life; however, the Word of God in the daily readings kept reminding us the Redeemer was coming. It was 4.30pm that day when we finally arrived in our first village, Yambi-Yambi. Scores of happy children became even happier at our arrival, but once the cargo was put ashore they were disappointed, as Father did not bring along a movie film for Christmas. I had to explain the projector was out of order due to the rats which ate away a part of it. Then one by one they took our luggage up the mountain to the bush house where we stayed that night. The rest of the evening was spent preparing the programme with the Catechist Henry for the following morning. It was not surprising to have nearly everyone in the village for Mass, as three people had died within three days of each other and there was a growing suspicion as to what was the cause of it. The big men had held an open Confession in the *houseboy*[10] and exposed a lot of wrong doing in the community, but they did not find the cause of the deaths. The people told me no one had anything to fear, only the guilty ones; the people were suspicious of sorcery being carried out in the community. Next morning, we hit the road again to the next village two hours upriver. Now the mountains appeared to be getting larger, and trees towered over the river at either side. After one hour on the water, our motor was making slow progress against a river that showed all the signs of anger. The water was churning, and white suds suggested it was either raining heavily on the mountains or we were close to a water fall. We had just arrived when down came the rain. I thought this would be a quiet night on account of the rain, and everyone was in their houses. This area is known for its lightning storms as it is close to the mountain wall where temperatures rise and fall, causing this great discharge of energy. The lighting storm was all over by morning, and the silence was broken once again by the beating of the *garamut* to call the people to Mass. After the third *garamut*, about 120 brown faces crowded into a little bush church.

10 A building where only men gather.

They were all barefoot, and they were anxious to sit and talk and make up for what they had missed out on the night before.

During our conversation after Mass, the people told the Deacon and me not to go to the next village as they had moved to the other side of the mountain in search of their god. It was not the God we had come to tell them about. Instead they were digging for gold. They had found one nugget worth 500 US dollars, and this has given them new urge to dig for more. The change of plan meant we were going downriver one day earlier than planned. When we arrived unexpected at the next village, most people were out making sago or out fishing. I could see confusion coming already, and Christmas was fifteen day away. I told them I would wait an extra day and Deacon Tino was only too happy, as this was his home village. He went off hunting with his *wantoks*, and I passed the day away talking with a few old people and listening to their stories about old times. There, my ears were opened to all sorts of stories whether true or false. I would be foolish to dismiss them as little or of no significance, because these men had found in these legends a support for their material and spiritual lives.

The following morning, I was the last one to roll up the mattress and fold my mosquito net in the large bush house where over twelve people had spent the night. Three old ladies had each an open fire lighting, and I made it one more when I lit my oil stove to prepare breakfast, which was coffee, a packet of chicken soup, and biscuits. Then I asked where everyone was gone to. One old lady was only too anxious to tell me that the Deacon had shot a wild pig early this morning and the men had gone out to the bush to bring it in. When the pig arrived with its four legs up and two men carrying it shoulder-high on a pole, I knew they were taken up with their new kill and the thought of Baptism and Mass was far from their minds. There would be no time to spare as the day was getting warm, and then it was suggested the Deacon should get the pig as a Christmas present, and six hours later we were back at the main-station to deliver the bacon to the Deacon's wife and family.

Life is quite another matter back at the main station. The church had already received its "face-lift" for the holy season, and several people were returning home from the towns via Middle Sepik to spend their annual holiday with their families. For the Sepik Fathers who were trying to make pastoral visits to all their communities there would be no holidays for two weeks more. One of my last villages to visit was Tambunam, which is by far the largest community on the river. It is thirty minutes downriver from the main station by speed boat, and it was only fitting that I would go there on Christmas morning after midnight Mass here at the main station. The church at Tambunam was removed three years ago to the other side of the river. It was thought the whole village would follow as the river was changing course, but so far only a few families have moved house. It is no surprise to see a hundred canoes crossing the river on an occasion like this. Today was no exception; there were single canoes, double canoes, family and motor canoes, all parked in a lagoon side by side and head to tail. After Mass, I watched three or four hundred people manoeuvre their favourite mode of transport out to the river, each person with a paddle and each canoe displaying on the brow the skilful carving of a crocodile head. It was a traffic jam with a difference, but once they reached the main water there was ample space and each one headed in the direction for home. Just one more village to visit, and I will be heading home as well to join the rest of the Maranatha community for our Christmas dinner with the sisters. There I will leave you by wishing you a happy New Year, and I hope you had a happy and peaceful Christmas. God bless.

February 2, 1985 Many thanks for your letters and donations I received last month. The month of January is probably one of our most relaxed times on the river. The schools are closed, and several people are home on holidays. It is also the middle of the wet season, so travelling is curtailed to a minimum.

At present, Timbunke village is standing in two feet of water. This is just part of life for the Sepik people, and if they want to visit their neighbour, they do it in their canoe. Very soon I will be making my first appearance to the village in my *pull-canoe*. There are three disabled people living in the village that I call to see them regularly, and two clerical students from Timbunke decided to make me a pull-canoe so I can continue to visit the village during the high-water season. I called once to the bush to see how the canoe was taking shape, and I took along some betel nut as it is the custom to appreciate their hard work and to thank them for providing such needed transport. Then the makers of the canoe asked me, "What clan do you come from"? I told them I come from the monkey. "Oh!" they said. "You are from the Dog clan"—so they will carve the head of a dog on the forehead of the canoe instead of a crocodile.

I went crocodile hunting one night with Fr. Cherubim Dambui, a local priest from Timbunke. It was a dark night and a group of young men armed with spears came along, or rather I went along with them. We had not far to go as a number of crocodiles had been seen in a small lagoon beside the mission farm. There wasn't a word spoken as we crept up to the side of the lagoon. Fr. Cherubim took over from here, and he began surveying the waters with a flash lamp. Then out of the dark shone two red eyes, and the hunt was on. We watched the crocodile move up and down the lagoon hunting for food. Sometimes he disappeared and surfaced again. All we wanted was one clean shot and we would be taking him home with us, but he kept his distance from us all night. A few boys tried the mating call to lure him or others in our direction, but to no avail. Finally, the moon came up and the crocodile had survived another night. Fr. Cherubim has been a priest for ten years, and eight of these were spent as Premier of the East Sepik Province. He had a big influence on his home village, and he gave me a lot of new insights into the lives of his people. For example, I was at a traditional marriage ceremony in his village, and he explained the different dances and songs which the people were engaged in. When the people went into a long chanting *singsing*. he told me that was a song about creation and it was just like the psalms we say in church, when we praise the Lord of all creation.

At the moment too, we feel like praising the Lord, not so much for creating the deadly *salvinia* weed which is clogging up the waterways, but for the introduction of an insect which is devouring it happily. The Chambri Lakes were like green fields before the insect finally took over. A New Zealand aircraft is now dropping more insects where other means of transport is unable to reach. The Salvinia, which doubles its growth every eight days, is a real pest for water transport, and it is the opinion of many that a European brought it into the country ten years ago. Water birds could also have brought the *salvinia* to the Sepik area, or ships going up and down the river; no one really knows.

It is almost ten years since PNG received its independence from Australia, and to celebrate the occasion, the government is introducing television to the four major towns: Port Moresby, Lae, Mount Hagen, and Goroka.

Over the last week, we were making up a pastoral programme for 1985 with emphasis on the local church. We will hold a number of short Bible courses and Prayer Leaders' courses here on the station over the year. We have decided to make the community schools one of our priorities for 1985. I really should tell you more about our pastoral work. We take it so much for granted, that it seems the more unusual events come to mind when I start writing. Just now I am attending to several jobs. Tomorrow I go out to the farm to repair the grass cutter, and there are always little odd jobs popping up that need attention. With that, I will close for now, God bless and take care.

March 9, 1985 This letter is long overdue and, with Easter approaching, I better start now. Saturday evening, I had a European-style wedding, not that I encourage this type of ceremony. The groom had seen a western-style wedding in Port Moresby and bought his bride a long white dress, and the groom came dressed in a long black trousers and white shirt. Br. Mathew provided a pair of shoes for the groom and Sr. Angela did likewise for the bride. They really looked a lovely, happy couple, and the church was nearly full of village people as they had come to see what they call a white man's wedding. I was excited myself. I started the Mass in English, and when there was no response from the people I realized my mistake.

There was excitement of another kind to come the following day. For three weeks the Timbunke area was a hive of activity with the arrival of Shell Oil Company to explore the Sepik Basin for oil. They asked me if they could use the air-strip to set up a refuelling base for the company. The locals got angry when they heard several men were employed from other villages, and once the helicopter arrived on Sunday morning the Timbunke people showed their frustration by pulling down their camp, smashing their radio, and threatening to blow the place apart if the company would not employ more men from their village. Shell took their threat seriously, and at 3pm, when the Stations of the Cross was about to begin, one helicopter after another air-lifted the fuel and all their equipment to a new site five miles away. The company ran into further difficulties over Easter when a tree fell and killed one of the local employees. The Europeans left immediately for Wewak as they feared a "pay-back." Pay-back is one of the several traditions which are still strong in PNG. It is the customary law, an eye for an eye and a tooth for a tooth. The government has stepped in and talks are going on between the two groups. If you kill somebody in a car crash in PNG, you don't stop; instead, you go to the nearest police station and report it. If you stop, you may get killed.

On a lighter note, Sr. Anne-Marie, superior general of the SSpS sisters, paid a visit to Timbunke last month. I had the honour of driving her from Wewak to Timbunke. If Sr. Anna-Marie was looking for a missionary experience, she sure was not disappointed. It was the middle of the wet season, and the road was like a skating ring, and the bridges we had to cross had to be repaired before venturing over them. When we eventually arrived, Mother General was greeted by a million mosquitoes all anxious to get a drop of her blood.

Some things are getting a little easier in the parish. Last year it took three days to visit one school in the parish called Boru—a full day to get there, a day at the school, and a day to return, and you can add another day to recover. The school has now moved to a more central area, and the government has pushed a road through to its location. I can now reach the school in one hour by car during the dry season.

Bishop Leo Arkfeld celebrated his seventy-third birthday last month, and he is still flying his mission plane. Bishop Leo is known as "The Flying Bishop" in PNG, and several parents have given the name Leo Arkfeld to one of their children when getting baptised. Recently in Lae city, the name Leo Arkfeld appeared on a notice board outside the court house. It read, "Leo Arkfeld due to appear in court at 10am on charge for been drunk and disorderly." If anyone wants to write to Bishop Leo, be sure to put Archbishop before it; otherwise there are several here with the same name and no relation to the original Bishop Leo who might not get your letter. I hope you are all well in Maynooth, and no doubt you are all busy with the studies. So, I will sign off for now, God bless and take care.

May 30, 1985 The dry season has already started, and I have decided to start painting the station. It will take about two years, as I will take one house at a time and do it in my spare time.

At present we have lots of lemons. I took the children out one day to the farm, and we picked as much as we wanted. The sisters make soft drinks from them. Another day, one of my workers, Bernard Bowie, and I were digging out a root of a tree when we found some dynamite left over from World War Two. We were lucky because we had set fire to the tree several times and it did not explode. The US Army visited PNG and recovered the bones of several crew members from the Forty-third Bomber Group lost in World War Two. A Port Moresby bushwhacker discovered a B-17 airplane near Rabaul, and the search is still going on for 360 US aircraft which are still missing. Here on the middle Sepik there are three aircraft lying in the bush that we know of, but the army has already examined these.

My neighbour Philip Luki, who lives only twenty yards away from me, killed thirty-one crocodiles yesterday and sold their skins to a European buyer. The crocodiles were breaking out of the pens, and he did not notice it until the dogs were chasing one of his best ones into the river.

I am now making a desperate attempt to try and know most of the people by their first names. You know the feeling when you talk to people, and see them more than once a week, and you still cannot call them by their first name.

Another day, I was sitting at table, when suddenly a young girl about five years old started to scream. She had caught her first fish, and she was so happy that she called out to the rest of the family to come and see it. She then ran to tell her mother, at the same time trying to hold the fish off the ground. Her mother told me afterwards that it was a special occasion when a child catches its first fish, and they have a celebration to mark the event, as the child knows now how to get food for itself.

I may not have told you how I bought a fifty-two-foot canoe for transporting goods up and down the river. It cost 200 US dollars. The bow displays a beautiful head of a crocodile, and I have a twenty-five-horsepower motor on the stern to drive it.

One of our Catholic high-schools here got into trouble with *Time* magazine. A teacher gave the students the magazine, where they read "Order now and pay latter." The students ordered *Time* and it kept coming for three months. Now *Time* want their money back, and they asked the headmaster to pay. He has refused on the grounds he did not order the magazine.

I had a busy Easter with plenty of pastoral work to do. It was encouraging to see the churches full of people during Holy Week, although I am sure several of them will not make the effort to come again until Christmas. This year, we had the most unusual wet season which nearly drove us all crazy. The river came up and remained at the same level for four months. This caused the waters in the swamps to stagnate, which was excellent breeding grounds for the mosquitoes. All we could do was to look out at them through the mosquito wire. The local people light fires to keep the mosquitoes away. They know how to make a good smoke fire with dry grass and coconut shell, and the smell and the smoke keeps them at a distance. Luckily, these mosquitoes are not malaria carriers; otherwise everyone would be dying with malaria for weeks.

People on the Sepik often attribute death, sickness, and snake bites to sorcery. This is very hard to pin down, as there are so many forms of sorcery, and different clans have different forms of it. It's a custom that has survived the modern changes and centres around the spirit house or magic man. Out of fear of been punished, the whole village will carry out any major decision by the elders, especially if it is connected with the spirit world or a threat from their ancestors that punishment will follow. To bridge this gap between western laws and traditional customs, village courts were set up in the mid-1970s.

These courts have their own rules, and it is something like an open Confession where everything is exposed to the community. During Easter, in Timbunke village, the councillor and big men met to discuss how best to deal with the young boys who were causing trouble at the hospital. The big men decided they should blow the magic spell around the hospital grounds, and anyone who broke this *tambu*[11] would be punished by the ancestors. The people believe this, and it works. Well one thing leads to another; this year I had some beautiful oranges and the young boys from the village were helping me to eat them, so I decided to put a *tambu,* which was a rope made from dry grass, around the tree. The *tambu* worked until

11 Taboo.

the boys asked me who put it there. When I told him it was me, they were back taking the oranges again because Father's *tambu* had not this power. I am beginning to think, when you live and work with these people for a number of years, one starts to think like them too. Anyway, I had a good laugh at the experience.

While this was an exceptional year for mosquitoes, it was also an unusual one for St. Patrick's Day. I must have received over thirty cards this year. I gave them to the children as they love pictures to look at. I find the Sepik children very interesting and amusing at times. Last week, I watched a four-year-old boy trying to spear a butterfly and no doubt he was learning the art of spear throwing already. With that I will leave you, and I hope you will have a good summer and take care,

April 2, 1986 (after second home leave) I arrived safely in PNG after flying all the way from Cork to Timbunke. As I changed at Heathrow, I met a young man from Belfast. He too was returning after burying his father, and he was returning to South Africa. It seems I am getting used to flying now, as I board one plane after another. I had to wait four days in Wewak for the weather to clear before making the last flight to Timbunke. The village people saw the plane circling the air-strip, and when it finally touched down, there were two or three hundred on the air-strip to welcome me back, including a million mosquitoes. It was like summer had suddenly arrived, when I found myself in the tropics after experiencing one of the coldest Februarys for forty years. Somewhere between the Middle East and Singapore I had to replace my winter clothing with lighter garments, as the heat was beginning to make its presence felt.

When most missionaries return from home leave, they put on weight and the locals were surprised I was just as slim as when I left them four months before. I told them the weather was very cold and that was why I did not put on weight, and I had to sit beside a coal fire to keep myself warm, and I had to wear special winter clothes when going out doors. Now I am back at the main station and trying to put it all together. The pastoral workers and I discussed what had happened while I was away. One of my catechists got fed up after Christmas and left the village because the people were not looking after him. He is now back in his village, while I find out what the real problem was. Another catechist told the people the world was going to end very soon, and now he says they are all coming to church. So, you see they need someone all the time to keep things going in the right direction. With Easter only one week away, there was no time for home sickness or, as the local people say, "home feelings". We made out our Easter plans, and it turned out to be very encouraging to see so many people at the services.

Each village provided its own little incidents during Holy Week. One village gave me one hundred coconuts as an offering, one to represent each person in the village. At another village a young man came up to the altar to light his cigarette from the candle.

When I went to Tambunam village on Easter Sunday, the church was packed, and there was another 200 people standing outside looking in. I was not surprised at this but when I saw a young man with his dog in the arms and both looking in the window, I found it very hard to keep serious.

I made the most of my four months at home. Now that Mam and Dad have said goodbye to the world, I can put my mind at ease, as I was there on both occasions to see them off. The Lord was indeed very good to me, to think I was so far away and yet by their side during their final hour. The nieces and nephews are growing up, and I think most of them will remember me the next time I come home. Goodbye and God bless you for the present.

June 17, 1986 Well, there are lots of interesting things happening here, but nothing really startling. Last weekend a regiment of the Australian army camped at the mission station. They were accompanied by three helicopters and a number of trucks. They had their own doctor, mechanic, and chaplain. They asked me if they could help me in any way. I told them I didn't need the doctor or the chaplain, but if the mechanic could fix the car I would be grateful, which indeed he did. The soldiers were on a training exercise which involved making rafts and taking a trip down the river to test their endurance. It seems the Sepik is one of the best places in the Pacific for such exercises, as solders from Hong Kong, Britain, and Australia are coming here to the Sepik with the last number of years.

A millionaire came ashore one day to see us. He sailed up the Sepik in his 60-foot yacht after sailing from the States via Honolulu and Indonesia. He went ashore at Tambunam village and gave the people watches, shirts, bed sheets, and a number of other small items. He went crocodile hunting one night with the locals. The tourists are fascinated at the idea of crocodile hunting, and they are prepared to pay a good price for a successful hunt. The crocodiles usually surface at night and rest on the sand by the water's edge, and their red eyes can be seen easily by torch light. While the crocodile's attention is focused on the light, another canoe comes from the opposite side and someone grabs the crocodile. The method used to catch the crocodile depends in its size. Before the millionaire continued his journey upriver, he donated thirty dollars to the missions.

I have an interesting story to tell you about one of our Fathers, who over the years had ten cartons of empty beer bottles in his shed. The Father thought he might be giving bad example to his parishioners if they happened to see them, so he decided one night to dump the cartons into the Sepik, thinking no one would see him. About twenty minutes after the deed was done, there was a knock on the door. It was one of the local men with an urgent message. "Father," he said, "I have just seen a man take everything out of your shed and dump it into the river. I came to tell you, so you don't think I did it." Father told him he would check everything in the morning.

During the wet season this year, some youths at Timbunke killed four wild pigs and captured a number of piglets. The wild pigs were stranded on a grass island due to the high water. They cooked and ate the pigs here at the station, as their own village was under water. The young boys were really proud of themselves, and they shared the pork with all the village people, and they did not forget the sisters and the parish priest.

The community schools in the parish are going well this year, even though I often wonder where the education system is leading the children to. These young boys and girls give six years learning English, which is a foreign language to them, and then most of them go back to their villages and feel out of place in their own culture. However, the school does give them a greater scope to travel, and it gives them greater confidence in themselves when they visit other areas or towns.

There are three new churches being built in the parish at present, two from bush material and one permanent church at Yindkum village. There is a nice story attached to this church. The people cut eight posts in the bush for their church. They had the posts at the river bank but there was not enough water in the river to float the posts home. They were discussing what to do when down came the flood. It was raining all the morning in the mountains, and a few hours later the river was swollen, and the posts were in the village that evening. The people really saw the hand of God in this, and it has given them a new interest in building their church.

The parishioners are painting the church at Timbunke, and an old man has carved two posts of Adam and Eve, which are now standing at either side of the entrance. So, you see, a few Irish pounds are being put to good use in the parish. That's all for now. I hope you are in good form and enjoying life wherever you are. God Bless you and take care.

August 14, 1986 Many thanks for your letters, and I am glad to hear you are all well despite the bad spring and the late summer. We are having a long dry season at present, and the road is after drying up as hard as cement, and most of the swamps have dried out. If you were here today, you would not be too impressed with the size of the river. Millions of fish have died as a result of the drought, and by the time the dead fish drift down to Timbunke, they smell worse than any pig slurry. Despite the dry season I am keeping myself busy building the new church at Yindkum village. The building material arrived by road to Timbunke, and I transferred it from there by canoe before the water went down. I arrived in the village a few days later with the intention of doing a good fortnight's work, but the big men in the village had something else on their minds. "We must kill a pig first and have a celebration," they said. I thought it a good idea, the big men sacrificing their best pig for the new church. Two or three hours passed before I asked them "When are you going to kill the pig?" They told me the pig was gone off into the bush and when it returned would kill it.

It was four o'clock when they arrived back with the pig. That evening the pork was dished out to the different families to cook, and that night we sat down in the *house-boy* to celebrate the occasion. Only then was the building of the church ready to roll. The next day men and women came to work at the building, and after ten days we were ready to put on the roof.

My stay in the village helped me to know the people better, especially their names. When I heard one calling the other Peter, then I tried to remember his name. I have got to know a lot of Christian names this way. One night the village held a party to finish the mourning period for the family who had lost a loved one four months previous. The men had let their beards and hair grow during that time, and the women had covered their faces, arms and legs with clay. Before the party or, *Rausim Sori*[12], all the men shaved both their head and beard, there was no variety in hair style all had the same clean cut down to the roots. The women also got the same style of haircut. Then after a good wash in the river, all returned to their homes and dressed up in their best clothes, and this was to mark a new beginning and to get on with their lives once more.

There is a Father's house in this village made from native material. It is a house with one big room, one door. and four windows. There are no chairs, tables, or bed, just an oil stove and whatever food and clothing I bring along. Of course, this time I had a box of tools, and the portable generator to help with the church building.

Every evening, some village children would come to visit me. If I had some extra rice in the pot I would dish it out to them. In the end, the number of children started to increase so much that the rice was limited to those who cleaned the pots. There were lots of minor problems in the village. One woman's rooster was stolen; another man was worried because he could not find his pig. I thought we might have eaten it, but he was satisfied the pig we sacrificed for the church was not his. Others were complaining because it was the same people who were coming to work on the church every day.

After five days working on the church, the people were anxious to go to their gardens to collect some food. I decided to visit two villages which were about one-hour walking distance away. Two young men went with me, as I was going to stay overnight, and I needed my camping gear. On the way back, a young man came jogging along the bush track He knew Father would be on his way back the following day, and he relieved me of my rucksack and mattress. I was impressed at his kindness. What a difference

---

12 The end of a period of grieving (*rausim*, to get rid of).

it makes to be able to walk without twenty or more kilo on your back.

During this time in the bush, an earthquake occurred. I was travelling up a small tributary of the Sepik when the canoe began to swing from side to side. Then I saw the trees bending over and I thought for a moment they would fall over. At that stage everyone was screaming and running for safety, and then it all stopped. When I returned to the main station I discover the cups and plates had fallen off the shelves and several were broken, including the spout of the tea pot. My two book cases had tumbled over; otherwise no real damage was done. The supermarkets in the town suffered most as their displayed goods fell to the ground and were broken or damaged.

Some village houses also collapsed, but the people blamed the builder rather than the earthquake, as earth tremors occur often in PNG. I am sitting in my room now looking out at the Sepik go by. I have put my books back on the shelves, and I have got rid of the spiders in my room that took advantage of my absence for ten days.

I am keeping well, and I hope this letter finds you in good form also. God bless you and take care.

December 1, 1986 (Christmas letter) Another year is coming to an end, and it has brought its own joys, trials, sorrows and hardships. This year, we had one of the longest dry seasons in living memory, while I read in the *Star* that back home experienced its worst flooding in twenty years.

I am still doing a bit of farming in my spare time. The horse I broke is fully trained now. He is a four-year old brown stallion, and he can be easily caught with a few ripe bananas. We have seven horses on the farm. Two are work horses, which help to round up the cattle in the paddocks. The mare has a foal every year, so the number keeps increasing. Jack the old horse is slowing down, and now Bobby will take his place. Simon Kevin, the farm manager, knows how to train horses now, which means he can break in a young colt in his own time.

At this time of year, the people are harvesting their tobacco crop. Most families grow their own tobacco and enjoy smoking it, while the town people feel there is more prestige attached to smoking Cambridge[13]. When I go into the houses, I am met with a piercing smell from the tobacco leaves hanging down from the rafters. It is left there to dry for a few weeks before it is packed neatly away in dry leaves. There is an art in getting the right amount of moisture out of the tobacco leaf, and if it is too dry it has lost its kick, as one native smoker explained.

For the past six days, there is a traditional dance in Timbunke village. It starts at sun- rise and ends at sunset. It is a fertility dance. You could call it a festival, as there is a lot of feasting and dancing going with it. There is also a lot of magic and superstition following it. The big men are blowing the flutes to bring back the voices of the spirits. I thought there would be no one for Mass the following Sunday, but to my surprise there was a big crowd. A few years ago, I asked some people why they don't come to Mass. They said, "We do not hear the *garamut*." To solve the problem, I asked two of the best carvers to make a really big wooden drum. The drum is much louder than the old one, and I am using it since last June, but it has made no difference.

The youth are very active in the parish this year. They painted the roof of the church, organised two sports days, one for the youth in the village, and one for the youth clubs in the area. They also gave two weeks working on the road filling potholes. I am continually filling up the mud holes in the road. If I don't organise it, we cannot get to Wewak by car, and it takes only one bad patch to close the road.

The government has declared all mission air-strips for commercial use. This gives the other airline companies landing rights, whereas before it was a private air-strip. Last week the first twin-engine aircraft landed with twelve elderly tourists on board. I went out to meet them, and the first thing they asked me, where is the office? "There is no office here," I told them, "but if you need the rest room, I will make one available." It seems more and more tourists are coming to the Sepik. Next Friday is a big day for the Diocese as Rudolf Mongali, a local deacon, is being ordained. He will be the sixth local priest in the Diocese. We are all going to it, I mean the church leaders, prayer leaders, sisters, brothers, and anyone who can find transport. There will be a big rush to get there, and then even a

---

13 A brand of cigarettes.

bigger rush to get back. All we need is a fine day, as the celebrations will be outdoors to accommodate the large crowd that is expected to attend.

I will sign off now by wishing you a happy Christmas and God`s blessing for 1987.

March 9, 1987 I had an easy day today. I wrote a few letters while the rain kept belting off the galvanised roof. It is *taim bilong ren*.[14] It is good weather for boating, and I am making the most of it. For instance, in the wet season I can take the canoe right into the village and there is no need to walk through the swamps or marsh land.

Last week, two catechists, two prayer leaders, a seminarian and I went to give a "Better World Retreat" to one of those remote villages. We took the motor canoe as far as we could go, and from there two young men came to collect us in a pull-canoe and paddled us through the small stream that ran between the sago trees. After half an hour, we broke into a clearance, and there stood the village on a small island. Right in the centre of the village stood the spirit house. It was about sixty feet long and forty feet high.

One old man knows the full story of the spirit house, but he was not sure if he should tell me the full story or not, because he says the white man doesn't reveal all his secrets to us. The villagers have built their own church from bush material, in front of the spirit house, and it is hard to distinguish how they understand the difference between the two buildings.

The people looked after us very well, and the retreat went very well. The six of us stayed in a large Sepik house on stilts. Over the main door was a shelf displaying the most precious treasures in the village. They were five skulls. The owner of the house went into great detail telling us all about them. He pointed to the small skull in the middle and said, "My grandfather was the first man to settle on this island, and when he came here, he brought his mother`s skull along with him. The two on the right are my grandparents and the two on the left are their sons." He added, "They are here to protect us from the dangers in the bush, and to ensure the land will be fertile, and that the people here will prosper."

Just to give you a brief history of the mission involvement in this village called Mangajigut: Fr. Laumann was the first missionary to go there in

---

14 Pisin for "rainy season".

1949, then he left in 1952, and it was 1957 before the next priest arrived, and Fr. Wand went there on regular bush trips up to 1974. The next ten years passed, and no priest paid a visit, and still the faith survived, and now they have their own prayer leader and Sunday service. This is not unusual in the remote villages, as the people know Father cannot come for long periods, so they take the lead themselves

Live television has arrived at last in PNG. At the moment it is confined to the capital, Port Moresby, but it is only a matter of months before it reaches the provincial towns. Up to now the church had very little competition in the village, but once TV is here it will be more difficult to get people to attend Mass or to get them to prepare for the sacraments, so one could say there are challenging times ahead of us.

Last month, Fr. Karl Junemann came to Timbunke to help me out at the main station. He is 75 years old, but he can hear Confessions and say Mass for the sisters when I am away in the bush. Fr. Karl gave most of his life in the bush, and he loves talking about all his adventures and the different experiences he encountered during his long life as a missionary.

We are having a general election this year. Polling day starts on the first of June and continues until July 26. I had better finish, especially when politics start coming up, and it's time to turn off the 6KVA generator which is dominating the many variety of night sounds that fill the air. Once again good health and God's blessing to you all,

June 6, 1987 My neighbour Philip Luki has bought a video recorder. It was nine o'clock one night when he called to the parish house to see me. A big crowd had come to see a video, but he could not get it to work. I eventually got it going, and a crowd of 400 sat down to watch the first video set that had come to their village.

A few years ago, I mentioned that another company was in the area searching for oil. They are now at the second stage. Last month, four barges, forty-five metres long and fifteen metres wide, went up the river with all sorts of equipment, including dumpers, dozers, mobile homes containers and cranes. They have set up camp 500 kilometres up the Sepik River, and they hope to confirm in a few months' time if there is oil there or not. At present the oil company is of no advantage to the area. They pass up and down the river in their boats. The captain uses his loudspeaker to tell the locals to keep out of their way, and the locals get furious at this. That's what development brings with it. The little native canoes will have to give way to the larger vessels.

My neighbouring parish downriver had a farewell party for Fr. Rudi Breyer. He was parish priest there for ten years, and to show their appreciation for his hard work in building up the community, the locals displayed one of their best traditional *singsings*.

Over fifty women in two large canoes went upriver to begin the celebration. Then they came drifting down singing one of their love songs to the beat of drums, and with the same rhythm they scooped up water with their paddles to splash Fr. Rudi, who was sitting between the canoes in his speed boat. As they came in sight of the entrance to the village, the men came forward and stepped into the water. For five minutes they danced there, and they kept striking the water, which created loud splashes and sent water in all directions. There wasn't a dry body among the crowd, as everyone had taken part in the water dance. The sun shone beautifully, and everyone was happy. The drums and the songs went on till daybreak the following morning.

I had a bit of bad luck after Christmas when my canoe turned over after hitting a log. I had my belongings packed well in rucksacks and they floated down river. We recovered it all, but the books and food were all destroyed, and as regards clothing and sleeping gear, the locals gave us everything we needed. The following day we returned to the station to dry things out.

It is the middle of the coffee season in the Highlands. The peak of the harvest is known as the coffee-flush. The country produces around 50,000 tons annually. For most highland villages, coffee is the main source of their income. And strangely enough, coffee has not caught on as a popular drink among the PNG people.

Last year, the country exported thirty-five tons of gold, and it is expected to double that by the year 1992. I was in Hagen town recently, and it is hard to believe how it has developed since Fr. Ross walked in there fifty-three years ago. The town was full of people, and it was hard to get a parking space for the car, and now with the gold deposits so promising, it seems the country will develop even faster.

I will sign off for now, and I hope this letter finds you in good form. God bless and take care.

September 14, 1987 It seems a long time since I heard from you. There should be a few letters and papers waiting for me by now in Wewak. Our elections went off reasonably peaceful last month. There were some disappointed supporters who caused a bit of trouble, but the police were able to control it. My neighbour Philip Luki was re-elected. I was pleased with the decision, as he is a good supporter of the Church, and he will help us to maintain the road between Timbunke and Wewak.

We had another long dry season this year. It was very hard to see all the cattle with no grass, and they were going into the swamps to find water. Some weaker ones got stuck in the mud, and Simon Kevin, the farm manager, had to pull them out with the tractor. Twenty-two schools in the diocese were closed because of no water. The heat was fierce, and there were bush fires everywhere; even the roots of the grass went on fire. We had plenty Sepik water for washing, and the rain water we had stored in tanks during the wet season was used sparingly for drinking.

I happened to be giving a retreat with my team at a village called Boru, when the people told me they had arranged to burn their grassland on the coming Thursday, and I must put off the retreat for one day and join them in the hunt for wild pigs and bush rats, and so I did. It was about 10am when the young men began to light a ring of fire around a large patch of grass land and trap the wild pigs inside. The fire burned for over two hours and every now and then a small creature like a rat used to jump out of the fire, and whoever was the nearest chased and killed it. It wasn't until the last ten minutes that the hunt really got into action. About 200 men and women armed with knives and spears, and at least a hundred dogs were waiting for the wild pigs to make a bolt out through the flames. Then one pig came chasing out, but when he heard the shouting he ran back into the fire again and went out at the other side to be speared to death in less than a minute. He was followed by another and another, and all met the same fate. Then several pigs made the last charge for their lives and at least ten of them escaped, but the people were happy they had killed four pigs and several hundred bush rats. I even saw one woman with a grass snake hanging out of her string bag. It was a very interesting hunt, and it was obvious they were not in it for the sport but for survival reasons; they needed some meat, and this was their traditional way to find it.

I am at present in a village called Tambunam, giving the same retreat. This is the sixth retreat this year. We started on Monday night and finished on Friday evening with a meal for all who took part. The meal varied between crocodile, wild pig, bush rat, cow, fowl, fish. and the Sepik dayfly. I think it would be hard to do better than that in West Cork.

British Petroleum have pulled out of the Sepik after three years' research work. The rumour is they found no oil, only salt water. They are now selling off their property, which includes cars and videos. The river will be back to normal again—no big barges or supply ships going up and down the river, at least for the time being.

You may have heard in the world news of the large deposit of gold found in PNG, and the locals are wasting no time in helping themselves. Last May, there was a highlander who walked into the bank in his traditional dress with two coffee jars of gold valued at 20,000 US Dollars. The bank manager called him into his office and told him he would reinvest his money, which he agreed, but he wasn't going to tell him where he found the gold.

For the last ten years, we were planning to build a new church in the village of Kowit, but now the village is moving to another area, because they believe the place is haunted. We had the posts ready to stand, when for some unknown reason the man who carved the posts died. Then his son died, and this was followed by three more deaths in the clan. The people believe if they stay there, they will all die. It is probably bad drinking water that is the cause of the deaths, but the people see it as a sign to move out.

On July 21 I took a trip down the Sepik, and then I went up the Biwat river to visit my neighbouring priest, Fr. Michael Fiedel. The bishop was opening a new health centre in his parish. The health centre is run by the Catholic agency, so I felt it was better to give it my support by being present at the opening. They had the usual celebrations. Eighteen villages took part in a traditional *singsing*, which was followed by a meal for the invited guests. The celebrations ended before night fell, as there was rumours a fight was brewing among the different clans, and we all moved off quietly to avoid any such conflicts.

I will sign off now, so God bless you once again from this side of the globe.

November 14, 1987 Christmas is approaching fast, and I had better start writing a few letters before I make my last bush trip of the year. At the moment I have an anthropologist and his wife staying with me at Timbunke. He was here twenty years ago, and he has come back to do further studies. He will be travelling around the middle Sepik for the next five months. On Monday, three Irish sisters are also arriving at Timbunke. They want to see the Sepik and its people while they are in PNG.

We had our family feast last week in Wewak. Over forty-five priests and brothers from the Society came together at our head-quarters in Wirui. We played some games of volleyball, and afterwards we had a good evening meal. We have this gathering once a year, and it gives us a chance to meet each other and compare life at the different stations. Most of our priests and brothers who went on home leave have returned, and a few of them are appointed to new parishes. I expect to be here in Timbunke for another five years, please God. I like it here; we have the farm, tourists, carving buyers, crocodile buyers, and a number of interesting travellers every year, and they all give the place a bit of variety.

Last week, some of my best Catholics were involved in a fight with a neighbouring village. It was a land dispute which has been going on for a long time, and this week two other villages started another fight; again, the dispute was over land. Land disputes occur on a regular basis as there are no proper boundaries. The people have only their ancestral stories to go by, and they have new stories to claim the land. The people are realizing the value of land, and they need cash crops to provide money to buy essential goods.

There is another traditional celebration going on at Timbunke village. It is something like our month of November for All Souls. Once every four or five years, each clan remembers their dead. Last year a different clan had theirs, so the "Pig Clan" are holding theirs right now. It is very interesting: the man who knew the deceased person recalls the dead person's life story, how many children he had, and who his wife was, what he died from, where he hunted, what his skills were, and where he lived all his life, who were his ancestors and where he is buried, and why he is buried in such a place. Then others who knew the dead person will fill in other good qualities he or she had. In this way, the story of his life is kept alive and passed on from one generation to the next. When this part of the celebration was complete, a number of pigs are killed, and finally the spirits of their ancestors were sent to their eternal resting place. I also sat and listened to their stories, as one speaker after another stood up to talk. It did not make much sense to me until one of the locals explained what was going on.

It is important to have a knowledge of the people and their culture if one is to work with them. It is amazing the things the people remember when they start talking. I was walking into a village a few months ago, and before I came to the village there was a sago swamp. To get from one side of the swamp to the other, you must walk on top on a home-made bridge made from hundreds of logs all lined up one after another. When I make this trip, I have to carry two long sticks, one in each hand, and this is the only way I can keep my balance on these logs. When we came to a bad spot in the swamp the people told me, "That is where Br. Terry fell down." I asked Br. Terry about the incident afterwards, and he said, "Do they still remember that? It happened over ten years ago." Once I had to crawl on my hands and knees to cross a bridge, and the elders in the village still ask me if I still do that when I cross the river to their place. I hope you will have a nice Christmas, and many thanks for the letters and papers which arrived over the year.

January 4, 1988 It is January the fourth and we have been on the road for the last five weeks. My helper, Luke Ming, who was also my driver and cook, accompanied me for most of the trips. He is a good fellow, but he loves speed, and I have to check him when overtaking small canoes or approaching sharp bends on the river.

Our first Christmas round was to the Chambri Lakes, where over 1,200 Catholics live in bush homes, all built along the edge of the mountain overlooking the lake. It was a pleasant trip as we made our way through the swampland and the water lilies. Around every corner, hundreds of water birds took to the air as the sound of the motor gave warning to clear the waterways. The first stop was at a village called Aibom, and it wasn't for pastoral reasons. We had a lot of mail for Professor Dr. Schuster and his wife, who are doing research work in the area, and they had every reason to smile when I told them what was in the bag. After a few brief words, they asked me to join them for a cup of coffee. I nodded to my driver to come along, and I hoped that the Professor`s wife did not regret taking out the tin of biscuits which had just arrived in the post from her mother in Switzerland.

Even though the company and the refreshments were nice, time was against us, as we had to reach the out-station before night. There were scores of happy children taking their evening bath along the shore when we arrived, and every splash and scream and laughter showed they were happy to be alive. Luke pulled ashore straight opposite the Father`s house and several brown bodies, mostly school children, offered their assistance to carry the cargo up the hill to the house. There was a scramble as to who would take the rucksack. It seems there is something manly about having such a sack on your back. There was confusion when it came to the box with the food supplies. That one was heavy, and only real men could carry it. It was also rat-proof and there was no doubt a few families of those four-legged creatures would be anxious to test it out or take advantage if one of us forgot to close it. The spiders had also taken up residence since my last stay three months ago. I have promised to do up the house for next Christmas and paint the outside yellow or "Kerrygold". I lit the Coleman lamp so there was no need to put on the door, "Father is home"; the light on the hill-top said it all. The Deacon and the pastoral workers were among the first to arrive, and we drew up a Christmas programme for the area. The following week, we visited all the Christmas communities, staying overnight in each one and moving on by boat to the next village until we completed the circle of the Chambri Lakes.

Since then, a new Polish priest has arrived in Timbunke. His name is Fr. Janusz Skotniczny. He has a master's degree in moral theology, and I am told he has a pilot`s licence for hang-gliding. I hope to give him his diploma for navigating the Sepik after twelve months. Now there are three priests in Timbunke. Fr. Karl Junemann came last year, and he stays at the main station. He keeps the station nice and clean and he keeps the house from turning into a mechanic shop. If you ever had the experience of fixing your bicycle in the kitchen, well, it is like that here some nights when I start working on the outboard motor. Fr. Karl was a medical soldier during the last world war and a prisoner of war for two months. He has vivid memories of the war and talks about it nearly every day, and he ends by saying, "Thank God, I never killed anyone."

I was comparing my pastoral diary with that of 1986, and I discovered I made five visits to most of the remote villages in 1987, and only four in 1986, so you see it helps to have Fr. Karl staying at the main station.

It's always hard to predict what the New Year will bring, but we do have a pastoral plan, and we hope to keep on giving the "Better World Retreat" to the rest of the villages for the coming year. Our parish team is very experienced now in giving such retreats, and I hope to keep them together for another year. That is all for now. God bless you and take care.

March 15, 1988 We have started our new school year once again. The first thing the parents and children must do on the first day at school is to cut the grass. The grass is always a problem as it grows so fast and there is always the danger of a child walking on a snake if the grass is not cut. Work has begun on our new road to Wewak. Twelve tipper trucks are dumping coral into the holes. The road is always one of our biggest worries during the wet season. Now it should be all right for another year.

I had my fortieth birthday too last year. The school children gave me a flower each and the headmaster gave me a rooster to celebrate the occasion. Bishop Arkfeld celebrated his seventy-sixth birthday last month. I happened to be talking to the bishop when one of the Fathers said to him, "I pray for you today that you live as long as your mother." The bishop told him not to pray any more. His mother was 98 when she died. Of course, he was only joking.

I told you last year how we were getting a hovercraft for the Sepik. Well the hovercraft has been assembled and tried out, but it is not practical for the river. In order to get it to lift, it has to travel at sixty kilometres per hour, and at that speed it takes half a mile to stop it, so it is too dangerous for the river, and besides, it would need a mechanic to keep it going. The country is full of new ideas, many of them foreign, and not practical just yet.

One of my good Catholics fell off a tree just before Christmas and died. He was deaf and dumb. I met him one day, and he was badly dressed so I decided to give him some second-hand clothes. From then he was always my best helper to carry my rucksack when I had to walk through the swamps. I called him *Amamas*, which means "happy" in Pidgin, because he was always smiling. I went to put a flower on his grave, but it was covered with water as it was the wet season, and the whole village was under water.

Sometimes, when I go to a village there is a young person dying or sick for days, and the whole village spends days deciding what is best to do. They think the person might get better if given more time or he might die, and it would be best if he died in the village. If the person is taken to hospital and dies there, then the whole village must agree to pay to bring back the body. You see, it is very difficult and expensive in the tropics to transport a corpse.

One night an elderly man knocked on the door, and he asked if I could help him. I said, "If I can at all I will." Then he handed me a two-*kina* note, local money, and asked me to work sorcery on the person who stole his pig. I thought for a moment about how I could get out of this one. I asked him, "Are you sure the pig was stolen? Maybe the pig got drowned in the swamps or has gone off with some wild pigs in the bush." He said he had searched the swamps and he did not see or smell anything and added that the pig was neutered, so he would not be in the bush. I asked him, "Would a crocodile have grabbed him?", but the man was convinced the pig was stolen and he knew the man that did it. In the end, I handed him back his two *kina* and told him I will pray for him. I discovered that night, this man was one of the chief sorcery makers in the village. He needed my prayers to make his work more effective. It is not surprising that these problems come up in a culture full of superstition and magic.

I will sign off here. Take care and God bless you.

April 10, 1988 I went to Kapamari parish for Holy Week, and Fr. Karl stayed here at Timbunke. Kapamari is a vacant parish looked after from Timbunke. Fr. Ben Jansen built the mission station, and at the moment the buildings are not in a very healthy-looking state. However, there are some very good Catholic villages in the parish, which goes to show buildings don't really matter. Kamanabit is one of the biggest villages in the parish. I went there for Holy Thursday. The first thing I had to do on arrival was to cover myself in mosquito repellent, and that was followed by three hours of Confession. Most people had arrived by then, and we started Mass at 4pm.

The church leader announced the previous Sunday that there would be a *bung kaikai*[15] after Mass, on Holy Thursday. After Mass all the food was brought to the side of the altar and blessed. The church leader stood up and told the congregation, about 200 of them, that if people had not brought something to eat they should leave. I felt it was like dividing the sheep from the goats, and I was just after preaching on how we must love one another as Christ loved us. Then those who were eligible to eat sat down on logs arranged for the occasion. The meal was typically Sepik: fish and sago, and not one person used a knife and fork. Then it was out to the Sepik to wash our hands, and the dogs were left to fuss around in the grass to pick up the pieces. We seemed to be a happy people lost in our own world as we sat and talked about the guys we all knew. On Good Friday, it was off to a village called Palembai. This is one of the well-known villages on the Sepik. The *Melanesian Explorer* had just arrived before me with eighteen tourists. Like most tourists on the Sepik, they had video cameras and cameras hanging from their necks. They were taking pictures for two hours of everything that moved, but the locals were more interested in trying to sell their carvings and string bags.

Fr. Adam, who is now in the Amboin area, told me he had a different experience with the tourists. He was preparing the Good Friday service when three river-trucks of tourists arrived. The locals told them, "Today is Good Friday, and we will not perform a traditional singing for you today." The tourists were very disappointed, but it was good for them to know that these people take their religious practice seriously. Tourists are getting very plentiful in the Sepik area. They are fascinated with these traditional places as unspoiled by modern civilization as they will ever see. It is the craze now to buy a pull-canoe in the Upper Sepik and paddle it down to Timbunke. The parish board is involved in a small way in providing lodging for them. The parish also supplies the Wewak Hotel,

---

15 A meal.

Windjammer Hotel, and BP with bags of lemons. The lemon trees were planted by lay missionaries on Timbunke Farm. It is one of the few fruits the locals don't eat.

At this time, we have some trouble in the diocese with the traditional landowners of Kaindi teachers' training college. The landowners are demanding a million *kina* compensation for the land. The Mercy Sisters and the Christian Brothers were ordered out last Christmas. The college was allowed by the landowners to reopen again, but only for six months if the demands were not met. The matter is now in the hands of the government.

The Charismatic Movement has also caused a few worries in the Diocese. It started off very well, but as it progressed it got caught up in traditional customs, and now we are worried because there is a danger of splinter groups starting up. It is not an easy job to be bishop these days, so do keep him in your prayers.

I am keeping well, I have taken up jogging again. I exercise up and down the air-strip two or three mornings a week, and I can feel the difference when I am out on bush patrol, as I am able to keep up with the elderly ones. Bye for now.

July 11, 1988 Today is Monday, and it is Laundry Day at Timbunke. The generator is on full-blast to drive the washing machine. I usually take Monday off from pastoral activities. I do some manual work, like cleaning up the station, or fixing an outboard motor or going out to the farm to see the cattle and horses. Today, I am going to break my routine and write a few letters instead. You know, I always found writing letters relaxing, and it was the same in the seminary. When I could do nothing else, I could write letters, so you see I have not changed much since those days.

We have just come to the end of a long mosquito season. The people say it was the worst they remember. I used repellent and Aerogard, but it was of little use. The locals used smoke fire under their houses, and it was more effective. Dry grass was heaped up on smouldering logs, and it produced a cloud of smoke. Everything I use for the bush trips has turned brown from the smoke.

The River Sepik is not so kind to some of its dwellers. The river keeps breaking its banks and changing its direction, and those villages in its new course must move their houses, which is a lot of hard work. Kamanabit is one such village. The river keeps breaking away the ground every year until it broke through to create a new course. Five years ago, we moved back the church, and now the community school has been moved back to a new position. I stayed five days in Kamanabit last month, and I found a great community spirit among the people. The young men were digging out the posts of a house that was about to fall into the water. The girls were giving a hand with the lighter work, and the mothers were doing the cooking. It reminded me of the thrashing at home, when all the neighbours came to give a hand to thrash the corn. The elders in the village told me the ground they were living on now was once a swamp, and over the years the river filled it up with silt when it was in flood.

During the dry season the river banks are very good for gardens, and the people like to live close to the river where they have plenty water all the year round, and they also go out fishing every day, so the water is their life. The people have a saying here, in pidgin, "*Sepik I bosim mipela.*" It means our lives are ruled by the river or we depend on the river for everything. The locals plant watermelons, tobacco, and crops that take about three months to grow. These crops will be harvested before the water comes back again. The watermelon only takes three months to grow, and there is nothing better to eat than a ripe watermelon after a long journey in the hot sun.

You may be wondering what goes through my mind when I set out on those long trips to the out-stations. The first worries always are: have I everything I need, is the motor all right or will it rain? As you can see, there is always a bit of anxiety taking off to make sure everything is in order.

After all that, the boat trip can be a pleasant one. On occasions, I come across some very interesting scenes. It may be an anxious mother duck chasing her young ones to safety if the boat is too close, or it may be a family of young gulls perched on a floating log taking a trip down river. They seem to be telling me take life easy and take a day off like us. Further up the river there is a family staying in a bush house, and when the old lady of the house hears the motor coming she is out to the water edge to give me some smoked fish. She is a pleasant old lady, and she always asks me to do something for her, like take fish to the next village, or could I give her some malaria tablets. I think of this bush house as my roadside restaurant. It's a place to pull in and take out my flask and have a cup of coffee and a few smoked fish. I don't think this will always be the case, as the Sepik is attracting a lot of tourists, and there are three tourist lodges already in the Middle Sepik. To stay in the Karawai lodge, which is the most famous of the three lodges, costs over 100 US dollars a night, and I can see it all for nothing. I have received my reward a hundred-fold already. I will close off here by wishing you well, and God bless you all.

July 25, 1988 We had a change of government three weeks ago. There was a vote of no confidence in the government and it carried fifty-eight votes to fifty. Next week the highland show is taking place in Hagen town. This traditional show attracts a lot of tourists from overseas, as it is a good opportunity to see some of PNG's best-preserved cultures. These tourists that arrive early are now travelling around the Sepik, and I expect it will be the same after the show for those who arrive late. I was out all last week in a village called Aibom near the Chambri Lakes. I often call to this village, but never stay more than a day. The houses are built around the foot of the mountain, and apart from this mountain the rest of the area is swamps and lagoons. It is in these waters that the people catch their fish and hunt for crocodiles. Now that it is the dry season, they are able to catch plenty fish in the shallow waters, and the men are out hunting crocodiles every night.

This village sold over 800 crocodile-skins last year, and last week alone they killed over forty. I saw one happy hunter sitting up on a large tree and beside him three large skins hanging out on a branch to dry in the sun, and at the same time he was on guard in case the ravens would come and pick holes in the skins. When I think of this village, I think of eternity, as there are large stones sitting deep in the ground, and they are about twenty feet high. When I see the children sitting on top of them they look like a nest of birds ready to fly for the first time. Aibom would be known more in the area for its clay pottery. It has a clay suitable for making all sorts of cooking pots and stoves which are still widely used by the Sepik women today.

There are many social problems in the villages. Scores of young men are going to the towns to find work, and the young girls who remain are finding themselves with no other choice but to become a second or third wife to the men left behind.

Drink is also a big problem. Many villages are turning to drinking spirits boiled in milk, as they cannot afford to buy beer or strong drinks. I have told them several times it is poison, and it will kill you; I even told them how they will die. They said, "No, Father, we know how to mix it, and those who have died did not know how to drink it." One day when I saw the pot sitting on top of the fire wood and one of the elders watching it boil, I thought of the play *Macbeth* and the witches, and the line, "Double, double toil and trouble, fire burn and caldron bubble."

I am back again in Timbunke and I am taking it easy for a few days. I am trying to start a parish youth movement here and I have bought two soccer balls, a volleyball, and a net. I cut the playing field and the volleyball court. I saw a group of children playing volleyball over a clothes line and for a ball they had filled a rice bag full of grass, so I thought it was time to give them the real thing.

On August 5, two Irish visitors, Pat and Claver Ryan, are coming to visit me. They are here doing voluntary work at an agriculture training centre in the West Sepik province. They have heard how I am looking after a large cattle farm, and we have agreed to exchange two bulls next year. The farm is going very well to everyone's surprise. The big danger at this time of year is bush fires, with the grass so dry one match could burn the whole lot. To avoid this, the workers burn off a few acres every week during the wet season, so the cows will always have new grass.

Speaking about cows, one very respectable gentleman comes to Mass on Sundays with a cow's tail in his hand. He uses it to keep away the mosquitoes. It looks very funny, but the people take no notice of it. Most people use a broom to kill the mosquitos or smoke fires to keep them away. On days when the mosquitoes are very bad, we light fires in clay stoves and put them in the church to create a smoke screen. The worst time for mosquitoes is at dusk, so we don't hold any services outdoors in the evening. I will sign off for now. God Bless you, take care.

January 1, 1988 The great feast of Christmas is over. And I hope you had a holy and happy one. Thanks again for writing about the more human side of Christmas with news and views from the homeland.

I finished off the Christmas celebrations on January 1, or you could say I started the New Year with seventeen marriages at Tambunam village. It was a beautiful morning to get married, and what was more beautiful was to see the brides arriving in their canoes across the river. Fr. Don Grant came upriver to assist me, as over forty couples were receiving marriage instruction, and I was expecting most of them to turn up. I knew most of these couples; some had grown up into men and women since I first came here. It was encouraging to see their young faces full of hope and confidence. I had a box of wedding rings, large, medium, and small. The rings created a bit of confusion when they tried to find the right size ring for the right size finger. Fr. Don blessed the marriages while I tried to keep the pairs in order. At the end of Mass, we wished them every good luck and blessing, and they went back to their homes in their pull-canoes for better or for worse.

On Sunday, November 26, Marienberg parish celebrated its diamond jubilee. This parish is in the Lower Sepik, and it was once the headquarters of the Wewak Diocese. The new road called the Sepik Highway has changed this situation now. The celebration began last July with the procession of a statue of our Lady from one station to another. On the morning of the jubilee, the statue arrived back at Marienberg after a three-hour procession on the river. A thousand people in boats and canoes followed it to Marienberg. This was something special, to see the procession moving at walking pace. Modern and traditional hymns were sung along the way. People from the out-stations were gathered at Marienberg for two days to meet the procession, and once it arrived you could feel that these people had a great sense of devotion and respect for Our Lady. There were no candles or religious stalls to be seen, but it had all the atmosphere of a believing community.

It was our turn at Timbunke to celebrate on December 4. The bishop was coming to give Confirmation at an out-station called Yindkum, and he was also to bless their new church. The biggest worry was how to get the bishop to this village in the bush. We arranged that a small motor canoe would take him over the swamps, as it would be easy to pull it through the grass if the channel was blocked with floating islands. The next stage was going through the sago swamps. A large canoe was needed and a four-horsepower motor and a few young men who were familiar with the area. This was a fast-flowing river and several sharp bends make it difficult to navigate. After all these precautions, we arrived safely. The locals had lined up along the inlet to the village and four strong men carried the bishop shoulder-high in a cane chair through the village. The locals sang and danced till dark just as if they were welcoming their own chief. I helped the bishop to make his bed and he helped me to make mine. I was complimenting myself for not forgetting anything.

Sunday morning came, and the people from the five neighbouring villages began to congregate. Some took the occasion to visit their cousins or their in-laws. The Mangajigut people took the opportunity to invite the bishop to see their village, so after all the celebrations and goodbyes at Yindkum it was down to the end of the village and into a waiting canoe to take us to this village.

There are no roads or rivers going to this village, just sago swamps. Three young men helped to paddle our means of transport through the sago trees, and it was a welcome break from the heat of the day as we moved through the green tunnel of sago palms trees. I have been down this water channel several times, and I would still get lost taking this route to the village. On the way, Bishop Ray Kalisz kept the conversation going by asking questions about different types of sago, and the locals were only too glad to point out the wild sago trees from the sago trees used for making commercial sago. They showed us the track of the wild pig, the baskets for catching crabs and the different waterways going through the swamps. Every ten or fifteen minutes we used to break into sunlight and then back into thick sago jungle again. I was wondering if the conversation would change when we came to a large rain tree. I always see this tree as a landmark. There is supposed to be a Japanese soldier buried there. Some say he died of malaria, and other say the locals poisoned him. I think the men in the canoe were waiting for me to bring up the subject. Anyway, I remained silent as I had heard the story so many times before, and the life and death of the Japanese solder was not touched upon. We must have been forty minutes sitting in the canoe, when one of the oarsmen called out to announce our coming, and at once the village drums began to beat, sending vibrations through the forest. Five minutes later we came to a clearance, and there it was, a neat little village with its hundred or more inhabitants. We stayed one hour in the village, listening to their worries, and then there was the long procession of people carrying baskets of sago out to our canoe as gifts for the bishop and myself. From here, it was another thirty minutes to reach our large motor canoe, which was waiting for us at the mouth of the creek.

The following week it was my turn to be chief. The leaders of the Chambri Parish had asked me to bless their Spirit House, which they had just completed. I was surprised and happy they had asked me to do this. I asked Fr. Karl, who is thirty-eight years in PNG, what he thought about this. He was not too happy. But I have blessed their marriages, baptised their children, heard their worries, so I went ahead and blessed their Spirit House.

The whole village had dressed up in their traditional attire for the occasion. They sang songs and danced to the sound of hand drums. It was their world as they knew it from their ancestors. The Spirit House would no longer be used for ancestor worship, but as a tourist attraction and as a historical monument of their culture.

It was a year of challenges with its up and downs, but its ups far exceeded the downs. The mission station at Kapamari was completely demolished last year. It was not a natural disaster, but a human misunderstanding. The station had no priest for almost two years. I was making a pastoral trip around the parish three or four times a year. During this time most of the items at the station were stolen, so I stayed in the village with the people. In the meantime, Bishop Ray told me to take one house down to Kamanabit village and build a Father's house there. The Kamanabit people did this, and a nice two- bedroom house is just complete. Seeing this, the surrounding villages felt they should also have a church, or a house built from the material from the station. So. the locals decided to take down the buildings and take the material back to their village and build a permanent church. Two villages, Karaua and Palembai, have built two churches since with the material.

Several people ask me when would I be going on home leave? I think next year at the latest, So goodbye, good health and a happy New Year.

February 25, 1989 I am here in Ulga Parish with Fr. John McCarthy for two weeks holiday. Fr. John was appointed here four months ago. It is like the Irish climate, with fog covering the hills in the morning and plenty of rain in the afternoon. It is a beautiful place for gardens and flowers. Fr. John's predecessor must have made the most of it, because the grounds around the parish house are surrounded with bananas trees and dahlias.

Last Wednesday was a big day for the Highlanders, as they had their first local bishop ordained for the Goroka Diocese. There were three or four hundred people there from Wewak, along with priests and sisters. We all knew Fr. Michael Marai (the new bishop) as he had worked on the pastoral team in the Wewak Diocese for seven years. During that time he had given retreats to most of the parishes in the Diocese and he had become well known.

Goroka is only three hours' drive from Ulga, which meant we drove down and back on the same day. We made an early start, and we had the road to ourselves for the first hour, but after that the countryside was beginning to move. The children were starting out for school, the women were going to their gardens with their pigs on a lead. There were pigs following their owners along the highway, and there were pigs walking about at random completely indifferent to the rules of the road. These creatures forced us to a sudden stop several times. It seems the pig has held on to his traditional rights in this area of PNG.

Goroka was full of life and activity when we arrived. The police were directing the traffic at the entrance to Kefamo where the celebration was held. The locals were busy changing from their everyday clothes into their traditional dress. Groups of highlanders were painting faces and they were making every effort that it would turn out right.

In the main building there were 110 priests and sixteen bishops vesting for Mass. The procession began through the Kefamo grounds, and the locals lined along the rough, the women on one side and the men on the other side with their spears and bows and arrows. Bishop Leo Arkfeld was the main celebrant, and who deserved it more than the 77-year-old bishop who has given his life on the missions, and now he has lived to see one of his own parishioners raised to bishop.

Bishop Leo is still flying his plane. There is no one to tell him when to stop flying and why should they? No one knows more about flying and planes than he does. His plane is to him like a bicycle is to a postman.

Last month we were returning from Wewak to Timbunke when we came across the unexpected. We were held up by masked men and robbed of our personal belongings. We were about one hour out from Wewak when there was a tree across the road. Two men armed with an axe and bush knife surrounded the car. We ran off and gave them everything. We later returned to the car with a group of men from the nearby village. The car and the cargo were not touched. They were after money. They thought I was carrying the payroll for the middle Sepik area. I had the usual cargo, which included a sack of brown and white flower, a bale of sugar, a gas bottle, fuel for the out- board motor, five boxes of medicine for the hospital, a new lawnmower, and house hold goods. Sr. Ancila and her niece were sitting in the front of the car with me and Alphones, a clerical student, and a nurse were sitting on the back. They also lost some of their belongings.

I have never told you about Alphones Saun from Timbunke who hopes to be ordained in three years' time. I was a new priest in Timbunke when Alphones knocked on the door one morning about half past six. He said he wanted to see me, and he thought this was the best time to catch me inside. I was about to say my Office, and I did not want to see anyone. Anyway, I thought I could get rid of him after a few moments and carry on from where I was. He took a chair and after a while he said, "Father, I want to become a priest."

I looked at him and saw his shaved head, and said, "I never saw you before, not even at Mass."

"That's right, Father," he said. "It was only yesterday I was released from jail."

I paused for a while to listen to his story. He told me he attended highschool where four other students decided to rob the school safe. They were caught, and each sentenced to one year. I told him I would see the vocation director and to call back in a few weeks' time. The vocation director told me that Alphones should work one year in a parish and that he would consider his application for the priesthood after that. That is seven years ago now and Alphones is still persevering. He stays with me during his holidays and helps out in the parish. All going well, he will be ordained in three years' time. Last year, our Society ordained 117 new priests for the missions. Most of these came from Poland, India, Indonesia, and the Philippines. We must give thanks to the Lord for this great blessing.

Some time ago I went down river to see my neighbour, Fr. Don Grant. On my way, I saw a large crocodile lying on the sand. Just around the bend of the river were several village children playing in the water, and when I told them about the crocodile, they said, "She has a nest in the grass beside the water, and she comes out to wash herself every evening." Recently I had to return from one of my bush trips as the swamps were drying up. We spent three hours digging a channel through the mud when some local people came along in a small canoe. They had pulled their canoe over the mud, and they told us to give up and wait until the rains come. The driver and I did not argue. We took their advice and turned back for home.

Regards to all and take care.

March 27, 1989 Now it is Easter Monday, and I am taking the day off to write a few letters. Holy Week went very nice. We were lucky with the weather and the mosquitoes also gave us a break. They missed out this year due to Easter being so early.

My workman, Bernard Bowie, is the father of a new baby boy. The last time I went to Wewak he asked me to buy a half dozen baby nappies for him. This is one of the jobs I get from the workers when I go to town. One Deacon has nine children and another Deacon eleven, while the catechists and manual workers average five between them. The girls in the supermarket see me coming and they start kidding me. You see, they know I am a priest, and I end up doing these down-to-earth jobs buying nappies for the new arrivals on the mission station.

Let me tell you something down to earth. While I was preparing supper one night in the village, two women were engaged in a verbal argument. It was insult for insult back and forth. The other members of the community kept their distance, but they listened to every word. The whole thing was sort of funny, but no one laughed. The next morning the two women were before the village magistrate. Most of the village were present and anyone could ask questions, and everyone involved was a judge. The magistrate was a real practical village man. During the court, he kept swinging his medal around in his hand, and he asked very down-to-earth questions. It turned out that one woman did not want the other woman to marry her brother. When a verdict was reached the two women exchanged coconuts and peace was restored. You could still see the signs of fury on their faces from the night before.

The opposite happens in a village sometimes, where it is impossible to start a conversation of any kind. I remember once trying to get a conversation going. I told them where I was the last two days and where I was going after this. Then I asked them if the dog lying by the fire was a good hunting dog, but even that question failed this time. It is hard to blame them as they have very little communication with the outside world.

You know, we have about fifty dogs that come to Mass every Sunday, and once the church bell rings the dogs go into a howling session. Apart from that, they don't cause much trouble.

A prayer leader and I went by car to an out-station to say Mass just before Holy Week, and on our way home we got stuck in a mud hole. We tried everything to get out. We even had spades and a bush knife, as this is part of our everyday experience. Then I told the prayer leader, Anton Tar, to go back to the village to get help. It was a tall order as it was an hour's walk both ways. No sooner had Anton gone when a group of schoolchildren came along full of life and vigour to help me. I told them they were too weak, and I needed some strong men as the car was down to the door in mud and water. The children were so anxious to help I thought it best not to disappoint them. Without any inhibitions they all stripped off and they got into the mud and water. They got around the car like a swarm of ants. I started up the car, and the four wheel-drive sprayed mud all over them. They kept pushing and shouting as if it was a toy car, and to my surprise they pushed me out with a great cheer of delight. While I was thanking God to be out of the hole, the children washed and played in a nearby stream before dressing up for the journey home. I still had to wait for Anton Tar to return.

Last February, I went to see Pat and Claver Ryan, two volunteers from Tipperary sent out here by Gorta. I knew Claver in Maynooth for three years, and it was a great surprise to see her here in PNG. They showed me around the farm. I saw the cows and the calves, the ducks and the geese, the hens and the guinea fowl. They kept up the good old Irish tradition by giving me two ducks and a drake. The ducks have settled into their new home on the Sepik. Claver and Pat enjoyed themselves here, and they did great work with the local people. So, from me, God Bless and take care

January 8, 1990 Another year has passed, so has another decade come to an end. We are all in good form after Christmas. It was nothing extraordinary, just simple and peaceful. The prayer groups decorated the church, and the school children cut the grass before they broke up for their Christmas holidays, and I was out on the highways and byways.

This year the weather was beautiful and dry, but much too dry for boating, as the swamps and the channels were dried up and several villages had no Father to visit them this year. I even doubt if Father Christmas got to these villages this year. This is where the prayer leaders take over when no priest can visit their place, and they can conduct the Christmas services quite well. I was up in the Chambri Lakes for the month of October giving retreats to the Christian communities. It was beautiful up there in those remote villages hidden between the mountains, and away from the modern world. The villages we stayed in have no school yet, but they hope to open a Catholic school there in a few years' time. I stayed in a large family house with three families living in it. At one stage, I counted fourteen children and two babies sitting around me. I asked them questions, like can you swim? Or can you make the sign of the cross? We hadn't a dull moment. Even the babies contributed to it before the night was out. Here at the main station, we have lots of children. The four teachers and the three station workers have forty-two children between them. Nearly every night when there are no mosquitos, the children come to the church to say the Rosary. I join them if I am there, or Fr. Karl. It all started when the bishop asked us to pray for peace in the Diocese when the highway bandits had the province living in fear.

Three months ago, Timbunke got its first radio telephone. My next-door neighbour, a member of parliament, received a radio telephone from the government. I was at his home when it rang for the first time, and it was if everyone shouted fire! fire! Nearly half the village came running to witness the first call. When the call ended there was a clap from all present, not because we had something other villages did not have, but because we had something others had. We are linked up now with the rest of the world. And we were there to prove it.

Our air-strip is open again. Four planes came today with tourists. The tourists no longer travel by road due to armed gangsters on the highway. The change has brought new life to the station. There are two tourist boats on the river, one is called the *Sepik Spirit* and the other *Melanesian Discoverer*. Both are like floating hotels. They have asked me aboard a few times for dinner. They hire the youth club to play the Bamboo Band, and they also hire the village elders to play the sacred flutes for the tourists.

On the pastoral side of things, the year went very well. Our main prayer group here went out to the surrounding villages to teach the other villages new hymns and give them some new ideas how to conduct prayer meetings. They call themselves the Outreach Group. They use the tractor and trailer to travel around the highway, and they use the canoe for the villages on the river. They love doing this. It is also a social event, meeting people from other places and making new friends. Most of the young people come to these sessions as we have no competition as yet from things like video or bingo. There is the exception: when one dies, or when one gets married, then the whole village comes to a standstill as regards other activities.

Mangijangut has its new village bell which once sailed around Ireland on a ship. We stood it up on a tripod, and it looks like it well never sail on a ship again. My brother Ted sent it out to me by surface mail, and it arrived after a few months on the road.

The bishop came again this year to bless a new church at Kowit village. The village people had been working at it for eight years, in fits and starts. In the end, I had to go and stay with them for two weeks and finish it. They have now built a nice bush house for me from bush material. Only the door has nails and sawn timber.

Two new sisters have come to Timbunke to help out at the vocation school for girls. Fr. Karl will be celebrating his golden jubilee next July, if the Lord spares him until then. The farm went very well this year. We started three cattle farms in the Sepik area. Two farms are going very well, and the other one, two of the heifers have run away and have not been seen since. They probably got stuck in the swamps. Such are the ups and downs of farming.

I hope you had a good year and a good Christmas, and may God bless you for the coming one.

August 10, 1990 (back from home leave) Greeting once again from Timbunke. It is three weeks since I arrived back from home leave. I could say I am back to normal again after having a wonderful holiday in Ireland.

After saying goodbye to you at Cork Airport I boarded an Aer Lingus plane to Heathrow. There was an elderly lady sitting beside me, and she was going to London for a wedding. She was nervous, as it was her first time flying. I had a five-hour stop-over in Heathrow before boarding the plane to Singapore. The plane to Singapore was full, not an empty seat. The pilot told us he was taking off with 294 tons. For this part of the journey, I was sitting between two elderly ladies bound for New Zealand and for Australia. These ladies slept most of the way as if they were on the Cork-Schull bus.

I had another five-hour wait at Singapore before boarding the Air New Guinea plane for Port Moresby. On this flight I had four seats to myself, so I pulled up the arm rests and stretched across the seats and went off to sleep. The same day I took off again from Port Moresby to Wewak. I stayed in Wewak three days before heading out to Timbunke. This part of the journey turned out to be the most difficult. You see, my car was standing idle for four months, and when I went on the highway I got two punctures which left me stranded half way from home.

I walked to the nearest village hoping they might have a wheel or anything that would get me home. As it turned out they had a bicycle repair kit and a pump. I knew they would have crowbars, as they use them for prizing open the sago trees, so I asked them for two crowbars and we went about repairing the puncture. The whole operation took four hours, but I was happy we were back on the road again. I arrived late in Timbunke, and most of those who had gathered to welcome me home were gone back to their village, but the station's kids were all there with flowers to welcome me back.

Timbunke station was really looking well. The place was cleaned up for Fr. Karl's golden jubilee the previous week. I had planned to be back for it, but Ireland were playing in the World Cup, so I stayed an extra week. The Fathers told me here when I arrived that they saw all the celebrations in Dublin on TV when the Irish returned home. I told them that if we had won, they would not have seen me for another month.

The holiday went very well for me. Perhaps I ate too much, not a bad complaint. I was home in good time to be with my sister Mary and family before Mary finally passed away.

We had a beautiful spring this year at home. I used to go down to the woods nearly every day for a walk. I used to meet a neighbour, John William, going and coming on his bicycle from his farm. Sometimes he would stop, and we would have a real good philosophical discussion about life. We discussed what was wrong with the world and how to put it right. He reckoned that the country is gone daft with the World Cup. I told him the World Cup had energised the country, and it would all settle down again in a few weeks' time.

It was my first time in nineteen years that I was home for the spring, so I appreciated it very much. The World Cup was very interesting until Ireland were knocked out by Italy. We are preparing for a big sports day here in Timbunke on September 16, Independence Day, when we will have soccer, volley ball and a few local games like throwing the spear. I hope it will go off without any trouble, because last year we had a fight which spoiled everything. Even some of my best friends lost their heads. Now they laugh at the whole thing when we mention the fight that erupted.

I have been on a short bush trip upriver to Kamanabit and Karau. The Deacon told me there is a lot of jealousy between the prayer leaders, church leaders and himself. This is one of our big problems, trying to get the locals to work together without one trying to outshine the other, or expose each other's weak points. Human nature is the same everywhere. With that I will sign off. Goodbye and God bless.

October 24, 1990 I arrived safe and sound after a pleasant trip across the globe which is becoming familiar to me now. It took the most of a month to catch up with what had been happening and to settle back again. I have spent the last five weeks out in the bush collecting data for the parish census. The people were very helpful, although the locals in one village got very worried as they thought this was a sign that the world was coming to an end. They told me that Jesus was born when the first census was taken and now that it was being taken again meant that he was returning. You see how they put things together. I had a difficult time trying to convince them that they had got it wrong, and I was taking the census to find out which areas of the parish needed the most attention. One question on the census form was, "Who is God?" I thought it a bit unfair to ask the people this, as theologians are struggling with this question from the beginning of time. They discussed the question among themselves for five minutes and then the big man answered. He said, "Father we don't know. The only answer we know is the one in the Bible—God in our Father in Heaven." I thought it a very good answer, the one I learned myself in national school.

Patrick Lotiak and I stayed three days in a village filling out the census forms. There is nothing in this village to suggest it has made progress within the last fifty years. The elders still believe in sorcery, black power, and magic. There is great rivalry between these people as to who has the most power. One of them challenged me, saying he had more power than I had. I ignored him as it is impossible to reason with such people and their beliefs. This village claims to have a rain-maker and a medicine bush doctor. Patrick was telling me about their successes and failures. These are the things that make news out here in the bush. I am becoming accustomed to their native practices at this stage. These men belong to their own time. We also discovered during the survey that the cargo cult mentally is still very much rooted in the minds of the people.

During the first two weeks of September, soccer was flourishing here in Timbunke. It had nothing to do with the World Cup. The youth were training to win the, "Luki Shield". Mr Luki is the member of parliament, and he has sponsored this game for the last two years to commemorate Independence Day. Both years the games have brought more division to the parish than unity, as the players don't understand the rules, and when an off-side goal is disallowed all hell breaks loose. Mr Luki had sponsored several teams with football shoes, and this sparked off another row between those who had shoes, and those who played in their bare feet. The spectators weren't long telling the players who had playing shoes that they were government shoes.

Now for a bit of general local news: Fr. Karl celebrated his 79th birthday on October 23, and he is still going strong; he loves going out every Sunday to say Mass in the different villages. I have bought a new fifteen-horsepower motor. I gave the old one to my driver, Bernard Bowie. He was delighted with it. His wife has another baby girl. He has five boys and two girls now. One of my prayer leaders is in jail for two years for armed robbery. His father thought if he became a prayer leader he might conduct himself.

The community schools had their government tests last Thursday. It is necessary to pass these exams to qualify for high-school. The construction of a new maternity ward at Timbunke Health Centre has just started. A man came to hospital yesterday after being attacked by a wild pig. He was at home in the village when the wild boar came towards him after being wounded by another huntsman. The boar was visiting the village pigs when the accident happened.

At this stage, I have visited every village in Timbunke Parish. My last visit was to a village called Kamangaue. The bush church had collapsed, so we had to gather under the shade of a tree for Mass. The people told me the new church would be standing the next time I come back. All they want from me is 200 four-inch nails and the rest of the material will come from the bush.

The Father's house too is ready to fall down. The white ants had eaten away the soft wood. When the church leader and his wife cleaned it up they collected a bucket of dust after the termites.

Recently I met an old man from Timbunangue village, and he came to tell me how Fr. Laumann was the first priest to come to his village. Then he opened his native basket and took out a large table spoon. He said, "Fr. Laumann gave me that spoon before the last war." It was one of those good old-fashioned spoons that you could step on and it would spring back into shape again. It is that time of year again to wish you all a happy Christmas and God's blessing for 1991.

February 22, 1991 Finally, I have got around to writing this letter; I think it is the wet season that is mainly responsible for me writing to you.

It has been raining for the best part of a month with the odd dry day in between. It looks like God has decided to really water the earth this year. Not a bad complaint when you think of the people of Iraq having to cope with hundreds of bombs dropping on them day and night.

Last year I took a picture of Santa Claus around with me in the bush. Not that the people have not seen Santa Claus. I wanted to tell them that Christmas was not just about Santa but about Jesus in the crib. I was saying Mass in one village when a shower of rain came, and half the women ran out of the church to collect the laundry off the line. We sang a few hymns and waited for them to return. You see how practical these women are. They come to Mass, keep an eye on the children, an eye on the clothes-line, and keep an eye on the altar, and they could have a pot of taro at home on the fire at the same time.

After Christmas, I went out to the farm for a few days. The workmen and I put a new floor in the trailer. We used mahogany timber, and it was beautiful the first day. Now it is a different colour from transporting stones and firewood. We even have mahogany for fence posts. It is very hard wood, so hard it has to be drilled before nailing it.

On January 4, I was in Wewak for the ordination of Charles Amia. We have three more seminarians getting ordained this year. Unfortunately, my seminarian Alphones Saun is not getting ordained now.

Timbunke is building a new spirit house. It is mainly to attract the tourists. The two tourist boats are contributing a lot of money to build it. Many tourists are postponing their holidays due to the Gulf war.

Just before Christmas a young man died in the village from drinking methylated spirits. They can buy a gallon of spirits for 17 *kina*, and it is enough to make twenty people drunk. I keep telling them it will kill them, but they laugh at me, saying, "This way we can get merry on a little bit of money, and if we were to drink the white man's beer we would need lots of money." I went to say Mass one Sunday at an out-station, and the church leader told me that no one would come to Mass today because a new spirit had taken over the village. And it isn't the Holy Spirit, or their ancestors' Spirit—it is methylated spirits.

Just before Christmas I lost my double canoe. I gave it to a lay missionary to transport cement upriver. He was gone about five miles when he came to a narrow bend in the river and the current was too much for it. It sank in thirty-five metres of water. We were lucky that no one was drowned.

Timbunke School was one of the worst in the province last year. Only one student went to high-school. One teacher is blaming me for not looking after the school. The parents are blaming the teachers, and the teachers are giving out to the parents for the children's conduct at school. It's the same old story when something goes wrong, blame someone else. This year, everyone will have to make a greater effort to see the school is running well and try to keep everyone happy; a tall order, but we can only get better. I will sign off for now,

August 19, 1990 On August 3 I was asked to attend a peace meeting between two Sepik villages. Five weeks previous, a man from Wambe village on the highway to Wewak was murdered by a Sepik man. A road block was set up banning all Sepik people access to the town. The Wambe village demanded 600 *kina*, plus a cow in compensation to wash the blood from their hands before removing the blockade on the road. It took a month to collect the 600 *kina* and the cow we provided here at the mission farm. When all was ready we headed off, about 200 of us, with the cow and the cash, and we lay them down in the middle of the road next to the barricade. Then some betel nut was placed on top of the cow. The cash was handed over to the brother of the dead man, and the road was open to all traffic again. Several speeches followed, and when they called on me to say a few words, I took the opportunity to tell them about the commandment "Thou shall not kill." I have been telling them a long time about love and not war, now I am stressing again the ten commandments. At least they will have something to think about.

Yindkum, one of our out-stations, opened its new aid post last July. All the neighbouring villages gathered for the official opening, and they gave me the job of cutting the ribbon. The women gave the day cooking the meal which followed the opening. One village failed to bring along a pig which they had promised for the occasion. The pig was after taking to the bush and could not be rounded up. When it came to meal time, and when those who failed to deliver the pig realised there was no share for them, they immediately turned for home. One could see they were angry by the long steps they were taking. But everyone kept saying what good is a pig in the bush, when one wants to prepare a meal. It wasn't a seven-course meal, but a good meal for hungry men.

One morning, at 9am, two prayer leaders and myself were paddling a canoe through a sago swamp when we heard laughter and chat upriver. We kept going, and around the corner there were about fifty village women with their dipping nets. They were surprised to see us so early in the morning, and I was feeling a bit embarrassed as they were not dressed up for visitors, but they were doing what they were always doing, and they were happy that we had seen them at work. They were catching fish in the old-fashioned way, and they were happy doing so. It was fish for dinner that day.

One night, one of my co-workers, Francis Kemeken, arrived home from giving a Bible seminar with a young crocodile. Being a lover of such creatures, he put it into a bucket of water in the shower room overnight. The croc had other ideas and decided to take a stroll through the house, and we could not find him in the morning. The house cat knew something was terribly wrong. She had smelled the strange creature and she took all precautions necessary to avoid battle. She moved up-stairs with her kittens. It took us two days to locate the croc behind a built-in press, and now it is in an artificial pond, and it will probably be two or three years before its valuable skin will be exported to Paris. It should end up eventually in someone's wardrobe.

Snooker as a sport or a past-time has become a very popular game in PNG but not everyone can afford a snooker table. One village thought of a bright idea and made their own from a piece of chipboard. The side cushions were made from rubber bands cut out from an old car tube. This was stretched on nails from pocket to pocket. The ball gave a good bounce when it made contact with the rubber. They seemed every bit as happy and as serious when playing as the neighbouring villages that have a real snooker table.

Menswat, a village in the Chambri area, is a place I always look forward to visiting. Moses is a big man there. He has held several titles. His latest one is that of church leader. He has three married sons and wives and seventeen grandchildren, all sharing the same, large Sepik-style house. By day the house acts as kitchen, dining room, and parlour, by night it is the sleeping quarters. Mattresses are rolled out and mosquito nets are tied up one to another. The following morning each mattress or mat is neatly rolled up and tucked away in the corner, and a new day begins. The women are the first up and out. They head off in their canoes to check their nets, and a good breakfast often depends on their lucky catch. I will sign off now, and I hope all is well at your end of the globe. God bless.

March 26, 1992 This year Fr. Liam Dunne has joined us at Timbunke, along with two seminarians, Andrew and Emel, who are settled well and should be a good help in another month or so. Last week, Andrew, my driver Bernard Bowie, and I went to Kanengara on a pastoral trip. We took the speed boat and a forty-horsepower motor, and what a difference, as it took us only two hours instead of three. We arrived just at school break to see all the school boys taking their mid-day swim as we pulled ashore.

From the top of the hill, a group of schoolgirls rushed down to help us. The boys did not like this and told them to go back, but the girls told them to shut up, saying "We have come to help Father take his things up to the Father's house." The Fathers house is about 300 feet above water level. There is a beautiful view from the top. The problem is to take everything up there and down again when it's time for home. On the right, looking down the river, it is all swampland, and on the left, it is all mountain jungle. We had only arrived when the driver from the sub- health centre asked if he could use the boat for an emergency case—a woman in labour for two days who could not deliver. I asked him could he drive. Had he petrol? And could he manage? He said yes to all three questions. I gave him the boat and the forty-horsepower motor, and they took off for Timbunke Health Centre. The mother is now recovering in hospital, but the child died before they reached the hospital.

Usually, the first thing we do on arrival at the out-station is to clean the house and get rid of the spiders. Once the glass louvers were covered with dust, and nowhere could I find a cloth to clean them. Finally, I had a look through my seven or eight shirts in my rucksack and used the worst one to clean the windows.

The next day we drove up between the mountains, following the river until we came to Governmus Lake. This is a beautiful part of the world, with four little villages perched on top of the hills. Our first stop was at Anganamai. Only a small group came for Mass as they did not know we were coming, and most of the people were out in the bush collecting food from their gardens. Mamari was our next stop, and it was mid-day when we arrived there. A few children met us at the water's edge, and we headed up to the *house-boy* to find some men resting there after their morning work. Six or seven men woke up to see who had arrived and went back to sleep again.

I tried to keep the conversation going with Frances, the most travelled one. I tried everything, even pig talk, dog talk, it was no use, and they were just in no form for talking. It seemed that even though we were under the one roof we were in two different worlds. I started talking about the forty-horsepower motor we were using on the speed boat, and how it was very fast. Frances came back to life again. He said, "Father, you have a new motor. I will buy the old one from you." Suddenly, there was new life in the *house-boy*; nobody wanted to miss out on a cheap motor. I had to tell them it was not for sale, and I would use it for spare parts as it was worn out and not reliable for long journeys.

On the morning of February 16, I arrived in another village to find everyone gathered around the body of a dead man. I thought first they were having a prayer meeting as there was an outreach group due to visit them. Then one grade six boy told me, "Petrus has died, and we want to know who killed him." Petrus was a young married man and a poisonous snake had bitten him the previous morning and he died as a result. The village leaders thought different and they were convinced someone worked sorcery on him. The big men in the village had Petrus`s body wrapped in a dry bark of a tree and placed it at the door of his house. Then the elders gathered around the body and asked the dead man to tell them who killed you.

I said nothing, as it was one of those times where I had to respect their customs and keep serious. Taman, one of the big men, kept asking the dead man to talk and tell them who it was who killed you. He kept asking until he was out of breath. At one stage, he bent down to the head of the corpse as if to say, "If you don't want the others to hear, you can tell me." There was no response, and then the next big man tried to persuade the corpse to reveal the killer. While this was going on, another man was tapping a bamboo with a small piece of timber. He kept tapping the bamboo, and then stopped to listen if he could hear a voice. It went on and on, and it was noticeable no one got up and left as he or she might be the guilty one. I asked one man why they had the body placed at the door of the house. His said that was where his spirit was moving right now and once it came through the door it would enter the bamboo and reveal the cause of his death. Again, I said nothing but wondered which direction they were going. It revealed one thing to me, and that was that they are still where I found them ten years ago.

I called to see Mari Kingin one day, as he is from the same clan as Petrus. Though Mari Kingin is not a big man in size, he is known as a big man in the area for his power over poisonous snakes. He was also called upon to help Petrus the day the snake bit him. He said he died because they did not send for him on time, and the people of a neighbouring village are suspected of making sorcery on him.

Years ago, Mari Kingin asked me to pray for him and his wife, so they could have a baby boy. At that stage he had seven daughters. I arranged with him to visit the Family Planning Clinic in Wewak and seek advice from Sr. Caia. I made one mistake: I left him off at the door of the clinic and went off to do my shopping for the day. When we met up in the evening to return home, I asked him how he got on. "Father," he said, "I was too ashamed to go in and talk to sister about such matters." I should have known better and introduced him to Sister and explain the situation to her. Mari Kingin has now nine daughters and one grandson. I have baptised them all, including his wife. Mari Kingin has decided not to get baptised, because he feels this would take away all his hereditary powers.

Simon was another big man who died over Christmas. He was a local councillor for fifteen years. He never achieved much as a councillor, but as a husband he had five wives and a long line of children. Two wives left him a few years ago and went back to their own clan. He was a kind man and always gave me something when I called to see him be it a rope of bananas or betel nut for the mission workers. He was the councillor, so I had to see him often about the road or school when something had to be on the government side. During Simon's latter years, he used to read the Bible and quote his favourite passage to me.

You may think that most men have two or three wives. This is not the case; over eighty percent of men have only one wife. It is just the men with all the wives are the ones we all talk about. World news is still not an important issue to these people. What is happening in their village is usually the topic of the day.

When I started this letter, the rains were pouring down; now the sun is coming through the clouds. The birds and the roosters are coming back to life again.

That's it from me. Goodbye and take care,

April 21, 1992 Many thanks for your letters and Easter cards; it was great to hear the news from the homeland. I am home today—that is what one says after being out in the bush for a week. On April 11, my driver and myself took off upriver to Amboin Parish. We stayed eight days going around to the different villages saying Mass, hearing Confession and listening to the people's worries and stories.

All the rivers were flooded, and so was half the parish after a month of heavy rain. We arranged the Easter programme to take advantage of the flooded rivers, to visit the remote villages behind the mountains. A dinghy and an eight-horsepower motor were our means of transport. The first day we travelled up to the head of the river where over a hundred people lived. Everything was so green and fresh after days of heavy rain. The jungle was alive with insects, bird song and the rushing of water down the side creeks. A pair of kokakos flew from mountain to mountain with their family of four flying behind them. Dozens of cockatoos were making the loudest clatter of the lot. It was their territory and they were letting us know. Even though the River Sepik was in flood, and the major tributaries were high, the head waters were running off quickly and we had to pull the dinghy the last half mile up the stream as it was too low for the moto. We pushed and pulled until finally we arrived at the village before night. I lit the Coleman lamp and we had a nice Mass with about forty people taking part. The rest of the population were either non-Christian or scattered about in the jungle. Once Mass was over, we prepared our meal which was lunch dinner and supper combined. It consisted of rice from China, pork from Denmark, and baked beans from Australia. Two men came in from the bush while we were eating. They shook hands, and as they went to sit down on the floor they put their bows and arrows down beside them. They told us they had killed a wild pig, and it was down by the stream, and a group of boys were cutting it up. One of the men showed me the arrow that he fired with. It had the blade of a butcher's knife inserted in the top of it. I praised him for his deadly shot, and he went on to brag about all the good shots he ever had. The night passed peacefully as we told stories about home, and away, and before we retired for the night the church leader told us to make sure the boat was secured well, as there was more rain coming, and the river could push away our boat during the night.

The next morning, we drifted downstream with a piece of smoked pork for our next meal. It was so easy going down, and the noise of the motor broke the morning silence as we headed off to the next village, who were waiting for us as we pulled ashore. The next three days were much the same, going from one village to another until finally we ended up in a village called Kaiwaria where eight villages had agreed to come together for Holy Week. It was the only village in the lowlands that wasn't flooded, and it could not boast too much as there was no more than an acre of dry land left. The young people were preparing a drama and others were preparing the readings when we arrived. The host village did a good job in providing meals and accommodation for the visitors. On Good Friday, the Stations of the Cross were being acted out in the village square until the rains came down. There were at the fifth station when the heavens opened, and Jesus was the first man to head for the church door, with a full-size cross on his shoulder. When he came to the church door, he had great difficulty in getting the cross through; it was the funniest part of the drama. We finished the Stations and the rest of the Good Friday services in the church.

On Holy Saturday the women were busy cooking, and every man and child were to bring a piece of dry fire wood for the Easter fire. By evening, a horse-load of firewood was ready to be sacrificed. I think the lighting of the Easter fire was the highlight of the Easter services. The fire was lit in the traditional way. The big men dressed in their traditional attire and led a procession around the firewood. A string of children joined in behind. It was like marching around Jericho and waiting for the wall to fall down. When the drums stopped we all turned towards the fire maker: whether he succeeded or not depended on how well he had prepared the material. He had dry fibre from coconut and a dry piece of timber with a splint through the middle of it. He had a long vine with two pieces of stick fastened to both ends of it. He put the dry fibre on the ground with the vine across the top of it. Then he put one leg on top of the timber and pressed it down on the fibre with the vine in between the fibre and the timber. Then he pulled the vine up and down as fast and as hard as he could. The vine snapped but the fibre was already smouldering. That was followed by one gentle blow after blow, and the fire took off. We all gave the fire maker a loud clap. From there on, I took over with the usual blessing of the fire and decorating of the Easter candle. The church was lit up with three Coleman lamps, so we let our light shine on Easter night. I am back at the main station today, and its mission in the flood. The mighty Sepik has once again shown its ugly side, as it did in 1973 and in 1983. It seems it floods every ten years. I will stop here; otherwise I would need another page to tell you about the flood.

December 29, 1992 It's December 29, only a few days left in the old year. It doesn't seem too long ago since we welcomed it into existence. Well, I am still here, doing the same things. I don't know if I am doing them any better or not. I did hear one parishioner saying recently, "If we keep Father happy, everything will be all right." Our main events this year in the parish were the Sepik flood, administrating the sacraments, promoting the Rosary, and visiting the villages.

At the beginning of 1992, Kanengara Parish called a parish board meeting to discuss their problems and worries, and their main concern were the sacraments. They told me there were lots of people ready for Baptism in the remote villages and I should not let them wait any longer. After listening to their worries, I said, "Give me one year and I will see what I can do." The bishop provided two seminarians for their pastoral training, and I sent them to these places to prepare the people for the sacraments of Baptism, Confession, First Communion, Marriage and Confirmation. Angarami was the first village to receive the sacraments. I stayed there for three days, had forty-five baptisms, nine marriages, and twenty-nine first Confessions and communions. I had to get all the names right for the parish register book. When I asked one man what name he was giving his child, he said "Ham". I told him you cannot call your son that name, it is the hindquarter of a pig. "Oh," he said, "Father, that is the name of Noah's second son." I had to tell him I did not know Noahs family at all, but if that is so the name should be okay for your son. It was obvious he read about Noah and the Ark.

The following week, I went to the other side of the mountain to a village called Taragai. Their main concern was how many got baptised at Angarami. When I told them the number, their number for Baptism increased from twenty-nine to forty-six. There was a dispute among them when I told them that I had only twenty-nine on the list prepared by the seminarian.

When I came to a village called Kambraman for Baptism, the church leader, Bruno Kambre, asked me if I would put on traditional dress. I had never done this before, so I thought why not. They put shells on my legs, dog's teeth around my wrists, and pig's teeth around my neck. The two-foot headdress which was put on my head was made from animal skin and feathers. If you see me in my full regalia, you would be wondering who was converting whom. To make matters worse, Bruno had informed the tourist boat the *Sepik Spirit* about traditional celebrations taking place in his village, and fifteen tourists with five video cameras arrived to record the whole lot. Bruno was using his head, and the church offering went up from the usual two *kina* to fifty-seven dollars.

On October 24 Bishop Ray Kalisz arrived at Kanengara Parish for Confirmation. The local people cut the grass on the station, painted the Father's house, and cleaned up the church. Everything was just fine until the bishop fell and broke his wrist. It was already dark and the thought of going back to the main station was out of the question as the river was blocked with floating islands in several places. The bishop decided to wait until morning to make a decision whether he could go ahead with the Confirmation or not. The morning came, and the mountain was alive with people. Seeing this, the bishop decided to stay. He gave me the book and said, "Michael, you will have to take my place today." I confirmed over 200 people, and the bishop confirmed as many more with his left hand. The bishop's hand was in plaster up until last week and the strength is gradually coming back to it again.

1992 was an election year here in PNG. It was also the year the River Sepik flooded. The politicians made an issue out of it for the election campaign. They received 200,000 *kina* in aid from the Pacific Nations to help the flood victims. The government health workers were assigned to distribute the food and clothes bought by this money. It created terrible aggravation as to who should get what. In the beginning the people were happy with the flood. They were able, with the assistance of the high water, to float logs to build their houses right to the building site. We all thought the waters would go down after a few months; instead it lasted three months and the people became depressed and agitated as it went on and on. The church workers and I spent the best part of five weeks collecting vegetables from the Sepik highway and delivered them to the neediest families. Bishop Ray Kalisz's finance covered the cost. The year of the Rosary was a great success. We had a statue of Our Lady taken around to all the villages, and the Rosary was said each night in a family home.

When the flood came, the Rosary had to be abandoned for some time, so we were not able to finish as planned on August 15. The procession of canoes on the river from Tambunam to Timbunke is something the people talk about to this day. About 500 people made the trip and another 500 welcomed them to Timbunke when they arrived. The whole experience is still fresh in their minds and the demand for Rosary beads is still greater than ever. Our Lady has something which these people like, and the people are talking about building a statue to her at the main station.

In all, I made nineteen bush trips last year. One evening in the bush one of my pastoral workers, Francis Kemekan, and I were having lunch together, I said to Francis that the fish tasted good. He had a look at the tin, and to my surprise, he said it is a product from Ireland by Gallagher Brothers Gold Fish. I had to explain that I asked for a carton of fish in Wewak, and this is what I received. We both agreed it tasted better than the Chinese and Japanese brands. What has become one of our favourite dishes is "One Minute Country Stew". It's easy to prepare and it's good.

This year I came face to face with an eight-foot crocodile. It was no zoo. The crocodile was taking a nap in the middle of the river, and I was going full speed around the corner. I took a fast swerve to the right and brushed him off with the side of the boat. It was like a rugby player cutting through the back line. Peter Markus, a pastoral worker, was with me at the time and we both got a good fright. Peter told the people afterwards that Father nearly killed him and not the crocodile. So what surprises have 1993 in store for us all? I hope they will be happy ones, I wish you God`s peace and blessings for the New Year, and I hope to see you in 1994

January 20, 1993 The village of Krimbit was alive with activity yesterday morning as I made my pastoral visit. After tying up the boat in a little creek, I walked across the marsh and everyone that could hold a grass knife was mowing the grass around the village grounds. It was a major clean-up, preparing for a village workshop to be held the following week. They had received word I was coming, and there was the usual handshake on arrival. Everyone seemed to be in a happy mood. One particular little girl was singing her heart out as she swung from the branch of a tree. She was composing her own song which did not make sense to anybody only to herself. She stopped abruptly like a frightened thrush when she noticed I was listening to her song. She ran off to her mother and hid safely behind her skirt. Her mother was probably the only one not swinging a grass knife, as she was about to give birth to her fourth child any day.

The community had tidied a large family house where I was to hear Confessions and say Mass. Two chairs and a table were all in order. From my position in the house, I could hear the grass knives mowing down the grass, and there were numbering sounds as to who would go first. The women obliged. After one hour a break came in the Confessions, but the prayer leader was alert and raised his voice saying is there anymore for Confession. It was a relief to be able to get up from the little carver stool when the voice came again saying, no more, Father.

The prayer leader and the church leader gathered around to prepare the Liturgy. When I gave them the reading of the day, they asked me about the young boys in the Spirit House who were preparing for a skin-cutting ceremony. They asked me to visit them as they were not allowed to come outside. After Mass I found myself with seven young boys in the upper deck of the Spirit House. They had one month of their nine-month period complete.[16] The signs were already beginning to show on their skin, which had turned a pale brown, while the palms of their hands were beginning to get soft and their finger nails had fresh sprouts a quarter of an inch long. My presence was of a different nature, although I did notice some of them had a Bible beside their sleeping net. I gave them a long homily about the meaning of life, and I told them not to waste this opportunity to learn something about their culture and customs. I thought there was no hurry as they had eight months still left to endure.

I had a sick call to make at the other side of the village and I noticed as I made my way there that the grass-cutters had changed from their good clothes into working clothes again, and hard at work, until a tropical downpour forced them all to take cover. I ran to take cover in a nearby *house-wind* where a group had already assembled. The *house-wind* is a thatched house with no walls, and the roof is supported by posts like a shed. In this way the wind can blow freely in and out. Here it serves its purpose well; the roof gives protection from the sun and rain, and it is here you will find most men resting during the midday sun.

The councillor spoke about the workshop. He said there was a white man coming from Port Moresby to speak about development, and a local health officer to speak about health, and another lady was to speak about nutrition. Several neighbouring villages were expected to attend. In all, they were expecting a few hundred people. All their energy and time was absorbed in this event, and they were determined to make this workshop a success.

While waiting in the *house-wind*, two church leaders asked me to buy a kilo of two-inch nails and a Coleman lamp. I wrote it down in my diary, but when the list started to get longer I had to tell them that it would be better you go to Wewak themselves and do their own shopping. With the talk, the rain, and the shopping list, I nearly forgot the sick call. When eventually I got to visit the sick woman, she was sitting beside her sleeping

---

16 This is part of an initiation rite that young men in PNG go through in order to be part of a clan and have a say in village affairs.

mat. An eighteen-month-old granddaughter was screaming her head off in the corner. The mother came to her assistance and put her behind the mosquito net out of vision. It worked for a minute, but the big sister had to come and take the child out and the crying faded away. I opened my Mass kit and the old lady smiled when a few drops of holy water touched her skin. The signs of her age showed on her little hands; her legs were too weak to lift her body. We prayed together, and she received Holy Communion and smiled again. I think she was ready to meet her maker and waiting for her last and final experience on this earth.

The rain had stopped as suddenly as it came. I headed back to the boat with four passengers who were taking advantage of a free trip back to the main station. The extra hands helped to bail out the water from the boat. I sat behind the steering wheel while the other passengers paddled the boat out to the deep water. Behind us the skies were dark and blue. I pointed the nose of the boat straight ahead, and we drove back to Kanengara before the heavens opened one more time that day.

I had one more day trip to Taragai to make before returning to Timbunke after Mass on Sunday. No shortage of passengers for the trip. Two were patients from the health centre. They were waiting around for a week to find transport to get home. Two more were Legion of Mary members; they wanted to start the Legion of Mary at Taragai. I always need a helping hand when I go to Taragai. Half a mile from the village there is a very sharp bend on the river and the current makes it very treacherous. On the way up there is no problem as I can hold and push with the motor, but on the way down there is no stopping in the river. Two passengers were ready with their oars to push the boat around the bend before the strong current shoved it against the opposite bank. They did it exceptionally well. They have been doing this so often with their own canoes that it seems only like fun to them. Three minutes and we were back in smooth waters again. I could relax now and enjoy the rest of the journey back to Kanengara. I had made my pastoral visit, said Mass, heard Confession, delivered the two patients, and the two Legion of Mary members set a date for their first meeting.

I did not take off from Kanengara on Sunday as planned, after all. A heavy night`s rain delayed the Mass by one hour and, besides, we had a parish board meeting after Mass which wet on until three o'clock. With one night to go I have been very lucky, no lightning storms this time. We can get some fierce lightning storms on this mountain. I still remember one night ten years ago when I was here in the office filling in baptismal records when one mighty blow hit underneath the house. Just four months ago the lighting struck again. It ran along the aerial wire and blew a one-inch hole through the wall, partly burning the timber structure. The hole is still there filled with paper, ready for the next blast. The house was unoccupied at the time.

I was about five miles from Kanengara on my journey home when my attention was diverted by the revving of the outboard motor. I thought some grass may have got tangled in the propeller. On close examination I discovered one of the propeller wings had sheared off when it hit a submerged tree moments before. With two wings on the propeller it was all noise and no speed, but we made it back.

February 5, 1993 I am now in Amboin, having arrived today at 2pm before the rain. It makes me feel good to be inside from it. This morning Florien Koki helped me to load the boat. Florien is one of my new part time-workers. When his wife delivered her eighth child he came to me to find a name for his son. I told him to call him Michael and ever since Florien is giving a helping hand at the station. I employ him to do some driving; he is also a good cook, especially when it comes to native food. Today he got the balance right in the boat. He put the fuel in the back, and the food and the rucksacks in the front. Florien handed me three smoked fish to eat on the way. He is like that when he has something to share. Everyone in Timbunke has plenty of fish these times.

I felt good taking off, checking my watch, and three hours later I made my first stop at Manjimai. I had some Rosary beads and guitar strings to deliver. Sr. Stella at Wirui gave me ten beautiful Rosary beads with steel crosses. Every-one wanted the new Rosary beads, and no one seemed interested in the old ones Br. Jack had repaired and given to me to hand out. One girl picked out a nice black one and asked me, "Is that a sister's Rosary bead?" I told her I did not know, but something convinced her it was. While the Rosary inspection was going on a group of Italian tourists came ashore and most of the men and women hurried off to put on their traditional dress as had been arranged by the tourist guide. At this all the tourists came towards me. Their first question was if I had seen the Pope? They told me most of them were Catholics and they were happy to see me in this part of the world. They left me once the traditional group were ready to give a display of their traditional dance. One tourist turned back and started to pull something out of his bag, and then handed it to me saying, "Give them to the kids." It was a kilo of Italian sweets. I turned to the kids and spoke to them in Pidgin; I thought he was going to give me a twenty-dollar bill. There was a big laugh, followed by, "Thank you, sir. Thank you, sir." It did not take one minute to empty the bag.

A short distance away a healthy group of young men and women went into action. They were dancing to the beat of a wooden drum. The tourists loved it. Their cameras were flashing, and their videos were whining as if they were the first ever to get this rehearsal on film. These people were being filmed every week by different tourist groups. It's their way of living, and the tourists are paying to perform. I could see a few male dancers were embarrassed when they saw Father among the group. They had practically nothing on them except a large head dress displaying many bright colours. The women had their usual grass skirts and a few children were hanging on behind them—whether it was out of fear of all the foreigners or that they too wanted to join the fun, it was difficult to say.

The show lasted half an hour and the tourists boarded he river boat to continue sightseeing further up the river. It was back to European clothes again for those who took part in the show. I too was about to move on when a village lady asked me when I was coming back? I didn't know for sure, maybe the middle of next week, I said. "I want to know for sure," she said, "as my husband has fifteen *kina* ready for you. Then I knew she was the wife of the man whom I bought the hatchet for six months ago. I told her the hatchet cost only 13.50 *kina*. She knew, but they had agreed to give me something extra for keeping me so long for the money. I was taken by surprise as I had given up hope of ever receiving the money back.

At Manjimai I connected the fuel line to the third five-gallon tank and in less than one hour I reached Amboin mission station. There is something about Amboin that never changes. When I arrive the women and children come out to meet me as if I had been away, for five years. There are always plenty of volunteers to take my cargo up to the Father's house in the hill above the village. I asked them where all the men were. They would be back this evening, came the reply. The men had gone to the head of the Arofunde River to collect material to build a family house. They arrived about 6pm with their raft of logs. Half a mile upriver they were giving orders to each other on how to dock the raft. A pack of hunting dogs standing on front of the raft added to the commotion when they saw another pack of dogs on the river bank. A long line was attached to the back of the floating logs, and four men pulled ashore to fasten the back line to a tree.

William, a committee member, was standing on top of the raft like a policeman directing traffic. He knew exactly where he wanted to put the building material. His biggest fear was that the raft would get carried away by the strong current. Just one mistake was enough for the floating logs to be carried into the Karawari River, which was only twenty yards away. Two extra lines were fastened to the raft and William gave the final order, that it was safe now. I left at this stage as the men were not just looking weary; they were wet and tired from three day in the bush. There was a pile of green bananas, dry coconuts, and fresh betel nut stacked up on top of the logs. The whole village had assembled to unload it.

I have just been outside to see the night; it is as dark as a cave, no light, not even a heavenly light, no stars or moon. Plenty of life out there though. The crickets and the frogs seem to have a competition as to who can keep up the chorus the longest. They usually keep going for about two hours. The mountains creeks are silent right now; they have no set hours, just waiting for the next downpour to begin, and I don't think the creeks will be waiting too long tonight for it looks like the rains are coming.

It's time for me once again to sign off. God bless you and take care.

March 13, 1993 I hope you are keeping well at this time of year. My last trip to Chambri was mainly to repair the house. I seem to be always doing something to this house. Four years ago, I hired Luke Yamun from Chambri to put in a completely new ceiling. Two years later the ants had eaten away several sheets of masonite. It looks like it's a battle between me and the termites. This time the masonite is treated against termites and hopefully it should last longer. While Bernard Bowie and I were tearing down the old ceiling, we discovered a rat's nest between the rafters made from the baptismal cards. The rat had half the cards of Wombum village chopped up to make a comfortable home for her off-spring. What amazed me a little was that Catechist Frances Komari never missed the cards out of the box.

Banban is in bad form these days. Banban is a mentally disturbed lady who has spent the last six years living between Timbunke village and the mission station. She arrives here every morning before Mass looking for something to eat. She has a six-year-old daughter, Sara, who follows closely behind her, and both spend the day around the station. Banban is going downhill noticeably these days, and the opinion is she won't keep going much longer. Fr. Karl is very kind to her and Sara, and he gives them something to eat whenever they come to the door.

Fr. Karl is almost six years in Timbunke. Since he arrived he has kept the mission grounds neat and tidy. This morning again he is off with his rake and wheel-barrow to comb the lawn wherever he sees mown grass or fallen leaves. He doesn't push the lawnmower, but he has a new grass knife and he was seen using it yesterday—not bad for a man going on 82 years of age. Next week, he will have the place to himself as we are all going to Wewak for the Diocesan Evaluation Workshop. It is eleven years since Bishop Ray introduced a new pastoral plan for the diocese called NIP ("New Image of the Parish"). On Monday we are coming together again to take a look back and see how NIP is fitting into PNG culture.

Last Tuesday we had a violent storm that lasted ten minutes. We get these freak winds a few times a year, mainly during the wet season. It was four o'clock, and I was getting ready for Holy Hour when the winds started. The coconut trees bent like elastic bands under the strain of the wind. I had just sent the children to collect flowers for the altar and I was scared in case a dry coconut would fall on one of them.

Yesterday we butchered two steers: one for the station and one for the workers. Fr. Liam is cooking the fillet right now, and if it tastes as good as it smells it should be excellent. Ninety-seven years ago today, our first SVD missionaries arrived in PNG and this is also a reason to celebrate. Fr. Liam is going home next week to Ireland as his mother is not well. She will be 82 for her next birthday, so this will be our last meal together for some time.

Our road to Wewak is in shocking condition. It is two years since any maintenance was done and it has deteriorated so much that only one car has come to Timbunke in the last two weeks. Tomorrow we will try to make it to Wewak with our four-wheel drive. We will take along a few strong men and spades and bush knives. A few dry days would help a lot as it is a dirt road. It is hard to do any planning in the parish when we are cut off from Wewak, as we need some personnel to help with different courses, and we need supplies like petrol, spare parts for motors, and supplies for the kitchen to keep us going at this end. Our air-strip is open again, and if we fail to reach Wewak by road tomorrow, we will have to arrange for a plane to come, weather permitting.

It is Sunday. and I was surprised to see so many people in church this morning. Usually after a wet night the church is half empty, and those that come, come late. Fr. Liam gave a nice homily; he was anxious to be the main celebrant as he had to tell the congregation he was going home to be with his mother as she was not well. He spoke about the freedom to choose between right and wrong. It fitted in nicely with the situation here in Timbunke. Just last week some young boys went crazy from drinking methylated spirits. They got violent and upset the whole village. None of them were in church to hear the homily.

Another week has gone by. Twelve of us made it to Wewak and back by car, but not without a lot of difficulties. The passengers got out to help the car through the mud holes. When we came to a bailey bridge at Wambe most of the decking was removed from the frame by the swollen river. We retrieved a few planks and guided the car on to the timber and we crossed safely. A fallen tree held us up for another half an hour. Luckily, we had brought along hatchets for this very purpose. Experience has taught us that we need them in such conditions. We eventually reached Wewak after seven hours, rather happy to have succeeded. I think we were even happier to be back home again. That's all from me at the moment. Take care.

March 6, 1993 I arrived here at Kanengara today and I knew I would forget something. I always do. This time it was the tea towels. The last time it was the soap. On my way up here, I stopped at three different villages, Mamari, Sangriman, and Kambraman. All three villages were flooded. In Mamari the village had a little bit of ground above water, and there I pulled in the boat to deliver a few letters, and I also had to leave a message with the prayer leader saying I would be back next Sunday week to say Mass. My stay was short, and as I pulled away one man told me he would have fish ready for me next time.

Sangriman village was only half an hour trip further on. It was completely under water; however, a large part of the village was only ankle deep. When the village people saw me coming they sent the schoolchildren out to pull the boat into the *house-wind*. I got out of the boat there and sat up on the bench about two feet above water. A lot of people gathered to ask if I was staying the night. I said that I came to tell them that I would be back this day week and stay a night and have Mass and Confession and a meeting with the church leaders. Now I am going right up to the top of the black water and work my way down. I stayed in the *house-wind* and talked about all the recent events. They had one story for me, how an old lady died last week for one day and came back to life again. They asked me if I could go to see her. I headed off in a dug-out canoe with my oils in my pocket. Her house was standing three feet in water, so it was impossible to walk to it. The old creature was lying on a mat on the floor as all the locals do when they sleep. This lady was alive. I said the prayers for the sick and anointed her, and about thirty people including children recited a decade of the Rosary with me, and after that I continued on my journey.

Ten minutes by boat and I was out in the main river again and heading of for my next stop at Kambraman. Yes! I wanted to stop there, as I had some messages to deliver. Their village is right on the river bank. I told them to have a house ready for me on Thursday week as I will stay the night, and they told don't worry, the same house is always available. The whole trip took six hours because of all the stops on the way.

When I arrived in Kanengara, I was back on dry land again. And a whole army of boys and girls ran down the mountain to collect whatever cargo I had and took it up to the Father's house. It is now the yellow house on the hill, and it looks well since it got its new coat of paint. Tomorrow is Sunday, and I will have the Mass here at the main station. I have the bishop's

Lenten letter to read tomorrow, so I have no homily to prepare tonight.

Two weeks ago, Florien, my driver, and I went to Amboin Parish. The Sepik was flooded, which meant we could take a short-cut across the swamp land. We headed down the Sepik to discover it was the day the Sepik eels were surfacing. This eel is about two feet long and three inches in diameter. It is beautiful to eat. We were both giving out to each other, as none of us thought to bring along a spear to catch them. We could point them out to each other like school kids as we motored along. Once we left the main Sepik and turned up the narrow water-way behind Tambunam village, we saw no more of the eels. Florien kept full speed and he cut corners as fine as a carpenter's saw. I had to give out to him more than once to take it easy as someone with the same idea might be coming from the opposite direction. After half an hour on this river, we had to slow down anyway, as the river became more like an overgrown pathway. We had to bend down our heads to get under the branches which stretched over the water from both sides.

Florien asked me how long it took when we reached the main Karawari River. I told him, an hour and a half. He started complimenting himself for making it in such good time. True, we met nothing, not a human soul, and I often thought if the motor broke down in such a place how long would it take for a good Samaritan to pass by. For this reason, I always take a helper when going to such places. At the mouth of this river I had arranged to meet Francis Kemekan, one of my pastoral workers, who like me had forgotten to take along the key to the Father's house at Amboin. We arranged the pick up at three o'clock. We arrived at two o'clock, so we boiled the kettle to make a cup of coffee while passing the time away. It wasn't long when we heard a motor and then it faded away again. I thought it must be Francis winding his way through the jungle about one mile away. Fifteen minutes later the nose of a dug-out canoe came around the bend, and I knew it was not him. It was a local man driving two tourists. I lifted my mug of coffee to them and they waved back, and they disappeared out of sight around the next bend. Four o'clock, and no Francis so we took off for the village of Karawari about twenty minutes' drive. On our way we met most of the Kumbrambun people washing sago on the only piece of dry land within miles. We stopped to talk with them, and they agreed that I should come to say Mass the following day. A group of children were playing in the water beside the sago workers. They were splashing, screaming and laughing, as if the world was theirs. They must have inherited something from the crocodile, because these children seem to be always happy playing in water, and this is something they have in abundance.

When we arrived in Karawari they were all out washing sago. Only a few children helped us unload the boat. As Florien prepared the evening meal, the canoes came back to the village in ones, twos, and threes, and slowly life came back to the village as the women lit their fires to cook their meals. Three months ago, I came to this village to hand out certificates to the grade-six students. It was the first grade six to graduate from the Catholic school. When the students enrolled six years ago, some of the boys and girls were already ten to twelve years of age. Now they had grown into men and women during their school years. The men would easily have qualified for any senior football team—that is if the selectors were looking for size. Some of these boys and girls joined us when they heard the local radio station broadcasting the PNG news. One or two from this class were already preparing for marriage, and only one out of the class of thirty-five had reached the standard required for high-school.

There wasn't much on the news except that most of the roads in the province were in bad shape after all the rain, and we already knew that. Several bailey bridges were hanging from one side or the decking was washed off by flood waters. Yes! The whole Sepik plains are flooded, but tonight I am high up in the Kanengara Mountains and the bull frogs and the crickets are keeping me company from the swamps below.

March 16, 1993 The Sepik is still rising, and all the signs are it will repeat the 1973 and 1983 flood. The locals don't seem to be that worried, as they were born and reared here, and they seem to cope well. For the outsider, simple things we take for granted can become an ordeal like going to the toilet. At Kumbrambun, I asked the church leader where the toilet was. He pointed to a narrow waterway behind the village and said, "Father, you see that road there, you follow that and pull your boat into the bush and let go there." Before the sun went down I decided to make the trip, thinking nobody would notice me, but soon the village people were informed to stay where they were, as Father was going to the bush. Everyone knew what Father was up to, and between the informers and the awkward position sitting on the side of the boat, it was a difficult situation I found myself in. When I returned to the house I tied the boat to the door post and I prayed that night that I wouldn't have to make that trip until the next morning.

During the evening, several people called in with worries of different kinds. One old man asked me if I could buy him a handle for a hammer when I went to Wewak the next time. When he left a younger man came in with some dry fish and sago wrapped in a leaf, and he put it down on the floor beside me. "Father, it's no good if you are hungry." I took the fish in one hand and the sago in the other and I started to eat in the traditional fashion. We spoke about many things. Then came the big request that he was getting around to. He told me the people were short of clothes and asked if I could get him a bail of second-hand clothes. I had to be patient; it was his fish and sago I was eating. After a long roundabout debate the answer was no. There was a long silence. He could have been thinking that I might soften as we sat there, while I was kept busy avoiding the fish bones. A third man called; he was more ambitious and enterprising than the two previous callers. He had a brilliant idea, or so he thought. He asked me to start a business with him selling petrol on the Sepik. I told him I was too busy already. "Oh Father," he said, "you don't have to do anything. I will do all the handling. You buy it, and we will share the profit." I told him that I would prefer if it was the other way around. There was no deal made. As the night progressed, things were getting back to normal. A young married couple came to see me. They had lost their first child, and they wanted to talk about it. Another mother called with her brother. Her concern was that another girl was going to marry her husband.

After Mass that morning, we were to experience live drama on the river. A village woman went to lay her net to discover her cousin had put her net a few metres away from her favourite fishing place before Mass. The woman came down river in top gear, saying, "I'll kill you, I'll kill you." She dug her paddle into the water and splashed it on the river, as if every dig and splash was for her opponent who was standing as cool as a breeze at the door of her house. The village stood in silence to listen and watch the action. Would there be physical violence or a verbal quarrel? The husband of the river lady, a quiet man, came along in his canoe and both went back into their house together. A village man told me these two women are always like that. They have a dispute today, and tomorrow they will be out in the same canoe collecting firewood off the river.

It was after 2pm when I headed off to Sangriman village, which was also under water. On the lake in front of the village, the people had built their toilets on stilts during the dry season and bored them down to the ground with the bark of a sago tree. The toilets looked more like out-posts to guard the village against invaders than the humble purpose they served. The water in the back of the village was strictly reserved for drinking and other areas at the far end of the village were for bathing and doing the laundry.

I had my own four gallons of water, but I did make a trip to the sago swamp to have a shower standing on a log using a coconut shell to pour the water over myself. Life went on as usual in the village. Every village has its own worries, and this village had a young man whom they thought would make a good SVD brother, and I should take him along with me. I had to explain that the young man must apply in writing to the vocation director, who would advise him on the steps to follow. After Mass, I had a meeting with the church leaders to discuss the man in question. One after another spoke and said, "He is a good man, he listens to you, and does whatever you tell him. He cleans the church and goes to all the prayer meetings and Sunday services." They were convinced I should take him along and not to miss the opportunity as he might change his mind. I decided to ask the leaders about the young man`s health as he didn't look too healthy. After a long silence all I could hear was one man tapping the floor with his finger. No one was prepared to express their opinion, and I thought it best not to express mine too. That's how the meeting ended, and I continued onto the next Christian community, at Mamari. They were well prepared for the high water. In front of each house they had erected a small jetty and that was connected by a cat-walk to other houses. On the jetty lay some fire wood, and the dogs and the roosters rested there too. Mamari is unique in that it has its own private school mostly financed by

Sepik Spirit Tours and visiting tourists. The government refuses to give them a school on the grounds that Sangriman School was only one-hour trip away by pull canoe. Mamari refuse to send their children there because of long standing disputes over land rights. They hope the government well change its mind either this year or next, and I am one of the delegates to get this application through. Meanwhile, all the schools in the area are about to close as the Sepik keeps rising. I hope not for too long because it would mean the children would have missed out on some vital studies for life. After reading this letter you should have an idea what goes on during my pastoral visits. So, take care once again from the Sepik.

March 24, 1993 After three months on the river I took a trip out the road to Boyen yesterday by car. The youth of Timbunke and Simon Kevin, the farm manager, used the two tractors to fill the mud holes in the road, making it usable again.

I called first to Morris who lives at Boyen Bridge. Morris worked for the missions for several years, and he is still very helpful and generous whenever our paths cross. The first thing he did was to get a coconut drink to take the edge off my thirst. I stayed with him the most of two hours. We discussed many things, including the local elections coming up in May, the school problems, the Sepik flood and other events in the villages. He told me his foal had been stolen, but it has returned to the herd. The missions had given Morris two horses to get rid of them some years ago, and now he has eight horses. The horses are of no use to him right now, but he expects some day people will need them and they will have to buy them from him. There was a six-week old wild pig tied to the post of his house. The piglet had a vicious temper. It was attacking everything that came within its reach. Morris said his son caught the pig two days ago in the swamp and it needed a few days to feel at home.

Boyen School was only a two-minute drive away, and I stayed with the headmaster, Michael Tan, during lunch break. The school children were playing volleyball under the blazing sun. Another coconut was produced and drank. It is the custom in this area to give a visitor a fresh coconut to drink when one arrives. After school break, the children went to the river to wash, and cool down, and when all was ready we began our school

CALLED FROM THE FIELDS

Mass. The singing was hopeless, and I couldn't help them to improve it either. I must bring along one of my pastoral workers and let him stay at the school for a couple of weeks to teach the children a dozen hymns. It would make all the difference to the Mass and the children would feel more involved too.

The children helped me to put some stones in the utility car, and I put them into a pothole on my way back to Timbunke. After that I picked up four women who were laden down with betel-nut to sell at Timbunke market. They were delighted I took the load off their back and when I left them off at their cousin's house, they gave me four handfuls of betel-nut for my workers. One of them said, "Father, you baptised me when I was attending Buru school." I had forgotten, as it was over six years ago; anyway, I was happy she remembered and that the event meant something to her.

Yesterday was very warm, and one could tell it was going to pour out of the heavens. The sky was blue-black towards the mountains, and just as expected it poured down before sunset. I checked the boats at 10pm; it was too late, as one had already sunk. I got the car and pulled it out on to the bank. Today Bernard Bowie is cleaning out the engine and the carburettor. This happens occasionally, especially when we leave the motor on the boat and all the rain water runs to the back of the boat and motor and boat go under water.

I went out one day to the farm to repair the grass cutter. It needs new blades. We need the grass cutter to cut the grass every two weeks. With all the rain, the farm is water-logged also. The stockyard is like a lake with wild duck swimming around in it. It is three months since the cattle were put through the crush, and they get very difficult to drive into the yard if they are left too long without herding. Last week Simon shot one old animal and gave it to Connie here in Timbunke to feed his crocodiles. Whenever an animal is sick or old it is always useful for those who have crocodile farms. The farm helps in many ways; it provides the diocese with meat. And we collect the manure to fertilize sister's garden and coconut trees.

Next Monday I am going to Wewak for our first SVD meeting this year. We have a new District Superior, Fr. Freddy Kell. The car will need a service that week. The Easter shopping is also on the list. Once the meeting is over, I am sure all the Fathers will return immediately to their parishes.

It is necessary to let the people know on Palm Sunday the programme for Holy Week. I will be off to Amboin again this year. Last year, for the first time most people came together at Kaiwaria village and it was very successful. It makes it much easier for me as I don't have to travel from place to place during Holy Week. The mosquitoes are beginning to get plentiful this week. Holy Week is one of their favourite times. So, it's time once again to wish you a happy Easter. Take care for now.

April 23, 1993 The heads looked up to the sky to assess the weather. Will it rain, or should Father wait another day? It was already Tuesday of Holy week, and to lose another day would make the Easter programme very tight. The boat was loaded, and this was another reason why Florien and I were anxious to head off.

After half an hour on the river, the rain came down. There was no bush house in the area to take cover. The downpour lasted twenty minutes, and in that much time there were thirty bowls of water in the boat. We were drenched, and some of our cargo, though covered with canvas, was saturated. It was a bad start to a busy week, but we kept going, and at 4pm we arrived at Krumbet. It was too late to start drying anything; instead, we sorted the dry clothes out from the wet ones. The following day the teacher's clothesline had a nice display of liturgical colours. For the first time I was able to see them from a distance and study the cross and the stem of wheat on the back of the chasuble. There was no need to tell anybody who they belonged to. Our personal clothes were put on the grass to dry, and before noon they were all dry again. We had a good sleep the second night, thanks to the brilliant sun that dried out our mattress and bed-sheets.

Several villages were to congregate at Ambunwari for Holy Week. Each village had a part to play. On Holy Thursday the people led the singing, and they also did a drama of Jesus washing the feet of the disciples. On Good Friday I went to Imanmari, about forty minutes walking distance, to visit the elderly and to hear Confessions. We had a nice service in their little chapel on top of the hill. While there, some Yimas women came to buy betel-nut, and the Immanari men chased them away with bows and arrows as there were some unsettled scores among these two clans. When the Immanari men heard this, they set out fully armed for Imanmari. We met them just as they were swimming across the Konmai River. They had their weapons in one hand above the water and used the other hand to swim across the thirty-foot-wide river. A few people from Ambunwari were with me and persuaded the warriors to go back as they were out-numbered fifty to one and beside it was Holy Week, and a fight now would put an end to our Easter celebrations. They turned back, but the matter is far from over.

The incident, though small, did prevent the Imanmari people from further participation, and the Yimas people were too upset to get involved in anything serious. We had only a fraction of the crowd that we had the previous year. On Easter Sunday, 133 children got baptised, and there was great rejoicing after the Mass, and the tension that prevailed the previous days was put aside. I told the church leader afterwards that his population was growing too fast. He laughed at me. I counted six women in a row that day holding babies as they received Communion. Ambunwari has a population of over 800 people. They are all Catholic, though some only in name. They have never allowed members of their clan to join another church.

After Holy Week, it was back to Kanengara to prepare for the bishop`s arrival on the following Friday. Just six months previously, Bishop Ray was in Kanengara and broke his hand. Now he is coming again to give Confirmation to two villages, Sevenbuk and Kambraman. The Confirmation was arranged first at Angonmai, but the mouth of the lake was clogged up with grass islands, making it impossible to enter the lake. The people from Angonmai had to cross over the mountain to receive Confirmation at Sevenbuk. Peter Markus is the pastor at Sevenbuk and he did an excellent job with the preparations. He even took the walls out of the church and extended the roof at the two sides to accommodate the extra crowd. The roof of the church is supported by six posts, which mean the wall could easily be removed and replaced later without interfering with the roof.

When the bishop arrived, they welcomed him with a traditional *singsing*. They led him up to the centre of the village in front of the *house-boy* and handed him a coconut to drink. Welcome speeches were made by former catechist Herman from Taragai and other leaders from the nearby villages. I had to leave then at that stage as there were over one hundred people waiting for Confession. The bishop had to come to my assistance for the last half an hour. There were 154 people confirmed, ranging in age from twelve to sixty years. When it was all over, each of the five villages made a presentation of a carving to the bishop. The women's club and the Legion of Mary gave him baskets made from the reeds which grew in the marsh land nearby. A meal was prepared for both of us. There was no table cloth or silverware, but it tasted very good, and there was nothing left when Peter Markus came to collect the dishes.

The second day it was the people of Kambraman who welcomed Bishop Ray. They had ninety people for Confirmation. They decided to take the bishop shoulder-high in a procession into the church. The floor of the church is on stilts about four feet above the ground to avoid flooding. The floor swayed and swayed as the people danced from one foot to another. I thought at any moment it would give way. The church leader thought the same when he noticed the posts sinking into the water-logged ground. The dancing was stopped immediately for the remainder of the service. Bishop Ray was asked to bless a few sick children after Mass and several people asked for prayers, and the bishop was happy to see the people believed in the power of prayer. I was happy the bishop did not fall this time and break his hand, and that our pastoral trip went off without a hitch.

May 19, 1993 Today is overcast here in Kanengara. The heavy rain last night sank my boat and outboard motor. James Berry, Florien, and I spent the morning getting the motor to start again. We had to take out the spark plugs and pull the starting rope several times to blow out the water front the engine block. Then we had to dry out the carburettor and drain out the fuel filter. We then took it on a trial trip up the river, and it is running perfectly again.

At the moment we are having a parish retreat here at Kanengara main station. A team of six people came from Wewak to direct it. My job is to stand by if needed and to do the cooking for the team. I was expecting fifty people to participate in the retreat; instead, 130 turned up. Last week we had a course here on family life given by Frank Dime, and he had sixty married couples taking part. The week before, Sr. Columbia, a Rosary Sister[17], gave a workshop on cooking, so you see there is a good variety

---

17 The order of the Holy Rosary Missionary Sisters.

of activity going on in Kanengara this year.

During the wet season this year, we completed one of our long outstanding projects in Timbunke Parish. It took eleven years to complete. When I came to Timbunke in 1982, Br. Jack was renovating the church. He asked the local people then to carve eleven posts to replace the old ones, which were getting rotten from the ground up. They all agreed, but that was as far as it got. In the meantime, I had replaced rotten parts with pieces of four-by-four planks to keep the roof from collapsing. When the subject came up again and again about the posts they told me to get the trees, and they would carve them with Sepik designs. Where to find the desired timber was the next problem. Every village claimed to have their bush full of *kauila*[18] but when we went to find it, only Boyen people were able to supply and that village was over fifteen miles away. The Boyen people felt that they should give the trees free, but I insisted we should buy them at the going commercial rate. A deal was made, and the farm tractor brought the posts two by two into Timbunke where they lay for almost one year before they were carved and ready to stand in place up the centre of the church. The Timbunke people carved them into different designs. Each design is to represent each clan in the village. Now the church is on eleven carved posts made from hard wood known as *black kauila*. One clan carved a life-sized man, leaving nothing to the imagination. Some village people objected to this, saying it was all right in the Spirit House but not in the church. The artist got his mallet and tools and chiselled its private parts off, leaving the once mighty *Sepik Spirit* standing like a skeleton in the front of the church, and the people are pleased it's gone.

Fr. Karl has decided not to go on home leave any more. He wants to die here as he has given most of his life in PNG. He will be 82 in October. Several of the older Fathers have gone on home this year and last year for good, mostly for health reasons. One old missionary, Fr. Schulcz, is 82 and he went home on holidays two weeks ago, and he says he will be back as he has nothing to do at home. Here in PNG he spends most of his time making and repairing Rosary beads. At the moment we are having local elections in the province. Voting will be here on the station on Friday, and we must put off the retreat until Saturday to give the people a chance to

---

18 An extremely hard wood.

vote. The people have shown great interest in the election, and the results will be known in one week. Bye for now.

September 27, 1993 We are very busy, with various activities going on in the parish. The good news is work has begun on the Timbunke road. A team of ten trucks, one loader, and a grader have spent the last three weeks filling in the mud holes between Timbunke hospital and Wamba Bridge. The road works had a lot of trouble getting the coral rock from Kowit, as they had a disagreement over the price of the filling and this caused delays in repairing the road. The police made a few trips to show their presence and the work continued again. Now we have a good dust road all the way to the Sepik highway. We left Timbunke one morning at five o'clock and arrived in Wewak in time to have breakfast with the Wirui Community.

On August 15 we had Antioch renewal at Amboin Parish. Young people came from all over the parish for the occasion. John Bates gave the double canoe, which is called the *Karawari Queen*, to the Kunduman people to lead the procession upriver to Amboin station. Most of the youth were dressed in traditional dress and sang songs all the way, with the Antioch banner displayed across the front of the Karawari queen.

Last Friday, we buried Deacon Tino Kante at Baliwai. It was discovered he had stomach cancer and he was too far gone to have surgery. He spent a month in the SVD lower house and the Rosary Sisters and Br. Mathew looked after him day and night. He died on September 16. His body was brought to the Cathedral church for the funeral Mass, and the church was packed, as a large number of lay people, priests, and sisters, and three deacons attended. On Friday September 24 the body was brought by plane to Timbunke and we had a second Mass here at the station. By twelve o'clock the same day we were on our way to Baliwai to bury the deacon in his home place. The body was waked in Tino`s old home until evening, and as the sun sat we laid him to rest about 200 yards deep in the rainforest. As the grave diggers went to cover up the coffin, they gave me the honour of putting the first sod on the coffin as a last gesture of goodbye to a co-worker and friend.

Two weeks ago, the people of Mamari killed a large crocodile. The crocodile had lived for many years at the junction of the Karawari River. It used to swim around the *Sepik Spirit* at night when it anchored there, and the staff on the boat were worried it would attack one of them one night, so they shot it. I saw it more than once with its upper jaw jacked to the sky and its yellow tongue soaking up the heat of the sun. Brus, the manager of the boat, claims it was nearly fifteen feet long.

Right now, we are preparing for the sixty-year jubilee of the first missionaries arriving at Timbunke. Andrew Sanara and Patrick Virua from Dagua Parish are giving a 'life in the Spirit' seminar to about sixty young people. The jubilee is on of October 16 and 17. We plan to have a Bible drama, action songs and a Bible quiz. At present the youth are preparing the area where all the action will take place.

A young girl came looking for a Bible today, and Fr. Karl, whose hearing is not so good, thought the girl was looking for Michael. After seeing to her worry, Fr. Karl told me I should be careful when they start calling you Michael. I thanked him for his advice without any explanations; you see he is still giving me advice. That is all for now, God bless you and take care.

October 28, 1993 I am on Kairiru Island taking a week`s holidays. It is a beautiful island, like the one Robinson Cruise got stranded on. This place has it all, sandy beaches, blue waters, hot springs and forest walks. To add to all that, few people come here. I have brought along a video of the 1993 All-Ireland football final to watch at St. John's Seminary, where I am staying.

Before I came here on Tuesday, I visited the Wewak show and met many of my parishioners. Some are living in the town and hadn't seen me for some time and they introduced me to their friends as *Pater bilong mipela* ("This is our priest"). At 1pm, the heavens opened, and the rain poured down for one hour. Everyone got soaked and most people left the showgrounds to find shelter or find a new change of clothes. The traditional *singsing* groups came out the worst. The rain mixed up the dyes they had used to decorate their bodies. It was a day when everything got messed up. However, there were five more days left to display their colours and to dance.

Last Saturday we had another occasion to celebrate. It was Fr. Karl's 82nd birthday. The sisters prepared a nice meal the night before, and on the day itself seven priests celebrated Mass at Timbunke with Fr. Karl the main celebrant. We have Fr. Tony Saint Pierae with us for the last three months. He is a Benedictine monk who wants to take a break from the monastery. He is finding it a bit difficult, especially with mosquitoes and the language. He has hired a young man called Joe from Timbunke village to drive his boat, but Joe never arrives on time. Joe keeps telling Fr. Tony, "I have no watch so how can I know what time it is." I had to tell Fr. Tony that he was asking him to get him a watch, and then he would be on time. Fr. Tony was used to monastic life where time is time, but here in PNG there is plenty time, and there is no need to wear a watch.

During the dry season this year, I walked into a village called Kurop. This is a little village in the middle of a swamp with fewer than a hundred people. I tried for ten years to bring them out of the swamp and settle them near the main road, but they are full of superstition and they won't move. If one of them dies or get sick they suspect sorcery as the source of the illness. They always come out for religious instruction and they walk out to school.

On October 2 I went to Kamangaue village for baptisms. When I arrived, the village was cleaned up and decorated with sago branches. I was about to hear Confessions and prepare the Liturgy for the following day, but the locals were more interested in holding a traditional *singsing* from six in the evening to the following morning. At six in the morning I went out to see how they were after the night, to discover they were still full of energy. A few strong men hoisted me up on their shoulders and carried me around the dancing ring for ten minutes. They rubbed black clay over my face and said, "Father, you are one of us now." That morning we had Mass outside in the village square, where forty young men and women received the sacrament of Baptism. Afterwards we all gathered again for a meal prepared by the village women, and as we sat down in the shade to eat we shared jokes and talked about the good old days.

Another bit of good news: Timbunke Health Centre has got a new Land Cruiser. I was asked to bless it, and hopefully it will last longer than the last two, which were crashed. Davit Ming is the new driver and he has years of experience as he was a driver for the government and missions for several years. With that note I will end this letter. God bless you.

November 23, 1993 I hope this letter finds you in good form. Fr. Liam arrived on Tuesday, November 16. He was in good form after his holidays. You would never have guessed what he brought me—a beautifully designed envelope with six bags of Barry's Tea inside. We prepared a cup each to experience the golden moments; that is what was written on the envelope. Barry's Tea brought back another golden moment, the All-Ireland final when Cork had Barry's Tea displayed on their jerseys. Also, I thought of the two great goals Cork scored. The goals were as good as Diego Maradona ever put between the posts. Cork lost a great game, but Derry deserved it and needed it more.

We had our own golden moments here in PNG during the year. Bishop Leo Arkfeld celebrated his golden jubilee to the priesthood. Cardinal Josef Tomko, who is head of evangelization in Rome, was the main celebrant for the opening Mass on November 6. It was a five-day event and recalled Bishop Leo`s great contribution to the development of the East Sepik Province. Bishop Leo was known here as "The Flying Bishop" and during his forty-two years of flying he clocked up 8,653 hours, which amounted to about a thousand flights. Sir Michael Somare, the former prime minister of PNG, recalled one flight in one of his speeches. When Sir Michael was attending primary school at Wewak, he received word that his mother was dying back home in the bush. He went to Bishop Leo to ask him if he could fly him home to see his mother. The bishop told him to get his bag ready and that he would take him the following day. Sir Michael told the large crowd it was Bishop Leo who made it possible for him to be back home with his mother when she died. He said it was a moment he would never forget. Little did Bishop Leo know then that he would be flying with a future prime minster that day. Another story that came to light during the celebrations was how Bishop Leo had a shooting accident when he was a boy and shot off two of his toes. When I asked the bishop, about the accident, all he said was, "Let me have a look to see which leg it was." He obviously did not want to talk about it.

I am back in Kanengara once again. On my way upriver today, I stopped at several villages. The village of Mamari bought three Bibles and six copies of *Wantok Niuspepa* ("Wantok Newspaper") with Bishop Leo`s life story in it. I was only twenty minutes on the river again when a man from

Sangriman village waved me down and told me his troubles. His motor would not start. I told him to clean the spark plugs and check the fuel line. He did, but it still did not start. He thanked me for trying to help, and he was still pulling the starting rope as I moved off. I refrained myself from telling him it was time you thought about buying a new motor, in case he might ask me for a loan.

The next stop was at Jasenbit junction. A group of children waved me down with their shirts to come ashore. They handed me a letter to read on the spot. It contained nothing more than to call and see the pastoral worker. I did and arranged to stay overnight. The last village was Kambraman, and they were asking for Rosary beads and guitars strings. "Some Bibles and *Wantok Niuspepa* today," I said. And they were all anxious to get a copy of Bishop Leo's life story.

Eight days have passed since I started writing this letter. It was a bush trip where everything went right. There was no trouble getting through the channel or the mouth of Governmus Lake which most times is blocked with floating islands. The river going into Taragai village was running fast, but with the help of the pastoral worker Florien and advice from the local people, we managed to get around the double bend without turning over.

Each village in the area has its own characteristics including its night sounds. Kanengara must have a choir of a million frogs, and all they need is one shower of rain for a night of song. Governmus village has a ten-foot waterfall, and a night's rain is enough to keep it crashing down for half a week. One day after sleeping for eight nights in a row in different villages, I took a siesta, and I woke up to the sound of traffic. I thought I was in Wewak town. It was the tourist vessel taking a cruise to Kanengara. It is not easy rolling up the mattress every morning and hanging up the mosquito net every night. Looking back, it feels good to have reached out to so many people. I do ask myself from time to time, how long more will life go on like this? When the locals ask me, I tell them jokingly until the year 2000!

There is a lot of speculation and superstition among the locals as to what will happen in 2000. I keep telling them not to worry, but the other churches tell them that the time is close at hand.

What the year 2000 will bring to the parish of Amboin is difficult to say, now that they claim gold has been found in the area. At this stage all work is at a standstill due to land rights. A few hundred nomads live in the area, and nobody made any real contact with them, and now everyone is claiming their land to have a share in the real thing, and not just golden moments with Barry's. I think it's time for another cup of tea.

February 4, 1994 Today I am back in the frontiers after spending a month attending to more immediate matters. I was a month writing my Christmas letters and putting together the 1993 financial report for the four parishes, and making out a budget for 1994, and we had our provincial chapter in Madang for ten days. The Provincial chapter was very prayerful, calm and reflective. It was an occasion to meet many of our SVD confrères, and I met one SVD whom I never met before. I don't know how we kept avoiding each other for the past thirteen years. It was that type of chapter where the best hour of each day was given to faith-sharing in small groups.

I left Timbunke this morning at nine o'clock for Amboin station, and it was a blistering hot journey all the way. The rivers were very high with most of the water coming from the highlands. On my river journey today I saw a dug-out canoe tied up to a fallen tree. I kept my eye along the bank to see if the owner was in sight. Not far away from the canoe two little brown heads peeped out through the grass. When I waved to them, they ducked into hiding as if surprised at being seen. The canoe is always a giveaway that there is someone in the area. The locals will always send someone out to the river to see who is passing by. Though they guess most of the time, if it is Monday it is the health river truck. If it is Tuesday, it is the tourist boat. If there is trouble in the area it is the police, and if it is any other day, it is Father. Around another bend of the river two men were standing in two canoes, and they waved to me to come ashore. One was my work-man Gregory from Kanengara Parish, and the man with him was his brother-in-law. They wanted me to stop for a chat, so we pulled under the shade of a tree and filled each other in on the day to day events around the parish. I was surprised to see them so far away from home, but they told me during the wet season they can cross the swamps by canoe in less than two hours.

Here in Amboin Parish, we have a very good Antioch group. They are a group of young people who come together with their parents to pray and share their faith. I attended a few prayer sessions and I was impressed. They have many action songs, like "Father Abraham" and "Love is Something You Give Away". It certainly has brought new life to the parish. Catechist Andrew introduced it here at Amboin.

Right now, the most urgent concern in this area is the increasing number of new TB cases each month. Amboin sub-health centre has sixty patients on full treatment. and there are as many more cases out in the bush who will not come in to get checked or treated. The officer in charge thinks that the number could be as high as 500. In the village of Immanmari, which has a population of 800, forty died last year from TB.

Just four months more and I will be packing my travelling bag for home leave and hence to Rome for the Nemi course[19] for five months. It is a good feeling, and there is a lot to get done here in the meantime. Take care.

Fenruary 22, 1994 I have just returned from Amboin after seventeen days in the bush. Catechist Andrew Sinara and I went to Konjimai village, one of the most remote places in the Amboin area. The Konjimai people were busy when we arrived, and all along the last stretch of the river we could see the fruits of their work. They were logging timber for Angoram sawmill.

Each of the thirty-four families had decided to make a raft of thirty logs. It was a big undertaking, especially when every tree was chopped down by axe. Now they are ready to start drifting. Only a few rafts needed a temporary house to shelter the occupants for the five or six-day journey on the river from the sun and the rain. When they asked me how much money they should receive for the logs, I was careful not to give false expectations. They were expecting 20,000 *kina* and they needed it for all the nice things they were going to buy immediately after the deal was complete. As we sat and talked all evening, I was asked the price of several items, like an outboard motor, a chain saw, a video, a generator, and a radio. In their imagination, the money was already spent.

Andrew and I had come to give a seminar on the sacraments, and we were wondering had we come at the wrong time. Anyhow, they all agreed

---

19 A refresher course for missionaries.

they needed a break from chopping down trees, and the following three days were given to Christian instruction. Andrew and I took every second class, and it was interesting to see the reaction as we explained each sacrament. The men sat in the back of the church, and one was very noticeable by the red beret he wore on his head. If you saw him in Moscow, you could mistake him for a train driver. His name was Simon. He claims he was one of the first in the village to receive salt from the Germans when they arrived many years ago. Once in a while Simon used to nod his head as if he understood everything. Then he would turn to the two men at either side of him and all three would start bowing in a gesture of agreement. Before we left, we had the Ash Wednesday service, even though it was one week away. The next stop was at Krumbet, which was deserted when we arrived. However, we decided to sleep there overnight. It was nice to have a quiet night to ourselves in the bush. The first thing we did was to light a fire to keep the mosquitoes away. Then we cooked a meal and had a wash in the Konmai River. The following morning, we arrived in Imanmari at 8am The people had already heard we were camping in a bush house, and they had stayed back from their gardens, and some were already in the church waiting for our arrival. After Confessions and Mass, I distributed the ashes and had a long discussion with the church leaders and the problems they were experiencing in their community. I went to see Simon Yangus (no relation to Simon with the red beret). Simon claims he is between 80 and 90 years old. He talks freely about the tribal fights, and the men he killed and ate during his lifetime. He stretched out his hands as if to mark the land boundaries and said, "All this belongs to me." He makes sure his grandchildren hear him. There are no written land titles, so he tells the story one more time. He was still talking after two hours, and he would have kept going if we had time to listen to him. Simon is now living alone in a bush house next to his family home. His house is about ten feet wide and ten feet long. He has his bed at one side and the fire place in the centre of the room. He has eleven great-grand-children, but that number could be different the next time I visit him.

Simon Yangus also boasts about his rubber trees. He was the first man to introduce the rubber tree to the East Sepik Province. Now his people have a large plantation of 10,000 trees. It is a good cash crop, but when you are hungry it is no use, and many people think the community would benefit more if they had coconut and banana trees instead. The people of Imanmari live on top of a mountain. In former times, they were not on good terms with their neighbours and the mountain was the most secure place to live.

A group of children accompanied us down the mountain and I noticed there was a confrontation among the group. Two young kids who were too small for the journey ahead were determined to follow us behind. A big brother tried to persuade the children to go back, but they ignored him. When I asked the elder brother what they would do if they could not make the journey, he replied that they were too heavy for them to carry, so they would have to rest for half-an-hour along the journey. On my way through the rubber plantation, there was a muddy patch, and the bigger boy called my attention to the large foot-print in it saying it was mine. I turned around to check the foot-print and sure enough it was my foot-print from that morning when I walked barefoot. The children felt a measure of satisfaction in having it right. At about the half way mark the children thought it was far enough, and they waved us goodbye.

When we reached the base camp at the river where our boat was tied up, we cooked a good meal before taking to Ambunwari. That evening I visited a few sick people in the village, and later in the evening several people came for a chat. Most of them were inquiring about our local MP, Philip Luki, who was up in court for misusing 387,000 *kina*. The case is still going on.

On the last day of our bush trip, Andrew and I started singing hymns as we travelled along the river. A rumble of thunder among the hills cut short our pastoral visit at Konmai, and we just made it back in time before the rain poured down, and it continued for three nights. We were happy to return to Amboin for the weekend, and Andrew's family were glad to see him back.

While in Yimas village, William Murkue asked me to baptise his new canoe. What he meant to say I think was to bless it. It was a short canoe about thirty feet long and three feet wide at the stern. On the side was written *Amboin Lady* in Pidgin. I blessed it and named it and wished the lady safe travelling. I saw the *Amboin Lady* one morning on the river and she left a large v sign rippling in the water behind her, a sign she is very heavy in the water or maybe she is too short for her width. At this time of year, most people are out in the bush making canoes or collecting material to build their houses once the water goes down, so I may have more canoes to bless before the year is out. The people like to get their canoes blessed, as there is a certain amount of danger when travelling the waterways, such as strong winds, a floating log, or, worse still, a sharp bend on a fast-flowing stream. A few serious accidents have occurred with motor canoes during the last three years, and over-loading was the main reason. Once I saw a large motor-canoe full of schoolchildren turn over. They were going home for a school break, and many of them had never been in a canoe before and did not know how to sit properly and threw the canoe off balance. Luckily no one was lost.

March 13, 1994 I haven't been out much in the last three weeks due to all the meetings. We had an SVD district meeting, a priest's meeting, a district council meeting, and a deanery meeting. At our priests' meeting there were twenty-nine agenda items to discuss. It covered anything from personal problems to pastoral matters within the diocese. Forty-one priests plus Bishop Ray attended the meeting. The deanery meeting dealt mainly with pastoral issues, and we elected a new dean, as the former dean, Fr. Harry Jannisen, is going on home leave next year. After that I had to tidy up the office and make sure all the Baptisms and Confirmations in Kanengara Parish were recorded in the parish books.

Deacon August is now stationed at Kanengara full time, and we went out together to visit some villages. We had sent word to Taragai we were coming, and we arrived they were all prepared and waiting for us, otherwise we would have to stay overnight and wait for them to come back from the bush. We had a nice Mass in their bush church, and Deacon August read the bishop's pastoral letter after Mass we went to the *house-boy* and discussed various issues concerning religion and political matters. We were ready to leave when the village people advised us to wait, as dark blue clouds were moving over the mountains. We just made it back to the house and sheltered there for two hours as the rain poured down. We were thanking God for not being out under it or should we have thanked the village people for calling us back. In the cool of the evening we took off to Anganamai. There we stayed overnight. Again, we had Confessions and Mass and the bishop's letter was read out. The last time I was here I remember seeing five young boys walking down the mountain one morning at dawn. All five boarded a single canoe and rowed their way across Governmus Lake. They were on their way to school. The Anganamai people gave Deacon August betel-nut, tulip leaves, and coconuts for his family. They gave me a basket, and bananas, and half the village came down to the lake-side to see us off. They are a happy people and they love to see someone from outside coming, just to give a little variety to their lives.

Governmus has a new community school since the beginning of 1993, and all four villages in the mountain area are sending their children there. At Governmus it was the same again: Confessions, Mass, and the bishop's letter. I also left a copy of the bishop's letter in each village, so the people can read and discuss it again in their own time. After completing the mountain-villages it was back again to the flat land and swamps of Tuninbit and Sangriman.

At Tuninbit, I slept in their new spirit house. Several villages are building them again, as they feel it is the main tourist attraction in the area. If there is no spirit house the tourists will go to the village that has and bypass those who have not. There is also competition between villages as to who has the most attractive spirit house. I must say I slept very well in the spirit house, and I had many visitors in the morning to know how the night went.

Once my pastoral visit was complete, I took off from Tuninbit and two women joined me for the trip to Sangriman. One was going to the Aid Post to see the nurse about her heart beating too fast, and the other came to look after her. As we drove out of Tuninbit, the sick woman sat beside me. She kept telling me to keep to the channel, and I kept asking her where it was. The whole area was covered with water and it all looked the same to me. She started drawing zig-zag lines in the air with her finger and told me to go like that. I was gone ten minutes when the propeller picked up some water plants underneath the water. The woman spoke up again, "If you keep to the channel that won't happen to you." From there on she told me when to go left and when to go right. When we reached the main river, I took off at high speed and missed the turn off for Sangriman village.

Before I could slow down the women spoke up again saying, "When I go to Sangriman I don't go this way." She was telling me in a nice way I was after passing the mouth of the waterway to Sangriman. I turned the boat around and drove across the lake and straight to the steps of the Aid Post where the water was up to the fourth step of the ladder. The two old ladies thanked me, and I thanked them for piloting me safely through the swamps. All the village was under water, and those who had to go anywhere were going around the village in their canoes.

For Mass the following morning over a hundred canoes tied up outside the church. I noticed one old lady arriving late. She tied up her canoe at the far end of the line and stepped across the other canoes which were parked side by side right up to the steps of the church door. She was the first again to leave after Communion. After Mass, nine old people came together to a family house to receive the anointing of the sick and Holy Communion. I usually visited them in their homes, but this time the flood made it difficult to go around to every house. Their skin and bones revealed that they had lived the full span of life. Their faces portrayed a great sense and acceptance of old age. It was a nice experience to have them all together, one which made me happy to be a priest.

On February 12, a fire destroyed four family homes at Yimas village. The occupants were all out in the bush at the time and lost everything they had. On hearing about the fire, Catechist Andrew and I called to see if we could help in any-way. I was informed last Monday morning that the peace and justice office in Port Moresby has granted then 800 *kina*, that is 200 *kina* to each family to buy some essential items.

We have a new headmaster at Timbunke community school. We will all miss the outgoing headmaster, his wife, and their twelve children. They were all lovely children, and they were always helpful around the station. They used to load and unload the boat as I went and came from my patrols. The mother told me when she was leaving that she needed a twin-engine aeroplane to transport the family and their cargo to their new school. We haven't heard from them since they left. The last boy is called Liam, called after Fr. Liam Dunne. One day on the garden seat, Liam's big sister, Bridget, was teaching her small brother the names of all his brothers and sisters and it was fun to watch the reactions. On that note I will leave you too.

April 11, 1994 As yet I have made no plans for travelling home. You can expect me around the month of June. By that time, it will be all World Cup, I expect.

Easter has passed by. I was in Kanengara for Holy Week. Deacon August made out a schedule for the Parish Pastoral team, and we shared the work accordingly throughout the parish. I stayed at the main station where the largest number of people gathered. The church was full every day. Only a few mistakes occurred due to the lack of foresight. When it came to the first reading on Saturday night, the reader did not show up. We discovered after Mass that he was outside the church door trying to get his butterfly lamp to light up. On Thursday night the group appointed to do the singing failed to appear because the heavy rain the night before had made the bush track through the swamp unsafe for them to travel at night. There was no mistake when it came to the Easter fire. It took off in a yellow glow, throwing flames ten to fifteen feet into the air. Even the people in Kambraman, which is twenty minutes by speed boat from Kanengara, saw our Easter fire. Some villages downstream were not in the best of terms with me before Easter, because I drove past their villages without calling in to see them. Fr. Paul Kanda, who has come recently to help out, had Mass there two weeks before, and I felt they should be alright for two weeks more, so I drove past.

Three weeks ago, I received the sad news on the mission radio that Jack Maradie was killed by a wild pig. In 1972 when Fr. Ben Jansen was the parish priest, he brought Jack and two other boys from one of the most remote villages in the parish to a boarding school in Kanengara. Jack`s uncle told me how he spent two days crying when Fr. Ben came to collect him. Jack continued on through high-school, and he eventually qualified as an Aid Post Orderly (APO). The government opened an Aid Post in his native village, Amboin, and Jack was the obvious choice when it came to finding personnel to run it.

Jack was not just a good APO. He was also a good prayer leader and church worker. When I needed a good driver to take me to his village, I sent word to Jack to drive the motor, because he knew where every tree and sandbank was, and he even knew where the deep water was. We all were proud of him, as he was a model for twenty years of missionary work on the Sepik. Jack was an educated man, and the only person in the village with a government salary. Emboin is right on the border of the Enga Province, and it is almost impossible to get another APO to live there full-time and cater for the people in that area.

I don't know if I will be coming back to the Sepik or not after my holiday and the Nemi course in Rome. Right now, every bone in my body tells me to stay on. The people, the river, the farm, the trees and the mountains tell me I belong here. Maybe after one year away from the place my head and my heart might tell me something else and maybe the bishop too. Whatever the decision, I am prepared to move to "higher ground" and get away from the swamps and the mosquitoes. I must confess the Lord has been very good to me. I was happy wherever he led me. I think that is it for now. God bless you and take care.

April 23, 1994 Today I have a red nose. I got burnt yesterday while travelling for six hours on the river. The strong-protection sunscreen did not help either.

While travelling yesterday, I ran up on a sandbank. I saw dark clouds gathering ahead indicating a downpour. I put the motor into full power and cut some bends on the river to save time. Suddenly the boat came to a halt. I had run aground on a sandbank. Lucky no damage was caused to the motor or boat. A Timbunke man was on the river with his motor canoe and came to offer his assistance, but before he reached me I was back in deep water again. The Timbunke man smiled and shook his finger telling me I should have known better after all these years on the Sepik. I agreed with him fully and took off. The expected rain fell more on the Chambri area, and only a few drops were blown across my way.

Last night, Paul Api, a workman on the *Sepik Spirit* tourist boat, called to see me. He told me how the vessel was held up at gun-point before Easter, and he was anxious to talk about it. Paul was in the lounge room briefing the tourists on the following day's tour when suddenly the door opened and the barrel of two guns pointed towards him. The gang shouted, "Hold up! Hold up!" By this time John Bates, the former manager, had ducked under the counter. The tourists asked what was going on. Paul had to explain that it was a hold-up and to do as they were told. The tourists were ordered to lie on the floor. The gang leader again asked for John Bates. Paul had to roll over on the floor and tell the man with the gun that John was no longer the manager, and that the new manager was lying on the floor with the tourists. Then the gang asked for the manager's room and one staff member lead him there. After three knocks on the door, there was no reply. The gun went off, by accident or intentionally he did not know, but it left a big hole on the side of the door. Panic set in on the lower deck after hearing the shot upstairs, and the four gang members left, none the richer for their ordeal. The tourists stayed on the floor for another five minutes, and then Paul told them they could get up now, the gunmen were gone. One tourist asked what they were looking for. "Money," said Paul. "Why didn't they take our money? I have money in my pocket," said another. Paul had to explain that they were not after their money but John Bates's money. Half the tourists got the plane out of Timbunke the following morning. The other eight continued on the cruise.

Four men are now in Wewak jail awaiting trial. The police acted on a tip-off after some village women returning late from fishing saw a canoe and four men trying to hide in the grass when they saw the canoes approach them. At the time the women did not give any indication to the men in the canoe that they had seen them. I was glad to hear it wasn't Timbunke men who held up the tourist boat.

Yesterday on my journey to Amboin, the Karwari bush camp was completely abandoned as I drove by. Six months ago, it was a busy place on the edge of the river bank. That time they were logging timber for Angoram saw-mill, and I stopped off for a chat. I tied the boat up to the raft which was about half-way under construction. Tony Sapkai came down off the bank to help me across the raft. He must have concentrating too much on my movements when he misjudged his step, and only for my firm grip on his hand he would have fallen into the water. There was a laugh from the onlookers on the bank, as Tony was supposed to be helping me. Anyway, Tony is always very helpful when I go to his place.

When they asked me at the camp if I was hungry I said, "What do you think? I am all day travelling." They had fish, sago, and wild birds' eggs, and there was a large wild pig cut in a hundred parts smoking on a wire rack. The pig I thought would take too long to cook, so I opted for the fish and sago, and one old lady gave me two wild birds' eggs. One old man was sitting on a makeshift bench eating a chunk of pork straight off the bone. He must have cooked it in his own pot. While we sat and talked a group of young men appeared through the tunnel of trees pulling a large log behind them. The floor of the tunnel was lined with timber-rollers, so the logs could slide easily and less manpower was needed to get the trees out to the river.

In the course of our conversation, I told them that they had a great life. They were quick to tell me they would change with me any time. I was probably seeing them at one of their best moments. I wasn't in any hurry to leave, when Tony pointed to the black clouds gathering over Amboin station. I thanked them for their meal and left, half-regretting I had delayed so long. There was no need for me to cook that evening.

Since I started this letter two weeks have passed. I was out in the bush for a week along the Konmai River. At Konjumai, we had over ninety baptised, forty-five first Confessions and nine marriages. That was followed by a prayer leader course at Amboin station. Then there were the goodbye dinners at four different villages to wish me well on my home leave.

I must go into Wewak next week to arrange my air ticket for home leave, and after that it is one last round to Kanengara Parish. See you all around the first week of June.

Cappagh, Union Hall, Co. Cork, Ireland

August 27, 1994 Home at last, and it seemed at first that I have never been away, but when the nieces and nephews came to welcome me I was reminded by their appearance that it was four years since I bolted the old kitchen door. Time never stands still, and even the family home is beginning to show its age of nearly one hundred years. My first job was to repair the roof, and there was no shortage of rain during the summer months to test the work of a missionary home on holidays. It was holiday time or time-off for everyone during the World Cup. Our first win against Italy led everyone to believe we could bring home the cup. The two following games against Mexico and Norway brought us down to earth and the knock-out from Holland was like a sudden death. The mourning lasted for the most of a week, and what was worse, a month of my holidays had gone watching soccer. July was no different as regards the weather, but the World Cup was over as far as Ireland was concerned, and I could start visiting my relatives and friends. I went for long walks down to the woods and up the farm road. It was great to be home where a part of me still belongs. I helped out on the farm a few days cutting silage. It was like old times again driving the tractor in the same fields along the same roads as I did thirty years ago. Farming methods like religion have gone through their own "evolution". What it took in my youth to do one month's work, the same can be done now in one day without any hard work involved.

People's attitudes towards the Church have changed very much in the last few years. Parents are no longer encouraging their children to join religious life, and the sisters are suffering the mostly in this regard. The old structures in Ireland are dying, and maybe the Church can once again become the Church of the poor. On a more positive side, the faith is still alive, and the youth are looking for faith experiences and faith sharing rather than being preached at.

On August 1 I am off to Rome to continue my pilgrimage journey. There I will do a refresher course for four months at our SVD house at Nemi. I am looking forward to meeting the other SVD confrères and hear their stories about missionary life in other parts of the world. For now, I don't have to worry about bad roads in PNG or if I have enough petrol to get home from the bush trip. My new address for the next four months is Missionari Verbiti, 000-40 Nemi, Roma, Italia. So, the journey of faith keeps going as long as we live. May God's grace give you the strength to keep travelling on.

Missionari Verbiti, Nemi, Rome, Italy

October 1, 1994 Here at Nemi there are three courses going on at the same time. The SSpS sisters are having their "tertiate", there is a Bible course for lay people and religious, and a renewal course for brothers and priests. Those doing the Bible course joined us last week for Fr. John Fuellenbach's lectures. He addressed us each morning in his good Roman

Catholic humour as the Scribes and Pharisees, and he ended his class with an Indian bow. He gave us a beautiful explanation of the Kingdom, and three alternative views of Hell. His model of Purgatory was seen as a place of constant growth where the arrows of selfishness, and pride, etc., are facing into the self and had to be straightened and put facing out.

Fr. John made full use of the blackboard to explain God's love in the human heart. He told us to put our hearts on fire with the love of God and keep it burning. He said to put less emphasis on trying to fill up the brain with more information, knowledge and the latest theology. In other words, a shift from head knowledge of Jesus Christ to a feeling of love, compassion, and joy where Christ can make his home in our hearts. It is all explained in his book *The Kingdom of God*. His classes were very good, humorous and inspiring.

The name Cardinal Joseph Ratzinger came up a few times during the week. The word *paradise* never came up in class, However, Fr. Bernhard Rass told us as we turned in for the main gate at Nemi in our fifty-seater bus that we were now entering Paradise. I noticed immediately that Paradise had taken full advantage of modern technology, and there was a video camera stationed at the gable of a nearby house and focused on the gate which was operated by remote control. From my room, Nemi lake looks beautiful. However, when I had a closer look, I discovered it was heavily polluted. Every night the amber lights of Genzano lit up the skyline like a small city. A few nights ago, I noticed a beautiful golden haze covered up the whole valley below. It is amazing how peaceful it is here, and yet so close to the city of Rome. Maybe this is what Fr. Bernhard had in mind when he told us we were entering Paradise.

Among the twenty-eight doing the renewal course there are ten nationalities comprised of a vocation director, a doctor, a vice-Provincial, a lawyer, school teachers, a vicar-general, a cathedral parish priest, a tailor, a novice master, rectors, and bush missionaries.

One morning before the sun rose, I went out jogging through the forest and an owl started to hoot from a nearby branch. I don't know what the owl was trying to tell me, but it gave me a startle as I was in strange territory. Now the clock has been put back one hour, and the owl and I haven't had a close encounter since. There is a great variety of birds here, and I hear them sing a lot. I told one Father that the birds at Nemi were very happy, and he told me every bird in Italy was happy because they had plenty of fruit to eat at this time of the year. I joked with him and said that should also apply to the Scribes and Pharisees at Nemi, as there is plenty of fruit on the table for every meal.

The meals are excellent, and if I don't keep up the jogging I might need the tailor to adjust my trousers. It seems meal-time is the expected time for telephones calls. Not an evening goes by without the telephone ringing, five or six times. There is ice-cream on Sundays, feast-days, and birthdays. There is also wine every day with meals. I don't want to make you feel bad by telling you all this, but if I had a choice I would prefer my motor and canoe.

Fr. John Musinsky, SVD, celebrated his Golden Jubilee a few weeks ago. He said a nice few words during his homily and that he wanted to thank the Lord for his goodness to him for fifty years as a priest. Fr. John is still very active giving courses and spiritual direction. He also has his turn answering the telephone during meal time. I even see him cleaning the tables after meals. I think the former Superior General has given me a few ideas how to live community life.

We read reports in the papers that the Pope is in bad health. The Vatican keeps denying it. I saw the Pope on television one evening leading the Rosary, and he looked very feeble. Mother Teresa was in Rome this week and she also looks frail and is confined to a wheelchair. It's amazing the people one can meet here. Our Provincial from PNG, Fr. Francesco, is in Rome, and I have met several PNG missionaries here in Nemi.

The weather is getting cold, and one could do with a jacket these days, otherwise everything is above board. That is it from me. Take care.

October 12, 1994 Last Thursday we had "a desert day" here at Nemi. It is a full day of fasting set aside to journey with the Lord. After taking a cup of coffee for breakfast, I put two apples in my pocket and went for a long walk through the Nemi woods. One hour or so later I spotted a bare rock high above the walkway and I sat down there for a few hours until the sun got too hot. While I was sitting there in silence listening to the forest creatures a green snake, two-foot-long, crawled over the rock I was sitting on. After seeing the snake, I moved on to another location which was high above Nemi village where I observed some workmen erecting a crane in the village below. I ate my two apples at twelve o'clock and began to wander back to be on time for evening Mass. When I arrived in the village of Nemi I stopped to observe the newly erected crane. I was like a countryman in the city for the first time looking up at the tall building. A lady came up to me and spoke in Italian, and I asked her if she knew English. She said she was born in England. We got talking about the crane and the building. It was an old monastery, and she told me it would take four and a half years to restore, and when it was complete she will have a room in it. I didn't tell her I was on a desert day, however. When asked later how the day had gone, I said I saw a snake, ate two apples, and I got talking to an elderly lady, and it wasn't the lady who gave me the apples.

Every Tuesday we have mission presentation. It is a day where each missionary speaks about his own mission work. I spoke about PNG. It went very well. It helps us to see the problems and difficulties other missionaries encounter, and we also hear about their successes and failures. Some evenings when we are together we share funny incidents which occurred during our lives as priests. One priest was saying Mass on Sunday, and after the consecration, he genuflected, and the portable microphone fell off. When he stooped down to pick it up he lost his train of thought and started with the "Lamb of God", leaving out a part of the Mass. He did not notice it until one parishioner came to him afterwards and said, "Do we not say the Our Father now during Mass?" I remember one Sunday saying Mass, and I put the chasuble on inside out and did not notice it until I genuflected at the foot of the altar. I decided to keep going and maybe no one would notice it. Well, ten years have passed since, and to this day no one has ever mentioned it to me. Once I was saying Sunday Mass and a house parrot came in to the church and landed on my shoulder and the whole congregation were amused.

Another story was about a bush priest who was out in bush patrol when he fell off his horse. Being hungry and covered with mud, he decided to knock on the door of a particularly good Catholic family. When he knocked on the door there was no reply. He knocked again and heard some noise inside. Nobody came to the door, so he got angry. He decided to put a piece of paper with a note for the people of the house to read on the door. The note said, "Look I stand at the door and knock, if anybody hears my call and opens the door I will come in to him and eat supper with him and he with me" (Rev 3-20). When the lady of the house read the note she also got angry and quoted scripture, this time from Genesis: "I heard footsteps in the garden, I was afraid, so I hid, because I was naked—I was having a shower." One cannot win every time one quotes scripture.! It seems everyone is enjoying the course. There is no real pressure on us. It is a time to relax and tell our story and listen to others tell theirs, and it's amazing how enriching this can be. I well sign off for now. God bless you and take care.

December 10, 1994 Today I went for a long walk to Genzano and back. You know, my Timbunke shirts will not fit me now. It is the sign of the times, and the sheep will not follow. How are all the *sipsip* ("people") on the Sepik? I am sorry to hear Fr. Liam got kicked by a horse. There is a farmer's golden rule: never trust a bull's head or a horse's behind. The latter Fr. Liam knows by now. When I told the Sepik this rule, they told me another golden rule which they have, and that is, never trust a crocodile's head or his tail, as both are equally dangerous.

I have read two accounts of Sr. Agnes's mission and farewell in Tambunum village, which is an out-station of Timbunke parish on the *Word PNG* and *SSpS Worldwide* newsletters.[20] It made me feel good to read such positive reports and to know all those trips down to Tambunum were not in vain. She is now the second religious from that village. One such trip I will always remember. Sr. Agnes had just returned from studies to her village as a young girl, and the village elders thought it was time for her to get married. To avoid being set up that night with a husband, she asked me if she could travel back to Timbunke. I refused to take her on the grounds it was against the custom to travel at night with a young girl. The same night she hired a motor canoe in the village and arrived in Timbunke to sleep in the girls' convent, out of the matchmaker's reach. She joined the convent the following year. Now the celebrations are over and let us continue to pray for Sr. Agnes that she will be happy in her new assignment doing the Lord's work in Ghana.

20 Sr. Agnes was the first from PNG to take her final vows with the SSpS order.

PNG was in the world news a few times last month. The discharge of ashes from the Rabaul volcano was a magnificent picture on television screens and newspapers. For the local residents, it was a matter of running for your life. From now on, they will have more faith in modern sciences for warning them of future eruptions.

I have visited many churches in Italy. This month we hope to make the pilgrimage of the seven churches of Rome. It is not that I am growing in holiness. No, it is just a chance in a life-time to see these holy places. Sorry to say these churches are more museums than places of worship, as each day bus-loads of tourists visit them. Tour guides are more attracted by the magnificent buildings than the purpose they serve.

In Assisi, it is different. Many people come to pray and see the burial place of St. Francis. Last week we went on an excursion to see the uncovered city of Pompeii. We drove along the coast road between the face of the rock and the sea from Sorrento to Amalfi. The purple bougainvillaea we have in Timbunke is growing here in abundance. A four-lane traffic jam almost a mile-long outside Napoli also caught my attention. When I got up from my seat to take a photograph of the four lanes of cars that were at a standstill, the bus driver said to me, "What in the name of God do you want a photo of that for? That's what gives people heart attacks." I had to explain to him that where I live in PNG we would be lucky to see five cars a day on the Timbunke highway. Now I have an interesting photo to show the PNG people how others live

One day I saw a police chase. The hunt did not last too long as the police disappeared into the human jungle and out of sight. The pick-pockets are constantly on the prowl. Four or five of our course participants had their pockets emptied by them.

It is almost time again to take up the "tent" and move on to new pastures, and then in April it is back to PNG. There is great rejoicing in my home parish at the moment, as Castlehaven football club won the County Senior Final. Football has put our parish on the map of Ireland. I should have been at the match myself. Even the Taoiseach Albert Reynolds found time to be there. That is all from me. May God bless you all.

December 10, 1994 When I came here to Rome in August the trees were green, and now they are yellow and grey. It is like a time in between autumn and winter. One big wind and the leaves will scatter, and just one week more and our renewal course is finished, and we will all scatter throughout the world. Most SVDs doing the renewal have no fixed abode at this stage. They may have two or three addresses but let us hope that wherever they go they will bring new life and hope to their parishes. Then the course will bear fruit and all the effort will be worthwhile.

Coming to Rome and not seeing the Pope would be leaving something amiss. A day was arranged for a general audience, but it could be cancelled at a moment's notice due to his weak health. Eventually the Pope did improve, and we queued up along with 6,000 others from all over the world to see the Holy Father, Pope John Paul II, in the General Audience Hall. The fact of having so many people come together from different cultures throughout the world brought home the reality of the universality of the Church. The Pope did look very feeble, but he did wave to the different groups as their names were called out on the public address system. Just in front of us was a group of sisters all dressed in black, and when the Pope called the name of their congregation they all stood up and waved. It was all so perfect it couldn't but be noticed. Our group were in Roman collars, neck ties, and open-neck shirts. When the SVD were mentioned we stood up and waved and clapped to let the Pope know where we were. The Pope spoke for a few minutes in different languages. He told us to be faithful to our vow of celibacy which helps us to be more committed to Christ and he told the married people in the audience to be faithful to each other and the Church.

Every time I go to Rome I see many sisters, some still dressed in pre-Vatican II habits, and if one had to die on the street, I don't think it would take too long to find a priest to give you the last rites either. On November 25 we made a pilgrimage of the seven churches of Rome. They included St. Peter's, the Basilica of St. Paul Outside the Walls, the Basilica of St. John Lateran, the Basilica of St. Lawrence, the Basilica of St. Mary Major, the Basilica of the Holy Cross, and the Basilica of St. Sebastian. It was a twelve-mile walk, which we covered in seven hours. This pilgrimage is a Roman tradition. You must walk from one church to another, say some prayers, and move on to the next church until all seven are complete. After the pilgrimage we went to a family bar for a cup of coffee. When the owner discovered some of us were Irish he made it an Irish coffee free of charge, and we had a great chat with him while resting our bones.

During our introduction to peace and justice, our resource person, Sr. Christel Daun, SSpS, took us to visit the St. Egidio Community at Castel Gandolfo. This community was founded in 1968 by a group of students in Rome to look after the poor and the homeless in the city. Three days a week, volunteers from the community give a full meal to between 1,500 and 1,800 people. Each evening after work, the members of the community come together in a small church to pray and meditate. That evening before prayers we visited the soup kitchen and saw hundreds of people lined up waiting for their meal. Most of them were refugees from Eastern Europe. We shared a meal with the community workers afterwards, and they told us how God is very important to them, and through these poor people they discover God's love in their lives. Christmas Day is one of their biggest days, and hundreds of dinners are distributed to the poor in the Basilica on that day. I wonder at times are we priests and religious caught up too much in rules and structures and fail to reach out to people where the real needs are.

I visited St. Peter`s again on Wednesday. Before leaving the square, I took one last look around and prayed to St. Peter to help me keep the faith when I return to Ireland. The Church in Ireland is going through a bad patch. Some see it as a great liberation from the old image of power and control to a clergy that is human, weak, and need God. 'When sin increases grace abounds all the more' (Roman 5: 20).

Let me tell you another funny incident. Half way through Holy Hour on Thursday night, we had a great laugh and we could not stop. There was complete silence when someone's stomach began to rumble. The weird sound kept going up and down, petering out and then coming back on again to a high note. Some had to finish the Holy Hour in the adjoining room. Maybe we are not using the gift of laughter enough. We discovered it is the green kiwis which were eaten at supper that started the rumbles. It is good that the Lord has a since of humour.

Tomorrow we light the third candle of Advent, so I doubt if you will get this letter for Christmas. Just the same, I can wish you a happy Christmas and God's blessings for 1995. Many thanks for posting on the news about PNG and the people that live there.

Wednesday, we have our farewell Mass and dinner, and we all go back to continue life and experience a new passing over after the renewal course. Give my special greetings to all. Shalom! Or should I say "Ciao"?

PART II

AMBUNTI: 1995-2005

Ambunti, East Sepik, PNG

August 8, 1995 This new day finds me far away from home. I mean Timbunke, which has been home to me for the last twelve years. I am now stationed on the Sepik Hills, near the Hugstain range, as it is known on the local map.

Ambunti is the name of the Parish. It`s just six and a half hours up the River Sepik from Timbunke; so, whatever way you see it, it's a good step up from my former Parish!

Ambunti District is the most remote and least developed of the four districts in the East Sepik Province. The main feature of the district is the Sepik, its many tributaries and connecting waterways. The terrain varies from low-lying sago swamps, course kunai grasslands to rugged mountainous tropical rainforest. The population of Ambunti district is close to 30,000. People live in villages sitting along the banks of the Sepik and on nearby high ground. The largest village has 1,000 inhabitants while smaller villages may have as few as twenty people. Many people still hunt and gather in the forest. Ambunti Station is a large settlement with government offices, a high-school, a health centre, and small trade stores.

Ambunti Parish has ten primary (community) schools, a development centre for teenage boys and girls; it also has an adult pastoral centre.

The parish is connected to Wewak, our headquarters, by light aircraft, or by a two-hour canoe ride down to Pagwi, plus a four-hour road trip. There are approximately 8,000 Catholics in this parish.

When I arrived in Timbunke, after my ten-month break away from the missionary front, there were over a hundred parishioners dancing to the beat of drums on the air-strip to welcome me back. We danced all the way to Father's house, and those home feelings which I had brought with me from Ireland were soon fading in the background. However, I had to tell them there and then that I had been appointed to Ambunti Parish and I was coming to say hello and goodbye.

I had written to Bishop Ray Kalisz during my home leave for a new parish, as I felt it was a good time to move on. The parties and celebrations which followed affirmed my thinking was right. I told the people at Timbunke during my last Mass that one of my greatest moments in Timbunke was when Sarah, a homeless and neglected child, handed me a flower and a one-*kin*a coin as a farewell present. Sarah has grown up now, and it was my turn to receive from her little hand a gift of appreciation for the help she and her mother had received from the missions during her infant days.

Six parish leaders from Timbunke travelled with me by motor canoe to Ambunti. Though none of us had seen Ambunti before, we were given instructions to follow the main river. Nobody had told us about the long island near Avatip village, which divided the Sepik River in two, giving the impression we were at the mouth of two great rivers. There were no signposts to say go left or go right, so we asked a local man and his wife who were out fishing in their canoe for directions. Not even knowing the way to the new parish brought home the reality that I was beginning all over again. In this new territory I would have to fish out my own landmarks and familiarize myself once again with the tributaries and waterways, the trees and the mountains which were signposts in my former parish. They served their purpose well but now they were only silent memories.

One of my first tasks was to hold a Christian burial at a village called Yigai. Fr. Jan Czuba, SVD, the outgoing parish priest, asked me to go there as a young mother had died. Fr. Jan briefed me on the community, how only six years ago they moved out to the waterfront. When I arrived there the body was brought immediately to the church. It was enclosed in a homemade coffin made from a family canoe. After Mass, the body was taken back to the "old sod" for its final resting-place. I thought the grave was somewhere near the outskirts of the village. When we walked on and on, I asked how far more it was. They told me they were taking the body back to the old place where her ancestors came from. Though none of us wore jungle boots, the journey through the forest was striking. We were accompanied by jungle music from the thousands of insects that lived there, and the tall giant trees helped to preserve our energy by blotting out the heat of the tropical sun. When we finally reached the burial place, it was overgrown with nail grass. However, some coconuts and bananas were still producing fruit and a coconut drink was prepared for me the moment I arrived. Then there was the last talk, the last cry, and the last prayer before the body was lowered into the grave. They may have moved out from their ancestral place six years ago, but their spirits and bones are still there. The same thought surfaced in my mind as I travelled back to my new home in Ambunti. I also felt a part of me was still in Timbunke.

I am here three months, and—so far, so good— "no volcanoes yet". I mean I haven't encountered any difficulties, though from experience problems come when least expected.

Fr. Willbrord Kamion, SVD, from Zaire is here with me. He is very popular with the youth and a great soccer player. We also have some overseas development workers and four FMM Sisters[1] and three Rosary Sisters. Seven different nationalities in all.

April 4, 1996 I hope you are all keeping well after all the excitement Clare brought to the hurling world by winning the 1995 All-Ireland hurling final? Things will never be the same in the Banner County again.

As for myself, I want to say thank you for your Christmas gift and newsletter, Mass stipends, and the book, *Divine Word Missionaries in Ireland* by Father Walsh. I really enjoyed reading about the SVD history in Ireland. It was full of life and faith-filled experiences. On page 38, I got the best laugh from Norman Davitt's comment on original sin, and the story of Barney Wrocklage walking the length of O'Connell Street clad in clerical black with an unwrapped hatchet over his shoulders.

These events were before my time. However, I was present with a shovel in my hand when the "Lord of the Dance" was sung at Fr. John Lynch's graveside. That is over twenty years now, and one of those twenty I have spent in Ambunti, my new home.

From the mission station here in Ambunti I can look out over ten mountain ranges—that is, when the clouds move off. It's like looking over the rooftops of a jungle city. Down below and in between the ranges are

[1] Franciscan Missionaries of Mary.

swamps, wetlands, lakes, and waterways. There are no roads as yet, but it won't be long before the yellow giant bulldozers will move into the area and remove the hardwood from its virgin forest and the hard, yellow metal (gold) from the bowels of the earth.

Mount Garamambu, which is an Ambunti Parish, is known to have a rich deposit of gold and the people there are panning its rivers and scratching its surface in search of the precious metal for over forty years.

In my second trip to Garamambu I decided not to bring up the subject of gold, but when I asked the prayer leader Simon where Arnold, the prayer leader, was, he told me he had gone to Maprik town selling gold, and when I asked where all the young men were, I was told they were out in the bush with two white men taking soil samples for further testing. Just below Simon's house on the bend of a big creek was a hole. Simon told me there was gold in there; but it is too deep, and the water keeps coming in and that is why we are inviting the mining company in.

There are still a lot of objections to the mine from neighbouring villages, as they fear it will pollute their fishing waters and it could have devastating long-term effects on their lives. There is still a lot of talk about gold and mining at present and little talk of God and the Good News; it is one of the challenges in this parish. Getting to Garamambu is another challenge of a different kind. To get there, one has to travel by canoe for the first part of the trip and then the rest of the journey is across two swamps, which are divided by one mountain range. The last time I reached the top of the mountain, I realized it was no longer the morning of my life. I must keep fit if I intend to make this trip five times a year.

Overall, it was a fantastic year getting to know new people and new customs and at the same time moving on from Timbunke and letting people go.

On March 4 there was a workshop on the pastoral plan of the Diocese held at Timbunke. Fr. Willie Kamion, Deacon Andrew, Seminarian Willie Wonduo, Catechist Jerry Markius, and I represented Ambunti Parish.

The Timbunke people had a rather unusual story to tell me on arrival. Just after Christmas some young people from the village decided to have a party. They needed a cow to feed the guests. Just across the Sepik River were a herd of cattle on grassland, with no fencing, only natural boundaries consisting of swamps and wetlands. The cattle were never housed or domesticated, only hunted when needed. When the huntsmen arrived, the cattle took off in a run, and a few dogs gave chase, which made the cattle more nervous. The cattle never stopped. They kept going through the swamps, jumped into a deep outlet from a lake and a strong current took them out into the Sepik River. All fifty-one of them floated down the river with their heads up. When the Wombun people saw the herd approaching they went out with their canoes to guide the cattle ashore. The cattle were completely exhausted when they reached the water line and lay half submerged in the water like beached whales. Four or five strong ones took off into the bush and David Minj took two young calves back to Timbunke. The rest were killed before they regained strength, and the meat sold or given away to neighbouring villages. One Wombun man tied a cow to the post of his house; he had to get up in the middle of the night because the cow had found new life and was sending shock waves through the house every time the animal tried to leap for freedom. The Timbunke people are still trying to figure out what possessed their cattle to behave in such a fashion. They have not accepted my answer: the dogs gave chase and scared the life out of them. Thinking along the lines of Mt 8:28,32, Jesus sent the evil spirits into the herd of pigs and the pigs went over the cliff. It was not mad cow disease, but wild cows going mad.

This year we SVDs are celebrating our centenary in Papua New Guinea. We had our first big celebration in Wewak on January 13 and the celebrations will continue through the year in the different parishes. We are expecting Henry Barlage, Superior General, to join the celebrations in August.

So, do you think Clare will win another All-Ireland final this year on the first Sunday of September? Anyway, let us all celebrate the joy of Risen Lord. Happy Easter.

April 6, 1996 Today is Easter Monday and things are very quiet here in Ambunti at the moment. I am taking the day off, and it is just as well as my energy level is not very high right now.

The Easter services were good, though Easter was a washout here at Ambunti station. After the Holy Thursday evening Mass, I went upriver to Maio on Good Friday morning. Casper, the prayer leader, had prepared the

Stations of the Cross very well. All along the ridge of the mountain track he had placed fourteen wooden crosses. A group of women dramatized their traditional custom of mourning by rubbing clay over their faces, hands, and legs. As the women moved from station to station they repeated the words of the song "Sorry, sorry, Jesus is dead". Two men carried the cross while Casper read the Bible text at each station. They followed the track through the village, the path where they carry their own cross each day. The dogs and roosters were wandering around the village undisturbed while their owners were reliving the road to Calvary. At the twelfth station the wooden drum (*garamut*) was beaten to announce the death of Jesus.

Sr. Geraldine, SSpS, had given a course to the prayer leaders in the parish some years ago on the Stations of the Cross, and since then most villages adapt her style on Good Friday to celebrate the Lord's Passion.

On Holy Saturday it was back to Ambunti again for the Easter Vigil Mass. There was a great spirit of cooperation preparing the Liturgy. One group decorated the church with numerous tropical flowers and sago palms. Another group gathered firewood for the Easter fire. The Legion of Mary rehearsed the drama of the Resurrection, and Deacon Andrew Huafilong and his group prepared the Exsultet for the Vigil Mass. Massanbuk settlement was given the task to light the Easter Fire. As this group appeared behind the sago swamp with their bush torches on Easter night, heavy dark clouds moved in over the hills. The Massanbuks managed to light the Easter fire but it was as if there was a countdown with the rain clouds, as just then the heavens opened, and the rains poured down for two hours. In less than three minutes we were taking cover in the church to continue the celebrations. Though the heavy rain poured down on the galvanized roof and made it very difficult to hear the readings, the choir made up for it by singing Easter songs.

It was down to Avatip on Easter Sunday morning. The sun was shining once again. A new day had begun. The people of Avatip came dressed up in their Sunday best to celebrate the day. The same day back in Ambunti, I watched on TV Pope John Paul celebrate Mass in St. Peter's in Rome.

The TV has its good points. I know a bit more about the world since moving to Ambunti. For three months we could receive Sky Sports. The highlights of Steve Collins's fight and Eric Cantona's return to Manchester

United were some of the highlights of the sporting world seen at this side of the globe. At present we have lost the signal for Sky Sports, but Euro News and CNN are keeping us up to date with world events.

Now some local news on the Sepik. On January 4 a Timbunke man Theo Jue was grabbed by a crocodile, and his body has not yet been recovered. Theo and his wife Monica were out fishing in their canoe when he decided to take a bath. It seems that the crocodile was resting in that very spot and took Theo under. It is the first time in living memory that a Timbunke man has met such a fate. The elders in the village blame the youth for the incident, because they misbehaved themselves at a dance in Aibom by getting involved in a fight with the people of Shortmari. When the fight got out of hand the Timbunke youth took off with an outboard motor belonging to Shortmari. The Timbunke people have returned to Shortmari since with the motor and a bunch of betel nuts to settle their differences in a customary fashion. Timbunke people hope this will get rid of the crocodile spell, which has the village living in fear. It is part of Sepik culture to settle differences in this way.

Last year 16,000 live crocodiles were flown out of Ambunti air-strip to a crocodile farm in Lae City, plus 28,000 centimetres of crocodile skin. The money is good in this business while the crocodiles keep producing. The Sunday collection also depends on such creatures.

One of my old friends, Ambrise Lisan from Yindkum village, died last month. Ambrose went on a few foot-patrols with me when I was looking after six villages in Tringe Parish from Timbunke. On my visit to Yindkum last January, Ambrose recalled the day I nearly pulled him into a flooded river near Buckenbowi. Across the twenty-foot river was a fallen log acting as a bridge. When crossing Ambrose held my hand, but the log started to sway when we reached the middle. I lost balance and we both went see-saw on top of the log. Only Ambrose's life-long experience at pole-walking kept both of us on the bridge. Whenever we meet in his house afterwards, the day we did a river dance at Buchenbowi was sure to be retold. May Ambrose dance in Heaven today.

Ambunti received two radio messages from Timbunke this past week. One was from Florin Koki. The radio was not that clear, however. I understand Florin Koki broke his shovel and would like if I could weld it for him.

The second message was from Simon Kevin, the farm manager; he came to speak to me personally about the death of the farm horse Jackie. Jackie was a two-year old stallion when Simon and I broke him in, and as we were both new at the job we had some great laughs and new adventures. Who would be first to mount the stallion was one of them. It was amazing how Jackie adapted to his new job rounding up the Timbunke cattle. Simon and I got to like Jackie and we respected him for his contributions on the farm.

I am happy Easter is over for another year, although we have to clear up now and get ready for a parish retreat in two weeks' time. So, rejoice and happy Easter, Christ has risen! God bless you and take care.

June 7, 1996 Life in Ambunti is very agreeable these times. Deacon Aufolong and a seminarian, Willie Wonduo, are here in Ambunti with me and Fr. Willibrord Kamion. It makes a big difference to have a few more living in the house; however, we are not always at home. Fr. Willie spends most of his time in the Mersie area, and Deacon Andrew and Willie Wonduo are out in the village giving Baptism, and Marriage instructions. Andrew will be getting ordained on September 26 this year.

On May 22 I went to Welfian, which is a mountain village between Ambunti station and Chambri Lakes. Many people from the parish had gathered there to do a Novena to the Holy Spirit. Alex Kapuwan, a prayer leader, and the seminarian and I decided to go by canoe as we had a lot of cargo to take along. We chose to take the river behind Avatip and on to Yabak. This route proved very difficult as the grass islands had jammed the waterway and we considered ourselves very lucky to end up on Lukluk Island before nightfall. The big man on the island is Stephen Wingue, and he took care of us for the night. He has four wives, twenty-four children, and many grandchildren. Although the family was Seventh Day Adventist (SDA) they treated us very kindly with sago and fish, and we sat late into the night talking about what we had in common. Early next morning we left Lukluk with Stephen Wingue's son as a guide to show us the easiest way to reach our destination. Most people had walked in from Ambunti side after travelling by canoe as far as Yaragai village.

The Novena was a good opportunity to hear the parishioners share their faith experiences and to get to know them a little better. I thought the best part of our four days together was where we spent time in a prayerful atmosphere sharing and discussing the Word of God and knowing how the Word of God has touched each one of us in his or her own unique way. The Charismatic group hopes to make the Pentecost Novena an annual affair.

Back at Ambunti station, life is more at an advanced stage. Every Tuesday on our way to give religious instructions in Ambunti High School we meet the garbage men collecting the toilet buckets with their tractor and trailer. The tractor driver never takes his hands off the wheel, but the bucket handlers must be the happiest men in Ambunti town, as they are always waving and greeting people as they move from house to house. Perhaps it is a good way to let the householders know it is collection time, and not to be caught unawares in the "small house". These bucket handlers are not interested in power or fame; their main concern is to earn a few *kina* to meet their family expenses.

One Tuesday when we arrived in the high-school we noticed some students washing in the creek. The students called after us, saying there were no classes as there was unrest at the school and the water supply was cut off. A group of Chambri students were sitting on an old motor canoe under a shade of a tree, so I joined them, and we started a discussion on problem solving. The discussion was even better than in a classroom as they got more involved in the debate.

Teacher Ivo Mepoi from Aibom has two daughters going to Ambunti High School and they asked me if I knew Ivo was teaching in Sangriman school for a number of years. I failed to recognize them in class, and they kept laughing at me for some reason or another. After class they told me who they were and how I used to stay in their house in Sangriman and make them laugh with my funny stories and spelling tests. The things they remember; I often wonder what is really going on in their little young heads.

Teacher Rosa and Philip Tonokon, also from Aibom, have a daughter in grade 10. She told me how she used to bring me a bucket of water every morning for cooking when we gave a retreat in Aibom in 1986.

There are about one hundred Catholic students at Ambunti High School. They are all fine young men and women searching for God and a meaning to life. I call the non-Catholics my Christian friends. So far, we have not encountered problems in this area. You know, most of the Public servants in the town are either Seventh Day Adventists or Assembly of God.

Between the town and the mission station is a lagoon where the Sepik River dumps most of its driftwood when in flood. This year the river brought a new supply. It's in this lagoon you see half the women of the town doing their morning exercises breaking firewood with their axes, and they sometimes can be heard giving strong orders to their younger kids not to play in the long grass as a poisonous snake might be hiding there. There is no need for this town to have a gymnasium, not while there is a need for firewood, and the Old Sepik keeps up the tradition with its free supply of driftwood. Nobody does exercise for exercise sake because their whole way of life provides more than enough for the body than needed.

So, you keep up the good work and I am looking forward to seeing you again in 1998 Take care,

June 7, 1996 Hello once again from Ambunti, and I hope you had a holy and happy Christmas.

Last year in 1995 I helped out in two parishes without priests, Marienberg and Torembi, as we are two priests here in Ambunti—Fr. Willibrord and myself. Marienberg Parish is at the mouth of the River Sepik, and it was established 84 years ago. The people there are very nice. They have time for God and time for people. Early one morning I visited one of their bush churches to find a group of women saying their morning prayers. Then they took off in their canoes into the mangrove swamps to check their fishing baskets. At each village I said Mass, heard Confessions, blessed Holy Water, visited the sick and elderly, and in some villages the people asked me to plant a coconut as it is the custom when one visits the place for the first time. We went from place to place, stayed overnight and ate local food, and met the people. Fr Adam Kruczynski, their parish priest, is on holidays plus a renewal course, so come next year he may come to Ambunti to do the same when I am on home leave. The other parish was Torembi, and that was a different experience.

One thing that hasn't changed here is the barter system. The women walk three hours out to the Sepik with their garden crops and exchange them for fish from the river people. I brought along some Catholic newspapers to sell. I had to leave them behind in exchange for fruit from their gardens.

After Christmas a group of us went upriver to purchase a large canoe. If you take out the world map and follow the Sepik River right up the Indonesian border, you could put your finger on the spot where we bought it. I have plans to drive it with an inboard diesel engine. It would cut the travelling expenses by half.

The year was not without its ups and downs. Just before Christmas I lost my forty-horsepower Yamaha motor in the Sepik. The propeller hit a floating log and the motor tripped off the stand into the river.

Back in May we had a big fight on the mission grounds. For weeks there was talk of a fight in the villages over fishing waters. They came with their bows and arrows and axes, shouting like a pack of baying hounds. One group backed off and the chase was on. Eventually the leaders brought both groups together and the tension eased off, but these disputes over land and water go on and on.

Of course, the greatest event of the year was the SVD centenary celebrations. The locals got the idea to act out the arrival of the first missionaries to Wewak town. As the canoe came ashore, the actor stood up holding the pidgin Bible on his chest and stepped on solid ground. About a thousand people came to celebrate the occasion and many of them wept openly to think this was how it happened a hundred years ago. The celebrations continued throughout the year in the different parishes, retelling the story of how the Word came to their homes.

At Ambunti, the occasion was celebrated with Mass, action songs, Bible drama, and sports. One leader in the church read out the history of the parish. He named all the Fathers and Catechists who worked in the area, going back as far as 1958 when the parish began. After that it was a sports day for all.

Two young deacons got ordained last year and four more on the list this year. The catechists and pastoral workers are doing a great job. They hold their services and prayer meetings every week, keeping the faith alive and active until Father makes his next pastoral trip. Last year we had 557 baptisms and ninety-eight marriages in the parish, a great effort by all.

June 7, 1996 It's sometime now since I wrote to you, although I receive your newsletter on a regular basis.

Its National Election time again in PNG. The election campaign is starting to heat up; polling day starts on June 13 and continues for four weeks or more. At this stage it is hard to predict any winners as there are 2,124 candidates standing for 107 seats. The Catholic Commission for Justice and Peace has also launched a Political Awareness Campaign to inform PNG people about their freedom to vote and to make the locals aware that these elections are important for the future development of their country.

Easter came early this year, and it passed joyfully. I flew into Torembi Parish for the Easter Services, and Fr. Andrew Haufilong stayed at Ambunti.

Torembi is a large parish with six air-strips. Torembi, Slai, Yakiap, Yamok, Kosembie and Gekorbai, which is just outside the Parish, border line. Ambunti has also a long green field. Therefore, I can fly into any of these air-strips in less than fifteen minutes. Torembi is the main station, with four teachers, a Catholic school and a health centre run by Catholic Health Services. In a parish like Torembi, where human strength is of greater value than human knowledge, it is quite a challenge to keep teachers at school. They aren't prepared for this lifestyle after three years in college or before that four or five years in boarding school.

On Wednesday of Holy Week, I observed all the schoolchildren going to the woods. When they returned to the open country the young boys were carrying firewood on their shoulders like young men. The girls were even better organised. They emerged from the forest in single file with a *bilum* of neatly chopped wood across their backs. They have already learned the art of carrying cargo. This is how it is in Torembi, where swamps and wetlands have made it impossible for the locals to build roads; all cargo is transported by "shanks' mare," except of course those who can afford to use the plane.

Holy Thursday was nutrition day at the school. The parents, teachers, and students came together to prepare a meal from locally grown food, which the children had succeeded in growing on the school grounds. The firewood, which was collected the previous day, was arranged into little fires and several cooking pots were hanging over them attended by their owners while they bubbled away to boiling point. Everyone brought along their own plate and spoon and they sat down on the grass to enjoy a pure organic meal. It is a beautiful part of their life; there is no hurry, no stress and no hotel bills to pay. Everybody seems to enjoy the whole process from growing the food to cooking it and finally eating it. It makes up for the many hardships the people have to endure.

At Torembi it is the custom that all parishioners from outlying villages come to the main station for Easter and Christmas. They did, and they came with the traditional dress to display their action songs and Bible drama. I left them in a happy mood when the plane came to pick me up on Easter Tuesday.

Back at Ambunti, things are going very well. The people of the parish and I have reason to celebrate after our latest achievement. Though I cannot claim all the credit, it was Bishop Leo Arkfeld's idea to introduce the Yanmar Diesel engine to the Sepik River, and Laura Martin, a former member of the provincial government, who provided the inboard engine. Laura Martin and Bishop Leo tried for four years to find someone interested in trying out the diesel engine in a dugout canoe. When she asked me, I told her I was the right man, and that's how it all began. Bishop Leo helped with finances to find a suitable canoe, and there was no shortage of spectators and advice, once word got out that Ambunti Parish was working on a new transport system for the Sepik.

The difference between the diesel and the petrol is: going downstream from Ambunti to Pagwi, the diesel engine uses 1.5 gallons of fuel, while the twenty-five-horsepower petrol engine needs four gallons to cover the same distance; however, the diesel engine takes half an hour longer. Going upriver, both engines travel at the same speed when fully loaded. The diesel engine sits on the canoe, and a drive shaft is connected to the gearbox, which is geared up to the shaft. The canoe moves beautifully in the water and at half speed she glides smoothly and quickly along. It is definitely something for the future, and I am glad to be part of it.

I am keeping well, thank God. The change to Ambunti has given me new energy and new challenges. Sure, I miss Timbunke. I saw the Timbunke children grow up and I knew their parents and uncles and aunts, but there is a time to say goodbye.

September 7, 1997 I hope this letter finds you in good form. It's back to school and back to college again for the younger generation in Ireland, and I am sure they enjoyed their summer break. Right now, all our schools in PNG are having a short holiday before they start their fourth and final term for this school year.

Last Tuesday we had celebration here at Ambunti to commemorate Independence Day. The day began with a special Mass followed by different sporting activities in the town. The Catholic Women's club was involved in several amusement games and Bible songs. They are a great group of women. How they still find time to participate in church and sporting activities and at the same time rear large families is an indication of their commitment to the parish. Here in Ambunti we have a disabled young man, Simon Gimbai, who walks on his hands and legs as a result of the polio he contracted twenty years ago. Simon is making the best of it. He has an interesting life story, starting from the time his school pals took him to school in a copra bag. I came to know Simon when the parish received money from the poor and needy fund and through these funds Simon received some towels, bed sheets, a pillow, a mattress and a mosquito net. Some Catholics on the parish board objected to Simon receiving help from the mission, as he was not a Catholic. Simon and I have now started a joint venture. He told me he was bored from sitting down all day and wanted something to do. He suggested starting a chicken farm, and he would need my help to transport three bags of meal—one starter and two fatteners—from Wewak to Ambunti. The plane would bring the day-old broilers and the project could get started.

Last May the first fifty chickens arrived, plus two extras. Amazingly they all survived to reach the market place. Simon is now preparing for his second batch. He wants to have the broilers ready for Christmas.

The weather is extremely dry and hot all over PNG. If rain doesn't come soon in the Highlands, they will need some assistance as their farm gardens are drying up. Here on the Sepik, we always have sago to rely on when the going gets tough.

Next month the crocodiles will start nesting. This is a concern for the locals who depend on the young crocodiles for a living. If the crocodiles move to a new territory to lay their eggs, the owner of the land is the rightful owner of the newborn crocodiles.

The tributaries of the Upper Sepik are also drying up to a trickle. One village, Yaragai, just across the mountain from here has a large canoe. They call it the "Blue Bus". It's now in dry dock waiting for the rain to return. When I asked the Yaragais why they gave the canoe that name they told me the mountain, which the tree grew on, is always covered in blue vapour and is known as the Blue Mountain. Once when the canoe arrived here in Ambunti full of people, I started counting the passengers as they disembarked. A prayer leader, one of the passengers, observed what I was doing. "Father, he said, "we once had eighty-four people in this canoe." That day I counted sixty-eight people and I thought surely it was the limit. Luckily none of the passengers were overweight.

This particular village seems to enjoy travelling and doing things together. They not only have one of the largest dugout canoes in the area, they also have a new mobile sawmill, which a non-governmental organization has helped to provide. There are five sawmills in the Ambunti District, all with the same aim, to keep out the multi nationals from logging the area.

There is a small bird in the Sepik plains like a skylark who loves to perch on the tallest trees and sing and sing when the heat of the sun has made everything go silent. I don't know if this creature sings best when she thinks nobody is listening, or in the silence she thinks everyone is paying attention to her song. Even the leaves on the trees stand still under this tropical heat, while the singing bird enjoys every moment of it.

Piggy, our dog, died some time ago. She used to sleep on the veranda and guard the house at night. She was a stray dog who was happy to eat the scraps from our table, and she decided to stay. Two cats have now taken up residence. All our lay missionaries have moved out except two "peace workers" who are teaching at Ambunti High School. They are due to leave at Christmas.

Most of our brothers and priests who went on home leave this year are now returning, after a well-earned holiday. Some of the older confrères prefer to keep to the old rule, home leave after five years, but the younger generation are opting for a break after three full years.

Last August I made my annual retreat on Kairiu Island followed by a short holiday. One morning I saw a whale surface in the channel near the island. It was my first time to see a live one. The locals told me that one comes around at this time every year. He must be also on his annual break.

I haven't heard yet who won the All-Ireland. I am looking forward to the newspapers to see the result. I was watching Diana's and Mother Theresa's funerals on CNN. They were both very special occasions in history and in our own span of life.

Life is great at this end, plenty of sunshine, but a bit of rain would be more than welcome now. Take care, and God bless you.

September 8, 1998 I am back again in PNG after a wonderful holiday back home. I enjoyed the break very much, though it seemed short as I had a lot of people to visit. It was a summer of activities, between the World Cup, the Tour de France, club and county championships, under-age games, regattas, horse racing, and agricultural shows. It's no wonder people feel no need to visit distant cousins or near neighbours. One can meet them all at different functions or activities throughout the year—that is, if one is not house bound.

On my arrival the people were happy to see me back. Marie Wawi, a teacher from the local community school, organized the children to greet me at the river bank with a hail of flowers, a well-rehearsed welcome song and handshakes from those present. Now it's back to reality for another term.

The people of PNG are still coming to terms with the tidal wave disaster which occurred on Friday night, July 17 at 7pm. Three giant waves estimated to be ten metres high roared in from the sea and hit the coast of Aitape along a thirty-kilometre section. They followed two earthquakes that measured seven on the Richter scale. It is estimated the waves travelled at 100 kilometres an hour and struck at the worst time as light was failing. The survivors had to wait until first light on Saturday morning before anything could be done for them.

One survivor, a young child, was taken out to sea. He was desperately holding on to a box to keep him afloat when his parents arrived to pick him up in a dugout canoe. The box was the tabernacle from the nearby church.

It is estimated that 2,243 died in the disaster and about 1,000 were seriously injured, and over 100 children have lost both parents.

I am still on the "road", going from place to place completing two pastoral visits to most villages since returning. I was in Singiok for Christmas Eve. Singiok is one of the largest villages in the area with a population of nearly 600. They are all gardeners and live off the land. Their catechist, Jerry Marks, had prepared the Liturgy in great detail. There were three processions during Mass—the entrance procession, the Bible procession, and the Offertory procession. The schoolgirls were the main participants. After Mass, the choir switched over to singing charismatic hymns, and immediately scores of people stood up and danced on the spot, waving their hands in the air and swaying their bodies to the rhythm of the guitar. It was Christmas, and it took so little to make them happy. I danced too, though not for long as the church leader arrived with a saucepan of pumpkin soup for my driver Damien Anton and myself.

Amaki 1 (as it so called) was our next stop for Christmas night Mass. Roland Hoskins, one of Amaki 1's more prosperous sons, has bought an electric band. He had it all set-up in the church. There was a drum set, bass guitar, a lead guitar, a keyboard, three speakers and a mixer. A portable generator was humming a hundred yards away with a power line coming through a hole in the wall. When they played it was not a silent night any more. It was a lovely Mass, with plenty of life and signing, and twenty-six young boys and girls made their first Holy Communion. Again, once the Mass was over, the band played all the latest Charismatic hymns and young and old joined in with the song and dance. They were expressing their joy at the birth of Christ. I wonder what it will be like for the year 2000.

On Christmas day, it was downstream to Amaki 2. Both villages are all Catholic and growing in number due mainly to the Catholic health centre nearby. Every time I visit these villages the children are playing in the sand along the riverbank or bathing in the river. They call out "Apo, Apo." That is the way for greeting a visitor. Amaki 2 had no electric band, however, but by next Easter the parish should have a set of its own. We are in the process of putting one together. It will be only for liturgical functions.

Damien and I were in an area known locally as Black Water region. The water coming out of the swamps is as black as tar and that is how it got its name. There are thirteen villages in this area scattered along the hillsides and along the riverbanks. Nine of these villages receive regular pastoral visits.

Damien Anton has only one eye, but it is a good one. When we came to find the inlet to Urumbanj village, I told him to drive towards the big tree with the white egrets sitting on it. It was the wrong tree. Damien was here before only once and he was able to recognize the right landmark.

Fr. Andrew Lolo from the Philippines arrived here two weeks ago for his introduction year to pastoral work, my thirteenth apprentice to date. Fr. Andrew is a qualified electrical engineer and also a good cook.

Last October, the World Wildlife Federation (WWF) moved into Ambunti. They are building a new house in the town. They have rented a house from the parish for six months. They have plans to introduce several new projects to the area and at the same time preserve the forests and wildlife in the region. David F. Hassell, a Canadian, is their project manager. It is a six-year project financed by the Dutch government.

On November the 25^h to 29 the parish held a four-day Charismatic rally here in Ambunti. Over 1,000 people attended. We invited a team from Wewak to give the seminar. We now know all the latest Charismatic hymns. The most popular are," Holy Spirit Kukim", "Jesus is the Winner Man", "Nogat Narapela Rot igo", and "Get up and Sing a Song". The rally has put new life into the parish.

Our girls' vocational school has only one teacher this year and lots of young girls inquiring every day to enrol. All our schools open again next month, and it's back to the grindstone for another year. I hope you all had a holy and happy Christmas, and may you have full and plenty and Good Health for 1999. Take care.

January 20, 1999 It has taken me until now to get my house in order, I mean filling in the Baptismal and Marriage Registry for 1998, writing up my financial report for last year and making a proposed budget for 1999.

Life is moving along here, though not as fast as other parts of the world. It was January 18 this year before I received my Christmas mail. The postmaster took some extra holidays, and nobody collected his or her post until he returned.

After Christmas the diocese lost one of its outstanding missionaries, Fr. Paul Blasig, SVD. He was forty-nine years in the Wewak Diocese. Fr. Paul was a man full of life and energy. He was known as a preacher, a builder, a doctor and a composer. His *wanwoks*[2] called him a jack-of-all-trades.

2 Colleagues.

Between two or three thousand people gathered for his last farewell, and the people of Negrie Parish composed a song to him and sang it at his Funeral Mass. When Fr. Paul reached his eightieth birthday people were asking him when he was going to retire, Fr. Paul's reply was, "I will retire when the Lord retires me" and so it all ended for him on January 10 with a head-on collision on the Sepik Highway. Fr. Paul's *wanwoks* were his twelve apostles and I am sure they will carry on his mission in the same spirit.

On January 29, we SVD in the Sepik region held our area meeting in Kanduanum Parish. It's the next parish downstream from Timbunke. There were seven of us in number, and we were seven different nationalities: Fr. Paul Kanda, PNG, Fr. Levi from Indonesia, Fr. Ruben, Colombia, Fr. Richard, Poland, Fr. Wilson, India, Fr. Andrew, Philippines, and me, Irish. We hold this meeting at different parishes every year. Fr. Richard did a great job as the host. He is doing a big job on the old wooden church at the main station. The tower of the church was wrapped in bamboo scaffolding, Hong Kong style. I stayed at Timbunke on my way back for breakfast, and the locals gave me two boxes of smoked fish. At Ambunti I divided the fish among the teachers and pastoral workers. When they asked me where I got it, I told them, I called home (Timbunke) on my way back. When I call to my former parish, Timbunke, I receive a warm welcome and they never let me go away empty-handed.

Last week I received three boxes of second-hand clothes from St. Paul's Overseas Aid Group. Most of the clothes are as good as new. One box had some beautiful hats, baby kits, and a plum-pudding. As far as the clothing is concerned, it's very difficult to divide them among the people without complaints coming back.

St. Joseph's school here at the parish centre is back to normal after its long Christmas recess. The parents came with grass knives a week before the school opened and cleaned up the school grounds. This week it was the schoolchildren's turn, and I met them all yesterday going home with a three-foot long steel grass knife. Most schools have lawnmowers now. However, when the grass is too long the grass cutters are called up.

The new church in Ambunti is progressing slowly. Pius Balsan is now putting up the fascia board, and next month we should be ready to put in the footpaths. We hope to have it opened for the year 2000. I have two

CALLED FROM THE FIELDS

steers ordered from Timbunke farm for the celebrations.

This past year was a great year for fruit. We had boxes of mangos for two months, and now it's pineapples every day, not to mention bananas all year round. Last Sunday, Fr. Andrew Lolo arrived back from Mersey with a wheelbarrow of pumpkins. As with the fruit, we had to deal them out among the neighbours.

I have three meetings coming up in March—an SVD District meeting, a Diocesan Pastoral Meeting, and Sepik Deanery meeting. The number of meetings we have to attend is growing by the year. It's part of the modern trend.

So, with that I wish you a happy Easter, and I am sure you are all looking forward to the spring and a good summer. Take care.

April 6, 1999 I have been working hard for the last few weeks; only today everything seems so peaceful, after all the Easter activities. Yes! It's springtime again in Ireland and for the students it's heading up for exam time again.

I am sure you are all concerned about the War in Yugoslavia. CNN is giving us a full report of the atrocious deeds going on in that country. When will mankind ever learn?

We do have our own power struggles here, especially among the pastoral workers. Everyone wants to be boss, and when I arrive in the village it's often the first problem I am confronted with. I usually hear two sides of the story and go to the *house-boy* where everybody concerned will come and debate the issue in public. They expect me to make a decision there and then, but now I refer all these problems back to the Parish Board or the Parish Steering Committee. However, I tell them it is better to sort their own problems. It's only human nature that these power struggles surface once in a while.

On February 26-27 the parish held its first board meeting for 1999. There were twenty-four items on the agenda and four topics for general discussion, and two letters. Among the topics were a financial and a pastoral report from each Christian community for 1998, a pastoral plan for 1999, which included Jubilee 2000, and the new church building in Ambunti town. I put forward a proposal to buy musical instruments for the new church. This would include a drum-set, bass guitar, lead guitar, a keyboard, and two speakers. The Parish Board turned it down. The members from the Black Water area felt it would benefit only Ambunti town and not the rest of the parish. You see, committee decisions don't always work in your favour.

When the school opened in February I had four people in one day looking for credit. I gave them a line of the "Wild Rover"— "a custom like yours I can have every day". I have sponsored two students at Ambunti High School and the word must have got around.

The Easter celebrations were excellent this year. Fr. Andrew Lolo went to the Black Water area and he hasn't returned yet. I returned from the Upper Sepik on the Wednesday of Holy week to lead the celebrations here in Ambunti.

On Holy Thursday the teachers from St. Joseph's school made an artificial garden in the church. They collected trees big and small ones from the bush and stood them upright in pots and between concrete blocks. The Blessed Sacrament was exposed all night on a small table between the trees for adoration. It was the people's idea to stay with Jesus all night in the Garden of Gethsemane. I joined them at 4 o'clock in the morning. Over one hundred people were still there; some were asleep, most were praying, and another group were sitting around a wooden fire drinking coffee. I was invited to join the coffee drinkers. They told me they were busy all night boiling water. I should have stayed all night, but I was trying to pace myself for the busy weekend ahead.

Good Friday service lasted three hours. For the Adoration of the Cross we used the Cross that was taken to Wewak by a group of fifteen people from the parish who walked for five days from Pagwi to Wewak.

On Holy Saturday night, forty-four babies were baptised. When I made the announcement after Christmas about Baptism for Easter, I thought we would have at most twenty. The teachers from other parishes had ten children baptised.

Ambunti is getting ahead, and over the last twelve months a number of permanent houses have been built. The World Wildlife Federation (WWF) has built a lovely two-storey house. It's known as the White House—not bad for the capital village of Ambunti.

One day has gone by since I started this letter. Yesterday, the parish buried one of its good Catholics, Sara Mankunda, from Malu village. Sara used to come to church every Sunday in her pull-canoe. She was a woman of 68 years and she looked every day of ninety. The Mass was in the family house with no dividing walls to separate the kitchen, dining room or sleeping quarters. Over two hundred people sat on the floor. After Mass we took the body, which was in a nice wooden coffin, across the Sepik and buried Sara up on a hill facing the village where she brought up her six children.

Just at the beginning of the school year, one of the teachers, John Grace, was transferred to a new school. Before John left, his six-year-old daughter told his mother, "Granny to-morrow I am going with Daddy and if you want to die, you can die". The granny was not well for days, but she is still alive.

Yesterday, Fr. Andrew Lolo arrived back from his Easter trip in the Black Water area. He had one Baptism and twenty Marriages over Easter. Today the kitchen is full of pumpkins and bananas. This is the church offering Fr. Andrew received during his twelve days in the bush. I think I should try one of these bananas now. God bless you and take care.

June 18, 1999 I have done a bit of travelling since I last wrote to you in April. This week I returned from Madang after attending a two-week seminar. Madang is thirty-five minutes flying time by F28[3] from Wewak. Twenty-four other SVDs attended the course, which dealt with two journeys in life. one up and one down. The best part of the workshop was the picnic by the sea.

During Pentecost Week I was in Tongujamb, an out-station of Ambunti. Half the parish went in their dugout canoes. Every village contributed fish and sago, pumpkins, and bananas for the final Mass of Pentecost Sunday. The leaders of each village brought a piece of firewood to the altar where it was set alight and then given back to the leader again as a liturgical symbol to take the Fire of Pentecost back to their communities and put it alight. Then a church leader came to the front of the church with a live rooster inside a sago basket. He held up the basket and told the people of Singiok, "I give you this rooster and every time it crows it is to remind you not to

3 A Fokker F28 Fellowship, a short-range jet airliner

be late for Sunday services!" Very often we get flowers or a coconut to take back home to plant in the garden as a reminder for special occasions, but the live rooster is the best one yet.

I also spent five days in Timbunke at the end of April. Twelve pastoral workers and I went down in our diesel canoe, and it was wonderful seeing all the old faces again. I am now forgetting some of the names and I am also mixing up the younger children with the older ones. Next week I am off to Bangus village to open a new church, so you see I am on the move most of the time.

Life is good here in Ambunti away from all the troubles in the towns. Our tourist trade is drying up; they are afraid to come because the rascals are robbing them.

Fr. Liam Dunne went home in April as his mother was dying, and she died before he arrived. He is due back any day now. This year, one of our oldest priests, Fr. Hugo Schulz, went on home leave. He was born in 1910 and he is due back next month. Two other Fathers left together but they were only 80 and 84.

So, this is a fast letter from Ambunti. Regards to all. God bless and take care.

July 21, 1999 This is the latest update from the sights and sounds around Ambunti and district. On June 25 I blessed a new bush church at Bangus village. It was a marvellous occasion with great support coming from the main centre here in Ambunti. Their church leader, Ambunigi Aboran, gave us a short history of Bangus. He told us he was a young man when he organized the building of the first church in 1948. Fr. Kowalski came to open it and he brought along five rolls of cloth, which he cut and gave each person a piece to wear like a bath towel around them.

That was the first time the people of Bangus wore clothes, a turning point in their history. Ambunigi went on to tell us he joined the army in 1950 and after that the Catholic Church ceased to function in Bangus. He is 69 now and he wants to start again where he left off forty-nine years ago. In the intervening years the Seventh Day Adventists and the South Sea Evangelical churches have contributed enormously towards the development of this village, which has over 600 inhabitants.

After Mass the people gathered in front of the homemade grandstand to hear the nine guest speakers. I was the last to speak and there was nothing left to be said so I changed the subject. I told them to dress well, look smart and feel good about themselves, to educate their children, not lose their culture and look after their bush (ground). I don't know if they understood what the Irishman was trying to tell them, and I was wondering too. Which was the better world, theirs or mine? That night we held a prayer meeting next to the church, with the stars and the moon shining down on us. Before we left the leaders gave me a coconut to plant on the church grounds. It's their custom, a bit like signing the visitor's book, only the coconut has a much deeper symbolism.

Every week two old ladies, Margaret and Agatha, come here to clear the church grounds and its leaves from a sixty-foot mango tree. They bring along their lunch and make a day out of it. Both have their families reared and both have their husbands laid to rest back home in their gardens. When this tree is shedding its leaves, one puff of wind and it's back to where they started. I suggested removing the mango tree but there was a strong opposition. Fr. Toth told me he planted it in 1985 on Br. Stephen's feast day, and moreover, when it bears fruit every two years the local people reap 99% of the harvest.

At the same church one evening, a mother and her children came to Mass. The mother took the first reading, and two of her children went up to the lectern and stood by her, and then the third child ran up and held on to his mother's dress. The fourth girl went up to bring him down, but he wouldn't budge. The four children remained standing beside their mother until she finished the reading. I said to the mother afterwards, "You had some strong supporters today." It is not unusual for one or two children to follow the parent up to the altar of lector, but four is the record to date.

Children feel very much at home here in God's house. Nearly every week we have Sunday school for the children and they join the main congregation during the Offertory. One Sunday, I counted eighty-three children marching into the church; most were barefoot, though neatly dressed. One Sunday they brought a flower each and placed it at the altar, and at other times they bring a basket of fruit. If they have learnt a new song or hymn, they will gladly sing it for us before the closing prayer.

It's two laywomen, Lucy Waison and Leak Gunguai, who do most of the work supervising for the Sunday school. They must be doing a good job, because the children look forward to their own get-together. Once I heard a parent say, "They keep reminding us tomorrow we have Sunday school."

Speaking about children, I had a nice experience during the wet season when two little girls and a boy from the Sowaimbau family offered to take me across the flooded lagoon in the dugout canoe. When I accepted their offer, they immediately became anxious and told me to get in, sit down, and stay in the middle. They were Sepik kids, so I gave them full responsibility. The journey was no more than one hundred and fifty yards, but once we arrived safely across, the children were delighted with their achievement and told those who had come to see what the commotion was about— "We helped Father Michael." I thanked them for their good deed and the three happy children returned to the same spot where they picked me up to wait for their mother who had gone to the hospital for a check-up.

On July 14 we had a change of government in PNG and our new prime minister is Mekere Morauta. The people, and especially the politicians, told the former prime minister, Bill Skate, that he was the one causing the problems, so he gave way and resigned. The new government will meet again in August to form the new cabinet, and there is great speculation as to who gets the top jobs.

January 4, 2000 It's already four days into the Millennium and it will take some time to get used to the idea. I saw the New Year celebrations all over the World on television, including Ireland where over one million candles were lit to celebrate the occasion.

Here in Ambunti Parish, we celebrated the new Millennium our way. Young and old came together on New Year's Eve to share a meal, which was prepared by the women folk the night before. The menu consisted of one ton of sweet potatoes and taro, five meal bags of cooking bananas, five cartons of fresh fish, five cartons of chickens, and a young 500-kilo heifer from Timbunke farm. When the meal was cooked, it was all brought together, still in the pots and saucepans, and put on canvas at St. Joseph Community School. Each person brought along his or her own plate and spoon and we sat down on the grass to enjoy the last meal of the Millennium.

It was a real community experience. As the New Year approached, all knelt down in silent prayer to give praise and thanks to God for the moment it was. Then the church leader, Sailas Jrajumb, beat the wooden drum and we knew Papua New Guinea had entered the New Millennium. With that, we all stood up to recite our slogan, "Immanuel 2000", and the usual handshakes and good wishes were exchanged and went on throughout the night. Midnight Mass lasted until two o'clock and at that stage most of the children and babies were out flat on the canvas fast asleep. Several mothers who gave the night before cooking were unable to make it through the second night and they too were on the canvas sound asleep. As I said it was a real community experience and if you felt like sleeping it was the most normal thing to do at 2 o'clock in the morning.

A few coffee pots were heated up and more coffee and sugar were needed to get through the last four hours before dawn. Before the sun rose, everyone was on their feet again dancing in the Charismatic style, and at the break of day we turned towards the rising sun to recite once again the slogan "Immanuel 2000". This was it, a new day had dawned, a new Millennium had begun, and it was back to our humble homes to continue life as usual. The Apans crossed the river in their canoes and went upstream. The Malu people walked down to their homes along the riverbank of the Sepik. The Massambucks went up-mountain to their living quarters on the hill, and the town-folk walked back to their settlements. Most parents were still carrying sleeping children in their arms and over their shoulders. When the young children awake from their sleep and when the babies grow up, their parents can tell them how they celebrated the new Millennium with song dance and prayer and with a community of 800 people.

Our first millennium baby was born at a minute past nine on New Year's morning. The parents, John Kaba and Agnes Ganjui, they have called him Immanuel. I hope you too had a good celebration to mark the "rollover" from the old to the new, and the Y2K bug did not affect you. Here in Ambunti, it was HCC—Human Computer Crash. We had a hard time getting the message across to the people that it was a computer problem— and not the end of the world, as some thought. Now it is all over and we have to focus on something else for the year 2000 and beyond.

Our Christmas celebrating also went very well. On December 11 my driver, Damien Anton, and myself took off from Ambunti in our forty-seven-foot canoe, *Jona* by name. We also had thirteen other passengers. Peter Inbugus stayed with us all the twelve days, and I had to tell him I had only two plates and he would have to eat out of the saucepan. It turned out that Peter was good company and a great provider. He had cousins and friends in every village. He would bounce back in the evening with a rope of cooking bananas or a bag of yam over his shoulder, all for the cooking pot. On Christmas night I was back at the main station for Midnight Mass. Sr. Clothilda had prepared fifty-eight children for Baptism. It was a beautiful night with the moon shining brightly above. The parishioners had decorated the church and sealed off the door, so we too, like Pope John Paul, could open the door of the church as a symbol and enter the Jubilee 2000 year.

Another event of importance occurred on August 21: our retired Archbishop Leo Arkfeld died. He was better known as "The Flying Bishop". The government gave him a state funeral and, as we say in Ireland, "it was the finest ever seen". Ambunti people travelled in great numbers, and it took a week to get them back. All the other denominations were present in full strength, and the AOG (Assembly of God) let us use their musical instruments to play at the funeral Mass. There was a big clap when it was announced, and we were all happy to know that such tensions between the different churches are disappearing.

Bishop Leo spent forty-two years flying in PNG. During the weekends he used to fly out to the mission fields for Confirmation. Bishop Leo would load his plane with a 16 mm movie projector, a portable generator, some films and 200 feet of electric power line. When night came people gathered from all over the area to watch the movies. The movies were a great crowd filler as there was nothing else on in the district. Many people still talk about the first movie they ever saw, and that it was Bishop Leo who showed it. At that time in the sixties and the seventies most people in the bush were unable to read or write, but they enjoyed the comedies and cowboy films to no end. Now the projector is obsolete, and videos have taken over. Wirui Air Services has also stopped flying and only three of the forty-five mission air-strips are still being used and serviced by the Mission Aviation Fellowship (MAF).

It has been a marvellous year here in Ambunti, where there have been no floods or droughts like other parts of the world. It was also great year for Cork. I watched the All-Ireland hurling final on video and it was a close one. I also enjoyed reading all the good results during the summer. May God bless you with peace, joy, and good health for the year 2000.

May 1, 2000 The Easter celebrations went very well this year, as the rains stayed off and the people put a lot of work into preparing the Liturgy for Holy Week. Ambunti town prepared the Liturgy for Palm Sunday. The leader Paul Gomiar arranged with the town-folk to clean the route of the procession and line the road with branches of palm trees and flowers. The church was like a small jungle when everyone held up his or her palm branch for the blessing. I had a bucket of holy water and a good sprinkler and I made sure everyone got their share. When I finished blessing the palms, I asked if everyone got a drop. The children in the front row answered "Yes" quickly and were spared a second thundershower!

The village of Apan prepared the Liturgy for the Holy Thursday and Malu led the way of the cross on Good Friday. The teachers of St. Joseph's school and Massanbuk prepared the Liturgy for Holy Saturday night. A horse-load of firewood was stacked neatly at the school ground and fourteen bamboos were laid along the route of the candle light procession to the church. The bamboos were cut into six-foot lengths and stuck upright into the ground about twenty feet apart. The cavity of the bamboo was filled with sawdust and soaked in diesel to give off bright red flame.

The lighting of the fire was performed by Massanbuk. Over a dozen human figures came down the mountain dressed in traditional style, each waving a flare of light up and down to increase its burning power as they approached the pile of timber. They danced around the wood several times, before suddenly turning towards their target to set it ablaze. As the fire grew bigger and brighter, we stood about thirty feet away and sang hymns. The Easter Candle was lit and so were a hundred smaller candles. The fourteen bamboo flares were already in full glow as we headed up the mountain towards the church, and that was part of our Easter Vigil, the service of light. This Easter, eleven of our stations had tabernacles, which meant the communities had the Eucharist for Holy Week, even though they had no priest.

Pius Balson, one of my permanent workers, is a qualified carpenter. He made two beautiful tabernacles from hard wood; one is now down in Avatip and the other at Yambun. It is our plan for the Jubilee year to give each village a tabernacle that is up to the required standard. Pius is a tall lanky man, and nine of his ten children have inherited his carriage, while the other one, Sabrina, is short and stocky like the mother. They are lovely children. Last Friday I returned from Wewak and they were down at the riverbank to take all my cargo up to the parish house. Pius, the second youngest, took a big box; it was a carton of toilet paper.

Two months ago, one of my former workers from Timbunke, Florian Koki, called me up on the mission radio. He told me his wife had another baby girl. He has eleven children now. I told him that was a full soccer team. Florian has six sons and one is called after me, Michael Koki. His main concern was that Michael Koki was about to start school and he needed a new school outfit for him. Lucky for Florian, Sr. Felicia McCarthy from St. Paul's Overseas Aid group had sent me two boxes of clothes that same week, and most of his family found something that would fit them. Florian has promised he will help me out with the new church if the need arises.

I visited Timbunke on March 25. I travelled by road and took two large tyres for the Massey Ferguson 178 tractor. Simon Kevin and I mounted one on the tractor and the other tyre was too good to remove just yet.

My main reason for going to Timbunke was to say Mass for Catechist Paul Kambu who had died February 13. Paul and I worked for five years together and we travelled to the faraway places in the Middle Sepik, as well as helping in the neighbouring parish, Torembi. Paul was one of the lucky ones. He was born with lots of talent; he loved life and lived it to the full. He had an excellent voice and loved singing hymns. Sr. Mersie, SSpS, stayed twelve years in Tambunum and she supported Paul and trained him to be a catechist for his home village. Paul was also full of fun. He used to make us all laugh especially when he took part in Bible drama. Paul is now buried 200 yards from the Sepik River and about six feet above water level during the dry season. I planted a flower on his grave, but his wife later told me no flowers would grow there as the river floods in the wet season and can kill them.

Paul loved flowers and was always collecting new ones to plant around the catechist house in Tambunum, and he also loved the Sepik. He used to say to me, "Me belong Sepik, Sepik belong me", and there he has finally come to rest, RIP. Strange none of his six children inherited his singing voice.

It's five years ago today since I left Timbunke, and I still go back for different meetings during the year and it's nice to see them all again though the older ones are moving on and the young ones are growing up and life goes on and on.

At our first Parish Board meeting this year, the motion was passed that our parishioners should dress up and look smart when coming to church on Sunday. The announcement was made the following Sunday after Mass. And since then everyone is making that extra effort to look respectable, including myself. Another motion was passed that the village of Amaki should put up a public notice board to inform the community what is going on.

June 26, 2000 A few days ago, we celebrated St. John's Eve, which means the days will start to shorten again, and so another year goes by. I am on holidays at the moment and on July 10 make my annual retreat in Madang. Fr. John Fullenbach, one of our best-known SVDs, is directing it.

Lots of interesting events took place within the last few months in Ambunti. On Sunday, May 28, a Russian heavy-lift helicopter arrived just after Mass to unload the barge, the *Kadora Madang*, which arrived that morning with equipment for a new communications tower. It took two days taking material up to the mountaintop behind Ambunti town. The local people showed great interest in the operation and a large crowd gathered along the riverbank to observe the most modern way of doing things. There was a great cheer when the helicopter went into full power and lifted off with a smaller loader to clear the building site. Later, there was a greater cheer when a carton of biscuits fell off the sling and into the Sepik. Someone from the Prugunawi settlement went out to retrieve it, and several in the crowd suggested we should call to Prugunawi for coffee and biscuits. The new tower is expected to function within the next eight months.

From June 8 to 11, we held our Pentecost rally at Nagri, a village not far from the West Sepik border. It was a nice occasion for all the villages in the area to take part and enjoy each other's companionship. Each group received a welcome with flowers and song as they arrived at the archway on the air-strip that was made from sago palms. Those who came with me were sprayed with flowers.

A hundred and twenty people from Amaki walked through the bush. They started blowing bugles half a mile out from Nagri to let us know they were on their way, and a big crowd went to the edge of the air-strip to welcome them as they emerged from the green tunnel of trees. The organizing committee brought the group of people to Alex Kiasaka's house. Alex's wife is from Amaki, so the Amaki people felt at home in this patch of ground. The Nagri people had prepared well for this rally. They had built ground toilets for men and women, and every group had a place to sleep. Firewood was stored away for cooking. The hosting village provided food. It consisted of pumpkin, sago, and bananas. Smoked fish and wild pigs were on limited supply.

Teacher Alex Kawasaki had built a new permanent house and Johannes Steven and I were given a room on the first floor. There were at least thirty others sleeping in the same house. One night a child woke up screaming as if he had had a bad dream, and the mother began immediately to pat it on the back, calling "Pater, Pater, Pater". She was trying to tell the child it would wake Father. In the morning those who heard the mother calling were teasing her, and everyone was laughing at the whole affair. They saw the humour in little things like this.

The woman of the house, Mrs. Kawasaki, looked after Johannes and me very well. Twice a day she would send her children to our room with pumpkin and yam.

The grandstand for the rally was erected facing out to the air-strip and when the plane touched down the second day. Everyone moved to one side. The day began at five o'clock with Morning Prayer, followed by breakfast. Mass at eight o'clock was followed by two hours of spiritual input. Then there was a break until four o'clock to give the people time for a siesta and their mid-day meal. From four to five o'clock it was a sing-along and when everyone had gathered it was more input followed by a charismatic prayer meeting.

The people of Amaki were in charge of the Liturgy on Sunday, and they spent two hours preparing the entrance and Bible procession the night before. The entrance procession wasn't walking up the aisle but walking down the air-strip. It was done in traditional style. It was the Amaki people's finest hour, and what better way to display their talents than in front of their home crowd. What amazed me most was the amount of energy people had. They kept singing and clapping hands until the portable generator ran out of petrol. The musical instruments were the property of the Christian Revival Church (CRC) and everyone was happy that the Catholics and the CRC were now able to work together.

This year we had no real wet season, though we had a lot of rain just now. The Sepik did not rise much. It means the river people could plant their gardens earlier than usual, and we did not have a lot of mosquitoes—in all, a pleasant year so far.

Last Tuesday it was announced on the mission radio that the SVD had a new superior general, Fr. Anthony Pernia from the Philippines. We also have a new Bishop. He is Fr. Tony Burgess, a diocesan priest from Aitape. He will be ordained Bishop on September 27. I will be twenty years ordained on that day. So farewell till I hear from you again. God Bless you and take care

July 5, 2000 Fr. John Walsh has retired on his fiftieth Jubilee. I will be wishing him well on his retirement. Fr. James Coombes and Fr. Paddy Sheehy have passed also to their eternal reward. Here in Wewak Diocese we have seven Fathers who are retired. One is over 93, one in his eighties and one in his upper seventies. They have spent their lives here in PNG and they want to die here. Some of these Fathers do light relief work—like hearing confessions and saying Mass.

Within the last three months, three of our Irish SVD priests died at home in Ireland—Fr. Dermot Walsh, Fr. Brendan Murphy, and Fr. Brendan O Reilly.

Life keeps moving on too at this end. I recently made a trip to Walfain and I had to climb over a steep mountain. When I found the going tough, the local people told me I was getting a bit old now for mountain climbing. I think they will soon be right, though I always feel good after such trips when I return home.

Usually people come to meet me when they know I am coming to their village. On my last trip to Walfain a big group of people came to Yaragai Village to help me carry my cargo. I just walked free-handed all the way. Once we reached the mountaintop, Simon the church leader produced a fresh coconut for me to drink. It is always part of the trip to rest for half an hour once we reach the top. Our conversation is often focused on the people who live in the distant hills. Though once we discussed the devil taking Jesus up the mountain, today we spoke about Yembiyembi and, mind you, it was very positive, and why not. A Yembiyembi girl has married into Walfain and is taking a leading role in church activities. For some years I was looking after Yembiyembi when I was stationed in Timbunke and now we were able to talk about the people we knew there. With the passing of the years, (I was told) a few of those were now resting in peace somewhere in the distant hills.

When we arrived at Walfain, three teenage girls were playing hopscotch in the village square; they must not have heard us coming because we were walking barefoot, and when I returned to put my wet shirt on the line, they had disappeared.

Banocort, which is next to Walfian, has a new bush church. It was the people from Walfain who helped with the building. Very often the church made from bush material can mean more to the local people than a permanent one built by foreign aid.

Last month I gave a retreat to forty Communion Ministers in Kunjingini Parish. One woman at the retreat told us how she never went to school, and she could not read. She sent her children to school, and she asked them to teach her how to read. Now she can read the Bible at her own pace.

Some months ago, a bad gale blew the roof off the Ambunti Lodge. Since than a few of their guests are coming to the mission's guesthouse. It helps to increase the cash flow. I told one of the workers at the lodge that he didn't have to be in a hurry repairing the roof. We get very few tourists anyway, due to the law and order problem in the country.

The WWF is building a research centre in Ambunti. They are giving employment to more than twenty people now between canoe drivers, typists, builders, and security workers. This year WWF has used our parish facilities three times to give different courses on bookkeeping, small business, and environment awareness.

The parish has also given some course this year. Fr. Andrew Lolo gave a retreat to the Legion of Mary, I gave a prayer leader workshop, and Ken Charles, a layman, gave a workshop to the Charismatic leaders. This month, Sr. Marie is coming to give a workshop on HIV to three schools in Ambunti. We have several other activities planned for the year.

Could you guess what I received one Sunday for an offering? We have a collection every Sunday, and people also contribute vegetables, fish, and sometimes a live rooster. On this particular Sunday, there was a roll of toilet paper in the basket. You see how my parishioners think of all my needs. God Bless for now and take care.

January 10, 2001 The Jubilee year has come to an end, and I was in the land of the living to see it pass by. There was nothing extraordinary about its passing, though there were lots of events that kept the year 2000 alive and interesting.

The main event last year was the Eucharistic Congress. It was held at village, parish, and diocese level. Ambunti Parish used two monstrances to take the Blessed Sacrament around the parish, one for the Black Water area and one for the main Sepik River. The monstrance was brought in procession from community to community by the hosting village, and finally made its way back to Ambunti main station.

The Black Water people walked over the mountain range behind Ambunti station carrying the Blessed Sacrament. When they reached the mountaintop, they started beating their drums and blowing homemade bugles. The local villages around Ambunti responded to the call and went out to meet them. Each person was carrying a branch from a tree and it gave the impression the whole mountain was moving. They sang hymns and charismatic songs all the way to the church where finally the Blessed Sacrament was put back in the tabernacle after a ten-hour vigil. In the meantime, the Eucharist procession was taking place along the Sepik, and they were equally impressive when they arrived back in Ambunti in their decorated canoes. From here we began the parish Eucharist Congress and the following week the Diocese congress took place in Wewak.

In Wewak, the procession started in four different areas, each presenting the four corners of the Diocese, the Sepik highway, the North, the East Coast road and the island people. Just before dusk the four areas converged at Prince Charles Oval, and it was an impressive scene to see so many people carrying banners and flowers and lighting candles all coming together in a spirit of prayer and faith.

It was part of our Jubilee year program to install tabernacles in thirteen out-stations. The other out-stations were not up to standard. The people in Mariwai village also built a bush church after many years of persuasion. I had passed them by on a few occasions without calling in, and they asked why. I told them it's time you built a new church. The bush church was blessed last year in real traditional style. The elders dressed me like a traditional chief with ancestral headdress. The young children hung a big bouquet of flowers around my neck. They knew how to oil me up and make me feel good.

Four diocesan deacons were ordained to the priesthood during the past year. Three for the Diocese, and one SVD, Fr. Stephen Rex Simangi, is now preparing himself to take up his mission appointment on the Amazon later this year.

The weather pattern was very different to predict last year. The wet season came instead of the dry season and destroyed most gardens along the riverbanks. The abundance of watermelons, which we enjoyed in other years, was not seen at all in the market place. The Sepik Highway was also torn apart by the continuous rain, and several patches of the road were turned into red clay. The big tracks needed manpower to get over the hills and through the mud holes. Once I came upon a line of PMVs[4] trying to get over a steep hill. All the passengers got out of the trucks and pulled and pushed until every vehicle made it to the top. These exercises had to be repeated a few times more before reaching the town of Wewak. What struck me most about this task was the people's power—what men, women, and children can do when they work together to achieve an objective.

Last August Fr. Carlos Alberto from Paraguay was appointed to Ambunti

[4] Public motor vehicles.

for his introduction to Pidgin and pastoral work. Fr. Carlos spent some time in Ireland learning English before he came to PNG, so it wasn't a complete culture shock when he discovered an Irishman here before him. He can now drive the speedboat and go out to the villages on his own.

It rained most nights during the Christmas period. One night it rained so heavily that I complimented the owner of the house I was staying in for making the thatched roof waterproof. In other houses, I woke up more than once to find a waterfall coming straight down on the mosquito net.

Despite all the rain it was good year for mango fruit. Here in Ambunti the missionaries planted many mango trees and this year we reaped the fruits of their labour. At one out-station this Christmas, one man from Tangajamb, Alosi Wangasump, brought me five large mangoes and then he went on to tell his story: "Twenty years ago when I worked for the missions at Marienburg I collected mango seeds and brought them back to plant in my own land." He went on to say this particular mango came from Madang and missionary sisters brought it to Madang from the Philippines.

Last month the Salesians Missionaries of Mary Immaculate took up residence at Ambunti. Two sisters will teach in the vocational school and one will help with pastoral work. All three sisters come from India and their order specializes in teaching. Ambunti people are delighted with the new arrivals.

George Balan, one of my pastoral workers, has brought a gold dredger. I told him it would make or break him, but so far it has done neither; he had a few good days with the dredger, but he has had several bad weeks. I see less of George now as he is camping out in Yaragai near a creek hoping one day he will strike it lucky.

One evening there was a knock on the door. It was a little six-year girl, Natasha Wan, with four fish, she managed to catch. She gave me the fish and whispered in to my ear, "I would like a ball." I couldn't say no; it was, after all, a very small request. I gave her a tennis ball. St. Paul Aid Group has sent it on in one of their boxes. She felt so happy with the exchange and ran off to join her comrades down by the river. Since then many more children came with fish, but the tennis balls ran out!

On a lighter note, Ambunti is hosting a soccer tournament this week, between the Sepik villages, and hopefully it will go peacefully; that would be a good start for 2001. I will leave you here for the present. I hope you had a holy and happy Christmas and I wish you many blessings for the New Year. Take care and God Bless you.

March 1, 2001 Yesterday I finished answering my Christmas mail, so it's time to move on and fill you in on the more recent happenings on the Sepik.

On February 1 Bishop Ray Kalisz arrived by plane at Ambunti for the official hand-over of the Rosary Sisters convent to the Salesian Sisters. Our big worry was how to transport Bishop Ray around the station, as he had problems with his hips and finds it hard to walk or stand for a long period of time. We came up with the idea to use the tractor and trailer.

When Bishop Ray came off the plane the Catholic Women's club were there to greet him and a cane chair was arranged for him in the trailer. The women also sat into the trailer and sang a song they had composed that morning while waiting for the Bishop to arrive. Simon Conte was the driver of the David Brown 990 and Johannes Stephen held the umbrella over the Bishop to protect him from the sun. I was sitting next to the Bishop, and we jostled along the road, past the police station and on to the market place and then up the road towards the high-school and right towards the vocational school

Ninety-six teachers and students doing a crash course at the school formed a guard of honour for Bishop Ray and presented him with a bouquet of flowers. Three Rosary Sisters also came to Ambunti to witness the official hand-over of the sister's convent. The vocational school is now renamed St. Clara Technical High School. Bishop Ray was happy he came for this important occasion, but he did say it could be his last trip to Ambunti as he is retiring next year.

On Friday, February 9, I drove to Timbunke in my speedboat. Bishop Ray asked me to go there to oversee the running of the parish for two weeks, as there was no parish priest there. The two weeks were focused on preparation to welcome home Bishop Cherubim Dambui to his native village. Fr. Cherubim was ordained Auxiliary Bishop of Port Moresby on February 12 and only his immediate family and three clan members were able to be present. When I arrived in Timbunke, the village people wanted

Mass to be said on the same day and at the same time as their beloved son was being consecrated. A big crowd turned up, and it was a great feeling to see all the familiar faces again after almost six years.

Bishop Cherubim eventually arrived by speedboat and went straight to his village, where the entire community gave him a traditional welcome. The welcome ceremony was not complete the first evening, so it was back again to the village the next morning. This time Bishop Cherubim and I were taken shoulder-high towards the *house-boy*, and when the singing came to a halt, several speeches were delivered, including one from myself. The women remained outside the *house-boy*, as is the custom in such events.

After this, it was back to the Mission Station where Bishop Cherubim was to say Mass and the women had prepared a meal for the entire gathering. A small plane circled overhead that morning, but it had to return to base as the activities of the day were taking place on the air-strip. It was a great time to be back in my former parish, where I spent twelve years.

During my stay in Timbunke, I visited five communities and had Mass and Confessions in seven others. I was to return on February 26, but I received word that morning that Catechist Godfried Bettino's wife, Emma, died that night, so I had to attend the burial. The next day I returned to Ambunti with the boat loaded with fish and bananas. I also had gifts and letters to deliver to friends and relatives from Timbunke who are living in Ambunti.

On a different note, but still about the Bishop: last month we opened a new classroom here in Ambunti for St. Joseph's school. It is called the "Bishop Leo Classroom" after the late Bishop Leo, who was nearly forty years as Bishop in PNG. I am sure you must have read his book, *The Short Story of a Long Life*. Take care and God Bless you.

March 8, 2001 I hope you are keeping well. It is some time since I heard from you. The post at this end is often delayed by two or three weeks due to the closure of Ambunti air-strip.

Today the air is clear and fresh after a heavy night's rain. I have put the men to work around the station. Pius Blouson is cleaning the weatherboards around the guesthouse, Bernard Bowie is repairing the outboard motor for the health centre, and Damian Anton is digging a hole for the rubbish. Fr. Carlos is on bush patrol with Johannes Stephen and Sr. Jolly while we are in Wewak getting school material.

Down below me in the flat patch of ground is St. Joseph's School. This year there are 448 children enrolled. During lunch break the screams, laughter, and voices from the school grounds are the same as any other school. What caught my attention this week from one of the classrooms was the song "Old Mc Donald Had a Farm" coming from one of the classrooms. One teacher, Jerry Gongiwin, was drilling his students with a moo-moo there and a quack-quack there. I thought Old McDonald was out of date, but this week he was very much alive.

Yesterday I was down at Avatip for a funeral of a seventeen-year-old girl. She died in Goroka and her body was flown to Ambunti and taken to her home place for burial. The funeral service was held in the family house. There must have been at least 200 people sitting on the floor and as many more sitting around the outside. The coffin bearers were dressed in black trousers, white shirts, and neckties. Before the grave was closed, the family members put all her personal belongings into the grave. In the background, the Catholic youth sang a number of farewell songs. Finally, the grave was banked with native flowers and the crowd moved off in twos and threes.

Our new Salesian Sisters are settling in well in Ambunti. Last week I went to the High School in Ambunti to introduce one of the sisters to the students. I told them this was Sister Jolly. Sister gave a big laugh; she told me she was Sr. Alice. The students gave a big laugh too—I got the name mixed up. Anyway, the students know me well and they are a very good group. I am sure the laugh will do more good than harm.

The sister gave me an extra job last month. Just below the mission station is a creek with four logs spanning it, acting as a bridge. The sisters found it very difficult to get across. One morning Johannes Stephen and I arrived in our canoe with some planks to repair the bridge. After ten minutes on the bridge we had volunteers hammering nails and sawing timber. The sisters feel more confident now in making the crossing.

Just down below the Mission Station is a settlement. There must be five or six families living there. One boy from there, Edward Kunes, called one evening looking for a candle, as he had no light to do his homework. When

I gave him the candle, he told me that last one I gave him lasted three and a half weeks. I told him he didn't do much study if the candle lasted that long. Edward often calls to the house with some fresh fruit and vegetables. There are eight in his family, five boys and three girls. It's nice to see that a family that size with plenty mouths to feed can still think about one more.

This year we had lots of people at Church on Ash Wednesday. I used the formula "Repent and listen to the Good News". When I came to one man he looked up at me and said, "I will try, Father." He probably had tried and failed many times before, but he was willing to give it another go.

The last time I returned from Wewak, an SVD student from Vietnam, John Lae came with me for a week`s holidays. He is an "entertainer" who performs magic tricks. He performed several tricks here in Ambunti Parish and the people were amazed he could do such things.

Last month I was back in Timbunke for two and a half weeks. I visited several communities in the parish, including Mangajanget, where Jacob Sakai lives. Jacob has ten children and asked me to find a name for the last girl. The name I gave him was Verona. Verona is now nearly six years old, a lovely little girl. That evening, Jacob and Verona came walking hand-in-hand through the village. Verona was holding a cooking pot in one hand and in it was a cooked chicken for my evening meal.

Suimbo was another village I called to. They had built a new bush church since my last visit. Though it poured rain during my time there, most came to church. After Mass I planted two coconuts in front of the church to remember my visit.

The changes I noticed most was that the young boys and girls had grown up and become men and women. Several of the older generation had moved on to their eternal reward and every village had lots of children, which means the population in the Sepik is increasing and multiplying.

I think this is all for now, so I wish you a happy Easter and see you in September. No dates arranged yet. Take care and God Bless you.

March 27, 2001 At this side of the world we got a lot of rain in the last six weeks. The sun also shines but it is mostly overcast, and the solar power is working in fits and starts, as there is no charge going into the batteries. I expect the new moon will bring change to the weather.

On March 18 the parish organized a special day for the elderly people. Here in Ambunti over fifty people turned up for Mass. After the Offering during the Mass, the children and grandchildren hung bouquets of flowers around their necks, which they had picked from their gardens. I had Rosary Beads and a medal to give to each one at the evening meal. However, blue-black clouds moved in over Ambunti and only a few turned up. While we waited in the tractor shed for some others to arrive, one old lady took out a razor blade and another lay her long leg on her lap and the lady with the razor blade began cutting her toe nails. It was obvious that with the passing of years the old lady was not able to get down that far any more to cut her nails and now she had met a friend at the party to do the job.

At the other end of the shed an eight-year-old girl was searching through her grandmother's black curly hair and picking out any louse she could find. A few men and I were chatting about the first missionaries over fifty years ago and how things have changed since then. The rain poured down and nobody else arrived, so we took out our plate and spoon and went into the pastoral centre to dine. We enjoyed out little gathering immensely. A thought came to mind: what a natural and simple life these people were living, and there was a great sense of belonging and caring among them.

Last month I sprayed my two Yamaha outboard motors green, not because St. Patrick's Day was approaching. Three young men broke into the petrol shed and stole one of my twenty-five-horsepower motors. Bishop Ray said I should paint them orange. I thought green was more suited for the Irishman. Now, if someone decides to steal the motors, he will have some job in trying to hide their identity.

At present the Catholic youth officer for Wewak Diocese, Clement Paime, is here in the parish. Last week Clement was up at an out-station, Yassan, giving a seminar to the youth on drugs, sport, culture, and human development. This week he is in Mersei and next week he is at Avatip, another out-station. Next July the parish steering team hopes to hold a youth rally at Ambunti to cover the whole parish. Fr. Carlos is also out in patrol at the moment, so the house is quiet. Fr. Carlos baptised thirty-two citizens at Yambun village, his first in PNG.

Last Sunday I said Mass here in Ambunti. Before Mass we were short of altar boys and girls, and I asked where everybody was. One girl spoke up, "My big sister is at home washing her clothes, and she needs them for school tomorrow." I thought that was fair enough. The altar girls love this job more than the boys. In fact, we have only two boys and twenty-seven girls, mostly all under twelve years of age. They argue among themselves as to who is going to ring the bell and hold the candles. They give orders when to ring the bell and cough when it's time to return to their chairs. After Mass they tell each other if they made one, two, or more mistakes.

Last week I heard a sad story. A group of boys were out in the bush hunting when they found a World War Two bomb. The boys dug it out and lit a fire around the bomb. Then the boys went off to a safe distance to wait for the explosion. In the meantime, some other people attracted by the fire went to see what was cooking, and while they stood examining the fire, the bomb exploded, killing one and injuring a number of others. The case is now in the hands of the police.

Ambunti air-strip reopened again last week. It was closed because too many dogs were on the strip and made it unsafe for landing. There is now a wire fence three feet high around the strip; it's something like a sheep fence. Moses Wapai bought a three-cylinder Yamaha tractor to cut the grass on the strip, which takes two days. The following day his clan were out raking the grass to the sides. In a place like Ambunti, it's very important to keep a good air-strip and the government are prepared to put money aside to maintain it.

Just before Christmas, I was down in Marui Mission Station. That is where the Sepik Highway comes to an end, so I left my land cruiser there and transferred to water transport for the rest of my trip. This day a helicopter circled overhead and landed at the mission station. Within five minutes it seems the entire population of Marui had gathered around the helicopter. I must admit I was among the first group of investigators as I was on the spot when it landed. It probably was the first time most of the children in the area had been so close to such a complex piece of machinery and they made the most of the opportunity. The pilot slid back the door and asked where such and such a place was. The place he referred to had another name, so we had to consult among each other where it was; it happened to be only 500 yards further down the river, and the helicopter took to the air again. With that, John, the prayer leader, arrived and seeing the number of people at the station he said, "It took you only five minutes to get here today. Now, next Sunday for Mass you can do the same." I told John, only joking of course, that he could hold a prayer meeting now, and the only problem being that they would not fit into the church.

I take this opportunity myself to wish you a happy Easter and may God bless you.

May 19, 2001 I hope you are all keeping well, as this leaves me in good form. Yesterday your papers arrived after almost two months on the way. I am still looking over them, as there is a lot of news to catch up on.

It looks like Joe Walsh[5] is successfully in the battle against foot and mouth. It would be great if you could keep it out of Ireland.

Today is Friday, so the countrymen and women were in Ambunti this morning to sell some homemade flower cakes, vegetables, and fish at the market, and do some shopping afterwards.

The Department of Primary Industry (DPI) has introduced a new fish to the Sepik waters, which the locals have christened "rubber nose" because of its nose. DPI brought it to the Sepik River because it eats grass and it will help to control the grass along the waterways and in the swamps. The locals are not that gone on it, as it has no taste and is full of bones. A few days ago, tempers were not the best at the market place, as some people from Malue village had started a boxing match and it is lightly to erupt again any moment.

For Easter I stayed at the main station this year. It rained a lot at night, but the rain stayed off during the services. On Easter Sunday morning I went down to Avatip village where we had Baptisms and First Communions. The village people decided to have open-air Mass, as the church was too small for the occasion. To my surprise, one of their Communion ministers, Catherine Buto, had brought a big Easter Candle three feet long and three inches thick. The Easter Candle was proudly displayed next to the altar and under the blazing sun. We were half way through the Mass when I heard the bang. It was the Easter Candle; it had fallen over and broken in two. We all knew what happened, and everyone started telling everybody else the candle should not have been exposed to the sun. I was

5 The then Irish Minister for Agriculture, who was also a TD for Southwest Cork.

thinking of the two Greek letters on the end of the candle, Alpha and Omega, the beginning and the end, and the morning sun demolished it in less than one hour.

On April 29 we had baptisms at Bongus, and over fifty parishioners also made the trip. Bongus is one of those places you would not go to unless you had a good reason, and that might explain why no priest was there for fifty years. Our pastoral workers were going there for three years to prepare a large number of catechumens for Baptism. This was the first time for the Catholic Church to baptise people at Bongus. During the Baptism, one old lady forgot her new Christian name. Her sponsor kept prompting her, saying "Sheila". The old lady kept shaking her head, saying "It's not." I thought to move on to the next person when the old lady called out "Sara". I was told afterwards her husband took the name Abraham, and Sara and Abraham were husband and wife. It was a beautiful experience. Bongus village is right in the heart of the Watch Cook Hills. All the little hamlets from around the area came together. The first evening we congregated outside their bush church on top of the mountain ridge for a prayer meeting which went on for two hours.

After that some people sat and talked all night while the women prepared and cooked the meal for the following day. The six-day old moon gave us light until midnight, and two Tilly lamps kept the hilltop aglow until morning. When the dawn broke, the village rang out with bird songs, and other forest creatures were also making themselves heard, all welcoming the new day. After the Mass and Baptisms, the meal, which mainly consisted of fish and sago, was brought to the church grounds and shared out to the different communities. I thought we were the happiest people on the planet, as there was no stress or strain on anybody and the people were enjoying being together.

On May 12 we had six couples at the main station renewing their married vows for those celebrating their silver jubilee. Three of the husbands shared their life stories during the service, which was very enriching to the big crowd present. Afterwards we all gathered on the parish lawn for a meal prepared by the families, and some more experiences of married life were shared. A few couples thought they should celebrate their silver jubilee too. However, when we looked up the marriage records they had a few more years to go. It looks like we will make this renewal of married vows an annual event now.

Today I had a lot of people call to the Parish House after the market. Everybody has his or her own little worries. Michael Yagundimi from Brukgunwai was enquiring if I had some smoke paper. Michael is a Sepik dweller and you can see him sitting and carving in his *house-boy* on the banks of the river when you pass by. Both of us are involved in a humble business, and I think we both gain from our transaction. When I have old copies of the *Star* I give them to Michael. He supplies me with oars for my canoe and boat when the need arises. Very often the oars get mislaid or break, and they are an essential part of the cargo when travelling along the river. And so, the River Sepik keeps on flowing and life keeps on moving along, and it seems it is almost time for home leave once again. See you in September, please God.

August 12, 2001 Today is blazing hot. I expect the mood will change once the sun moves off and the children come out to play.

It was a busy week here in Ambunti. Bishop Tony Burgess gave Confirmation to over 500 people, and seven teachers graduated with a diploma in external studies at St. Clara's Vocational Centre.

Bishop Tony flew from Wewak into Nagri, an out-station of Ambunti, on Monday morning 13th August. When he arrived, the locals welcomed him in their traditional dress and customary ways. A signboard was up saying, "Welcome Bishop Tony", and a bouquet of flowers were hung around his neck, and flowers were hung around his large sun hat as well. Then lots of flower petals were thrown at the bishop and me as we walked behind the *singsing* group that led the way to the teacher's house.

The first day the Bishop said Mass at Nagri and blessed their new bush church. The following morning a *singsing* group from Waiawis paraded us both down to their village where Bishop Tony gave Confirmation to over ninety people, and he also blessed their new permanent church. It was the first time for a bishop to confirm people at Waiawis, so the locals put all their effort into making it something special. That same evening an MAF plane came to pick us up from Nagri air-strip and flew us to Merise Air-strip, where over one thousand people were there to welcome the new Bishop. At Mersie, over 300 people received Confirmation and over fifty schoolchildren received First Communion. The local people gave the Bishop a petition. They wanted to have their own SVD priest.

On Wednesday, August 8, Bishop Tony and I returned to Ambunti from Merise by motor canoe. It was Bishop Tony's first time to Ambunti as Bishop, so he received a warm welcome at Mino and Marawai villages as we made the journey downriver to Ambunti. At Ambunti the women had their songs and flowers ready for him when he stepped ashore. The following Thursday, 121 young people were confirmed, and Bishop Tony flew back to Wewak the following day after paying a visit to the Salesian Sisters at the vocational centre.

While the Bishop and I were out in the bush, over one hundred teachers from Ambunti and Maprik area were updating their studies and exams. Two-week studies were sponsored by the WWF. The course is the first of its kind in the country, and it is expected fifty or more teachers will graduate next year—that is, if they keep up their external studies during the year.

Last month I was down at Madang for a course on preaching and teaching given by two lay people, Adrian Commadeur and Nan Deaakin. The course was very good, and I hope to give it now to my pastoral workers when I return from my home leave.

During the month of May, Fr. Patrick Punwari, a local priest, helped me out with a Communion minister course. Thirty-five people turned up for it, mostly men. All the out-stations have Communion ministers now.

A Pentecost Rally was held this year at Apon, a village just up the river from Ambunti. It was held on the sports field and beautifully laid out with the grandstand in the middle and large camps at each side of the stand to accommodate the visitors. Colour ribbons were strung overhead, giving a carnival-like atmosphere to the place. I stayed at Apon for the three days, and it was a very nice spiritual experience for those who attended the rally.

On June 3, the Coffee Industry Corporation (CIC) held a meeting in Ambunti Council of Chamber to discuss the difficulties the growers are facing with the coffee industry. The price of coffee has dropped to an all-time low, and the C.I.C has offered some help towards transport costs to help keep the growers happy. However, many of the growers are now growing vanilla, which is a worry to the coffee board. One speaker at the meeting described vanilla as a second wife. He said he could grow both together in the same garden. Some onlookers were amused at the comparison, and said vanilla was much sweeter than coffee, and it had a better cash flow as well.

Pius Balson and Damien Anton spent two months repairing St. Joseph's church. They managed to complete the concrete floor before the Bishop arrived. The church looks much bigger now.

During the month of June, fourteen extra young men were coming to church on Sundays. They were inmates from Ambunti Jail. They used to arrive in a group like a football team and occupy two seats at the back. Two of the prisoners were giants of men. When I saw them, I thought they would be right fellows to have if the land cruiser got stuck in a mud hole.

The Salesian Sisters at Ambunti have a new two-way radio. Pius Balson and I put up the antenna last month, but the radio only works in fits and starts and must be replaced.

As I complete this letter, the drone of the evening insects is coming through the window louvres in full tone. They too must have felt the heat of the day, and now they are letting off some energy.

December 10, 2002 Our main event for 2002 was the hand-over from Bishop Ray Kalisz to our new Bishop Tony Burgess. Bishop Tony is new to the Wewak Dioceses, and his first job was to visit the parish out-stations and meet the people. Bishop Tony was here in Ambunti two months ago for Confirmation, and he showed a video on the large screen each night in different villages. The locals were delighted, and they would like to see him more often. Bishop Ray Kalisz has gone back to the States to retire after spending forty-eight years in the Wewak Diocese, twenty-two of these as Bishop.

This year we had three more deacons ordained to the priesthood. One was from the Chambri Lakes, Emmanuel Sagways. Ten years ago, I was looking after that area, so I went back to Chambri for the first Mass. It was a great weekend of celebrations for the local people. What I enjoyed about the celebrations was meeting the people I used to visit in their villages and hamlets, and now we were all together at the main station celebrating the ordination of one of their own priests.

We had a general election during May and June. It spoiled our pastoral plans for the parish as most of our church workers were involved in the campaign or standing for the local elections.

In Ambunti district, sixteen motor canoes were used to transport the polling teams. Each canoe had a team of five people, all the necessary camping gear, and polling material for their assignment. After five days the first polling team arrived back after completing the voting in its area. The last team took eleven days, and when they arrived back to base, they asked for a helicopter for two days to reach the remote villages in the Upper Sepik. The counting of votes took place here in Ambunti. I was an observer for the four days, and most people voted in block for their candidate. Tony Imo was the eventual winner with 4,313 votes. Tony's father was a catechist who invited the first missionaries into this area, and Tony also spent some time in the seminary. I think most people were happy that he got the Ambunti Drekakir seat. The World Cup created a big interest in the soccer here in PNG. All the games were shown on the local TV. For weeks after, the youngsters were playing soccer on any piece of available ground.

Here in Ambunti we have a very reasonable soccer team. Last September the team travelled to Wewak to take part in the Sir Michael Somare Shield. Our team were runners-up in the junior final. I had helped some players to buy their football boots. When it came to the presentation of the medals, the players did not want to come forward, so I went myself and the players and supporters followed. We are already making plans to win next year.

The first Tuesday in November was the big day in Australia for the Melbourne Cup. This year, an Irish horse, Media Puzzle, won it. When I told the locals how the Irish horse travelled by plane to Australia and won the Melbourne Cup they just thought it was "too good" to be true. Anyway, I think Irish eyes were smiling as a result.

In August we had a fierce earthquake, 7.5 on the Richter scale. It went on for thirty seconds and gave the province a real shake-up. Three people were killed in the Wewak area when their homes fell on them. Kairiru Island, which is off the coast of Wewak, rose two and a half feet out of the sea. At first the people thought the ocean had sunk. Experts from Australia are examining the effects of the quake on the local environment. In Ambunti no one was killed; only one of my pastoral workers bumped his head off a post as he made a run to get out of his house.

On Sunday, November 17, we had a beautiful Mass at Ambunti. The Sunday schoolchildren prepared the Liturgy. They dramatized the Gospel of the day and sang some action songs. After, there were light refreshments for the children, and over thirty graduated to make way for newcomers next year.

Our school year has just come to an end. Last week, eighty-seven students graduated from Ambunti High. Next week, St. Joseph's Primary School has over fifty students moving on to High School.

So, with that I wish you good luck and God's blessing for 2003, and may you have a holy and joyful Christmas.

December 30, 2003 It was one of the most enjoyable Christmases I ever had. Lots of people came to Confession and Mass; there was a great welcome in most villages and some great stories shared.

Fr. Adam Sroka took one half of the parish, and I looked after the main Sepik River. Nine days before Christmas, I took off upriver on our diesel canoe. I had a driver and a helper, both known as the "bus crew". We also had two passengers returning home after their Christmas shopping. We were supposed to leave at 6am, but the driver had no watch, so it was nearer to 7am. On our way up the river we gave the message to each village when we would return for Christmas Mass and Confession.

It took us eleven hours to make it to Owem Village, which is the last Catholic village on the Sepik. They did not expect us and most of the people were away in the bush attending to their gardens. We stayed the night and had Mass and Confession the following morning. Only the elderly and some children attended.

From now on it was downriver and being so far upstream the current was fast. It took only one hour and twenty minutes to get down to Kupkine Village. There were over twenty people there to meet us and take our camping gear up to the Father's house. They had cleaned the house, put flowers on the table, and opened the windows to let in the fresh air.

Matthew, the church leader, was among the group who welcomed us. He asked me if I was okay, so I told him my bus crew hadn't eaten yet today. After one hour he was back with two pancakes of sago for each of us.

After the meal, Matthew took my helpers to the garden. It was a half a mile upriver. When they returned, they had two bags of sweet potatoes in the canoe. They also gave us two baskets of smoked fish. That evening I went down to visit the village people, while my bus crew, Samson and Nelson, who were also musicians, prepared the Liturgy for the following morning. After Mass, we packed up, and on to the next village, Yessan. We drove nice and easy for two hours. At that stage I suggested looking for the shade of a tree by the bank of the river to have a picnic and make a visit to the bush—that is, the toilet. We had smoked fish and sago and some beautiful mangoes with us. For the rest of the trip, we met one motor canoe, and we waved to each other as we passed by.

We arrived in Yessan at 6.50pm. A group of children helped us to unload the canoe. What to do with the fish was our main concern, as it would go sour before morning, so I suggested we had to eat it. I asked the leader to get some firewood and a few big cooking pots. Everyone present gave a helping hand, either with the firewood, washing the sweet potatoes, pealing the pumpkins or scrubbing the coconut to get milk. The fish was reheated, and within an hour four pots were lined up and each took his or her share direct from the pot. Before the people left that night, I told them that there would be Confession the following morning at seven o'clock. One of the church leaders said, "Oh, very good, Father, the place is full of sinners. And now you can clean up the place for Christmas." After Confessions and Mass the following morning, we left early for more of the same at Mino village.

That evening it was down to Brukangaui village, which is only twenty minutes away by motor canoe. We stayed the night with Michael, the church leader, but when we arrived he told us he too had just arrived from Wewak and had nothing in the house. We told him not to worry, as the canoe was full of sweet potatoes, pumpkin, and fish; all he had to do was provide the pots and firewood. He did that, and another big meal was provided. It was the same again at Brukangaui: Confession, Mass and visitation of the sick, and onto the next village, Yambum.

Yambum is a big village, so after a siesta and a bath in the Sepik I started hearing Confessions to avoid a long queue on the Sunday morning. After Mass, it was back to Ambunti. What was left of the sweet potatoes I gave to the "bus crew". I thought my Christmas post would have arrived; it turned up the Sunday after. I stayed at the main station for Christmas Eve and Christmas night Mass. The following morning it was back on the Sepik and down to Avitip. Avitip is the biggest village on the Sepik, with over 1,000 people. We had a lovely Mass in their little church. After Mass, we sat around outside the church and told stories while the women cooked the Christmas dinner. When the women were satisfied that the food was cooked, I blessed it. The hundred-plus Catholics sat down under a mango tree for Christmas dinner. This is what makes Christmas special on the Sepik; it's having time for each other, talking, eating together, and without disturbance from the TV or worries about over-spending.

When I arrived back at Ambunti Christmas day, Fr. Adam Sroka and his helper Damien Anton had just arrived back before us after completing their fifteen days on patrol in the Black Water area.

I still had two more villages to visit in the Garamambu area, so it was off again on Saturday Morning at 7am. George Balson drove myself and two carriers, Alex Kapwan and John Kupai, to Yaragai. From there on we had to walk across the mountain. George went back to Ambunti and returned the following day to pick us up. We had just reached the outskirts of Yaragai village when Robert, a schoolteacher, asked us in for a cup of coffee. I thought it was a great idea and Robert boiled the kettle. We had a long chat about all the local events such as sports, problems between villages, people home from Christmas and beer clubs. Eventually Robert advised us to go as the day would be getting hot, and it would be much harder to walk.

My two helpers had two rucksacks each, and I walked with hands free. When we reached the top, we stopped for a good rest. I went to one of the rucksacks, took out five mangoes, two each for the carriers and one for myself. When I had finished my mango, I found a stick and planted the seeds of the mango a few yards of the main track. I noticed Alex and John did the same with theirs.

From here on it was downhill. Alex went first and reached the bottom long before John and me. We rested again and had a lovely cool bath in a mountain creek nearby. We changed into fresh clothes and we looked nice and fresh when we arrived at Walfain. Word was sent to Banacort that

Father Michael had arrived and come for Mass tomorrow. Walfain were delighted to see us as they had a big problem on Christmas night. The Communion minister had refused to give out Communion because he said he was tired, and the other Communion minister said it wasn't his turn.

After Mass, we had an open meeting to hear the two sides of the story and hopefully it is now finished. I picked up one of my best stories at Walfain. Two young men were out fishing at night when they saw a crocodile resting in the water. One jumped on his back and squeezed his legs around the croc's waist. The croc and his companion went to the bottom of the river, but his companion gave the ground a push up and both came to the surface again. Then he grabbed a knife from the fellow in the canoe and both went to the bottom again. This time the croc tried to take his companion under the bank. He gave one more push to lift the croc off the riverbed and at that moment he cut the croc across the back of the neck. There was one last final slash from the croc and he turned the rider upside down. The croc was dead and floated to the top when his companion put his head above water. I am sure this story is true, because they spent the night talking about it and I have heard stories like this before.

Back at the main station, we had to get ready for New Year's Day, and a farewell party for Fr. Adam, who has received his new appointment to Timbunke, my former parish. On January 2 we drove him down to Timbunke and stayed with him four days. I visited the farm, Tambunam Village and Timbunke Village. Now I am here in Wewak writing a few letters and taking it easy. Fr. Liam Dunne is returning home on January 14, so I will stay to see him off. With that, I will sign off. God bless you and take care.

February 28, 2004 Another year has gone by and I am still at the Sepik River. The year had plenty of unexpected events, though these events did not hinder our pastoral plan for 2003.

A new seminarian, David Bakio from PNG, was assigned to me for the pastoral year. We were returning one evening to Ambunti after doing our shopping in Wewak when we saw wild pigs swimming across the Sepik. David grabbed an iron pipe to push the pig under the water. In doing so he broke his right wrist, which put him out of action for a few months. David then spent most of the year at the main station giving religious instructions at the high-school and working with the youth of Ambunti town. He is now going to the Philippines for two years for his novitiate. In the meantime, Fr. Peter Wasko from Poland is here in Ambunti doing his introduction year to pastoral work. On November 12, Fr. Andrew Aufalong, one of our diocesan priests, died when he failed to recover from an attack of malaria combined with asthma. He was our first local priest to die. Fr. Andrew did his pastoral year with me in Timbunke, and he spent another year in Ambunti after his ordination. His death came as a shock to us all as he was sick only a few days, and he was only 49. Also this year, Fr. Tony St. Pierre died. Fr. Tony was returning to PNG after his holiday in the States when he got a heart attack on the plane and died. Fr. Tony and Fr. Andrew are now buried side by side in our SVD cemetery in Wewak.

Last October, an old man in New Ireland[6] was dying. Before he died he told his family he saw the Japanese army during the Second World War taking several bars of gold up the mountain and burying it in a remote mountain cave. Police and army were quickly sent to the area on a training exercise. The government said it would claim any such treasures as a war relic. To date no gold has been found. The whole exercise created a great stir in the region for a few weeks.

Last April I attended a formation course in India at our SVD house in Mumbai. For the last twenty years I have been introducing new seminaries and priests to pastoral work and culture and language, so the provincial council asked me to update my skills and share my experiences with other formatters from different parts of the world. It was a good experience and it added a bit of variety and challenge to 2003. It wasn't the best time for travelling, as the SARS[7] outbreak was at its worst in Asia and almost everyone in Singapore were wearing masks at the time. Travellers were scared they would catch the deadly Asian flu.

Our soccer team failed to impress this year in the Michael Somare Shield tournament. The selectors could not agree to pick one good team. They opted to send three teams from Ambunti instead. It was a learning experience. We are looking forward to putting on a better display in 2004. Clement Primary, our Catholic youth leader, is coming to Ambunti next

---

6 An island in PNG of about 7,000km2 with 120,000 inhabitants.
7 Severe acute respiratory syndrome.

March to give some coaching to our youth groups and to prepare our teams better for bigger occasions in Wewak Town. Our teams have a very good defence, but no game plan and no strikers, and they fell into the offside trap several times.

It was a year of grace for the SVD. Our founder, Arnold Janssen, and our first missionary to China, Joseph Freinademetz, were declared saints by Pope John Paul on October 5. A select few from PNG went to Rome to witness the occasion. A few weeks later, over one hundred SVD missionaries in PNG gathered at the Divine Word University in the Madang Province for further celebrations. It was our first time for such a meeting in PNG, and it was nice to meet the confrères from other dioceses and share about the past and present and come up with a vision for the future. The students were on holidays, so there was plenty of accommodation for all of us.

The Divine Word University has expanded at an alarming rate in the last eight years since Fr. Jan Czuba took over as president. Just now the university has completed a huge library costing over four million US dollars. It is now recognised as one of the finest universities in the country.

Here in Ambunti we had some very heavy rain during Christmas week. Our air-strip is still closed, so no Christmas mail or visitors this Christmas. On Christmas Eve and Christmas Day the sun shone, and we had lovely liturgies on both occasions. On Christmas night the people danced in the church as if they had won the World Cup when the music group sang "Jesus is born in Bethlehem". Early on Christmas morning it was down-river to celebrate Mass at Avtip. We travelled by diesel canoe and several people came along to visit friends. After Mass, the community gathered on the lawn outside the church on the banks of the Sepik for a barbeque. There were no strong drinks, though cold water was provided for Father and his crew. The menu consisted of yam, taro cooking bananas, rice, and plenty fish from the lagoons nearby. During the meal, several children were playing games running around the lawn and enjoying themselves just being together as a happy family.

I hope this letter finds you in good health and happiness as it leaves me. I am keeping well. Many blessings for the New Year. God bless.

March 25, 2004 I am now in Wewak, having flown in on Monday for Fr. Karl Wand's funeral on Wednesday. The road is not good from Jamma to Marwai, which is almost six hours' walking distance. The people from the Upper Sepik are walking this stretch of road for the last four months. I hear a dozer is coming next week to repair it. I am staying for the weekend, as we have our priests' in-service meeting next Monday and our district meeting the week after. It's all meetings at this time of year. We had our Parish Steering Team meeting in Ambunti. Then we had the Area Steering Team meeting followed by the Community Steering Team meetings. Then there were the School Board meetings, two already this year. There is also a Deanery meeting coming up and a Vocational School Board meeting as well next month. In April we have our retreat in Madang and at that stage one third of the year is gone.

We buried Karl Wand at Wirui next to Fr. Andrew Aufolong. Fr. Karl had a nice Funeral Mass. Fr. Karl suffered a lot during his last few months, and everyone is happy the Lord has taken him to Himself. May he now rest in peace in the Lord where he worked for fifty-four years as a sower of the Good News.

Fr Henry Sollner and Fr. Hugo Schulz are still holding out strong and they have no notion of giving up just yet. Fr. John Vegvari, who celebrated his ninetieth birthday last month, is still using his chainsaw. I was sitting at table with him this week and he told me "I have letters in my room, I can show you, I was told by my Superior to give up using the chain-saw two years ago. I proved them all wrong."

Wirui now is very different from what it was a few years ago. Only a few people gather in the upper SVD house after evening meal. No more early morning rising at five o'clock. Brother Daniel is the only one who still has his cup of coffee at five o'clock, and he may have someone join him if they come in from the bush.

Bishop Tony is finding the going a bit tough at the moment. He is trying to make new appointments, but the local priests don't want to move. Bishop Ray had it easy in that sense, so the hand-over has its growing pains; otherwise the Diocese is going very well. Our pastoral workers are doing a good job. Even if no priest calls for months they still hold the Sunday service and prayer meetings during the week and many have been doing it for twenty or thirty years. At present I have a new SVD priest with me, Fr. Peter Wasko. He was in Ireland learning English. There is also a seminarian coming next month to do his pastoral training. Fr. Peter has just returned from Mercie in the Black Water area of Ambunti Parish. That means I don't have to go on the bush patrol as often as before.

The local people are now very busy planting vanilla. They are also stealing it from each other, and family disputes often arise as to who is the rightful owner of the ground. Several families have gone back to their home villages to plant vanilla gardens. This week the price has dropped from 720 *kina* per kilo to 550 for grade one. Sevond-grade vanilla second grade is 450; still the price is very good. I have planted nine plants in Ambunti, so the people call me a vanilla farmer also. The local people gave me the beans as offerings. A good pod is worth three *kina*. I have forty-three pods right now on my writing desk. I tried to sell them this week but there were so many people lined up at the Sepik Construction store, about 200, that I went away hoping the queue would get smaller, but no such luck.

This year we have lots of beautiful mangoes. I thought of you one day as I was eating one—what you would give to have one for dinner. At Ambunti Station the children took them to the market to sell. They had to sell them for 20 *toea*[8] each, as there were lots of mangoes already at the market place.

Yesterday I was talking to Br. Jack. He told me he nearly got killed during the past earthquake in Wewak. Over his bed he had a large statue of Our Lady made from cement. When the earthquake struck the Statue fell on the bed beside him. What a way to die. I am sure Our Lady made sure Br. Jack was at the other side of the bed before the earthquake struck.

If you happened to visit my room just now you would see that I have two bails of rice, two cartons of Hi-way beef, two cartons of two-minute noodles, one carton of Heinz beans, a bale of toilet paper, a carton of black batteries, a box of coffee, altar breads, a guitar, a new lamp, paint, and a carton of Besta tinned fish. I have kept them away from my bed just in case we have another earthquake.

Now this is my last page and I am writing this at a fast pace so excuse the scribble. I still receive the *Star* every week. My home team, Castlehaven, won the football county final. There was great celebration at home. I no longer receive RTE Radio 1, which is a pity as I used to look forward to

---

8 A coin worth one hundredth of a *kina*.

the sports results every Monday evening. I still get *The Harp*[9] and I see a copy of it here in the SVD upper room. All my family are keeping well. I had letters from them all and I phone home often too. Regards for now and God bless you.

March 26, 2004 It's good to be back home again after a week in the bush. You know the feeling, how one appreciates a good bed to sleep in, a good shower, and a good toilet to sit on when one returns to the main station after days or weeks on patrol.

I had Ken Charles, a pastoral worker, here for two weeks giving Bible seminars in the Black Water area of Ambunti Parish. Ken Charles is very good, and he has become a very powerful evangelist in the Wewak Diocese. Some priests don't see eye to eye with him as he challenges us priests to get out of the comfort zone and preach the Good News. Our first stop was at a village called Mino. It was when we pulled into Mino that I realised it was the wrong time for such courses. It was the wet season, and the mosquitoes were having a field day as we unloaded our camping gear. At this time the church was six inches under water, so the Area Steering Team chairman led the way for Ken Charles, his team, and me into the guesthouse, where we stayed for four nights. The local people looked after us very well, with plenty of sago, fish, and bananas.

The Bible seminar was also held under the guest house, as it was the only dry place that was not flooded, but as the days went on the waters got higher, and it meant the 200 people or so had to sit close together as the patch of ground was getting smaller each day. One day a large grass island came floating down the river and it brushed the side of the village as it forced its way downstream. A loud voice called out that the island was taking the canoes along with it. The Bible seminar came to a sudden halt as those with canoes made a dash to get back their only mode of transport. It was a ten-minute break to attend to the more pressing needs, and the workshop began again as normal.

It amazed me to see the people were so patient and understanding despite the mosquitoes and the floodwaters. Some village dogs and roosters also sat in for the workshop, as they had no other place to lie. One rooster

9 An SVD newsletter.

thought he had enough, got up and left his droppings next to the blackboard. Without a word one elderly woman got a spade and removed it from the earthen floor and disposed of it into the water. I thought to myself what a nice simple attitude these people have towards life.

After four days we moved on to Tongujamb to give the same workshop. This time we had problems with the river as it was jammed up with the floating island. We would have turned back only that a local man out fishing heard the diesel engine a long way off and he climbed up a tree to shout directions at us.

Tongujamb is a large village with its houses built along the foothills, and I could see only a few houses standing in flood waters. The church was high and dry so no problem this time where to hold the Bible seminar. Urbang, a neighbouring village, also attended, bringing the participants to well over 400. The last day ended with a prayer meeting, and a large crowd gathered, including members from the other Pentecostal churches. The seminar finally ended with *bung kaikai*; a meal, of course, was easy when everybody brought along his or her own supply of food. The headmaster's wife, Mrs Grauly, killed one of her roosters and that was served to the special guests.

Tongujamb, like most villages in the area, has planted vanilla along the side of the mountain. It should be in full production in two years' time, though some who planted earlier are harvesting already.

Three weeks ago, I went to Dagua to say Mass as there is no priest appointed there since Fr. Andrew died. Fr Andrew had planted two hundred plants of vanilla in front of the parish house. It is growing very well, but it needs someone to look after it. Sr. Agnes has also a vanilla garden and the first 200 plants should be ready for pollination this year.

So, what is happening to the sixty million *kina* which the province received last year from vanilla sales? Ela Motors sold thirty lands cruisers, for a start. PMVs head back to Maprik every evening loaded down with store goods. The roofs of the trucks are decked with mattresses. New bicycles are penned on the front to the bull bar, and buckets and baby baths are put into *bilum* string bags and tied on at the sides. What's inside the trucks is anybody's guess. One day I was in the BP store, and the floor manager was wheeling out a diesel generator on a trolley. I asked him where it was going. He smiled and said Drekikir, adding that this was the fourth one this week. So long may the boom last.

Last month a few shock waves hit the selling price, but it's because the beans were not properly dried and not of high quality.

Several people have given me their first harvest as a thanks-giving offering to God. No doubt you will be hearing much more about vanilla in the coming years—about its blessings, its problems, and how it has changed Wewak and Maprik towns in a matter of a few years.

To change the subject, I had a lovely experience a few months ago. I was returning from Wewak with a full load in the Land Cruiser. I stopped at the market near Kunginjini and a local man asked if I could bring him and his child as far as Burwi. I told him to climb on and don't fall off. When I stopped at Burwi to let him off, his small daughter came up to the window of the car and handed me a can of Fanta. I did not want to take it and the little girl explained: "My daddy bought this to help me walk home. Now you have helped, me and I don't need it anymore." Then the father added: "Father, you must take it, because if you did not help us we would never have got home today. My daughter is too heavy to carry and too weak to walk that long journey in one day." I took the can of Fanta. As they say back home in Ireland, "you should never discourage the art of giving." Anyway, it made my day and its little events like this that make it all worthwhile to keep going.

So for now, have a good Easter and look after yourself.

July 5, 2004 It's Monday morning here in Ambunti, and the mission station is very quiet. The schoolchildren have holidays and that explains why there is no activity around here at present.

Yesterday was St. Peter and Paul's feast day so Pius Balson and I went to Yambun village to celebrate Mass there as their church is called St. Peter's. Yambun is the first out-station upriver from Ambunti, about thirty minutes by speedboat. It has a population of 700 plus, and they all live along a two-mile stretch at one side of the river. Except for a few, all the inhabitants live in bush houses. Their school has three permanent classrooms and their church is semi-permanent. The church is called St. Peter's because Yambun has two large rocks at either side of the Sepik, known as the Yambun

Gates. The Sepik has to push through this narrow area when in flood and it can be scary for a newcomer to drive through there for the first time.

On our early morning trip we noticed several slicks along the water edge made by crocodiles during the night. One was a huge U-turn made by a full-grown croc.

The Mass was a special thanksgiving Mass for all the blessings God has given the community during the past year. The main emphasis was on the offering, which came to 1,064 *kina*, about 300 US dollars. The money is to help finish the building of their church.

Three weeks ago, I went to Wewak for a diocesan pastoral meeting and to do some shopping. The road from Morwai to the Marist Brothers' High School at Burwi, about five miles long, was in terrible state. We just got through with the help of the passengers pulling the Land Cruiser. On my return trip I left the Land Cruiser at the high-school, and the four-wheel-drive tractor from the school took our cargo out to the Sepik where it was picked up by the canoe. The same cargo had to be loaded and unloaded five times before it eventually reached Ambunti. We have enough supplies for two months now, and by then hopefully something should be done to the road.

During my stay in Wewak I met a local man who was a complete stranger to me. He asked me where I was from. I told him Ambunti, and I asked him where are you from? "I am Paul Pingo from Maprik" he replied. We kept talking and after ten minutes he went to his car, took out fifty *kina*, and gave it to me. I was really surprised, and afterwards I asked the parish priest, Fr. Bernard from Maprik, if he knew him? Fr. Bernard said, "He is one of my best parishioners!"

My time in Wewak was extended by the death of Fr. Henry Sollner. It happened that I was the only one with him when he died. Br. Luke who was talking care of Fr. Henry called me at 1am to give the last sacraments as he had taken a bad turn. I stayed with Fr. Henry and he died peacefully in his sleep just after five o'clock. Fr. Henry was forty-nine years in PNG, and it was his last wish to be buried there. Fr. Henry spent most of his life doing mission work in the Wasera area, the most densely populated area in the dioceses. Fr. Pat Horgan gave the homily during the funeral Mass, and the daughter of Fr. Henry's cook boy delivered a short account of his life. She said Fr. Henry was a tough man. He used to say first Mass at the main station; then walk two hours for a second Mass and walk three more hours to say a third Mass and then walk home that evening. I presume he was travelling on horseback, as most missionaries used horses in those days. I must make inquiries. Fr. Henry was 82. May he rest in peace.

We still have two retired missionaries here in Wewak. Fr. Schulz who is ninety-four and Fr. Vegvari who is over ninety. It was only last month Fr. Vegvari retired from cutting firewood with the chain saw.

At present the Sepik River is very low. The local people tell me the river is full of crocodiles as the swamps have dried up and the crocs have moved out.

As I mentioned it is school holiday time, and most of the schoolchildren are out fishing. I tried the hook and line one day myself with no success. The day after, some children brought me fresh fish and said they felt sorry for me yesterday "that I did not catch any".

The great vanilla boom is over, at least for the time being. The price has dropped from 600 to 250 *kina* a kilo first grade. Long lines of people queue every day in Wewak trying to sell it. It seems every tropical country that can grow it is growing it now. The supply has out grown the demand. Buyers are only buying the top-quality vanilla at the moment. In one sense it's good, as the local people were not able to cope with the sudden influx of large amounts of cash.

We had a lovely celebration here in the parish for Pentecost week. It's becoming an annual event, as it was something Fr. Jan Czuba started during his time and is still going strong. Each year we have a Pentecost Rally, and each out-station has to host the rally when their turn comes. This meant Mayo was the hosting village and they spared no effect to impress the neighbouring villages. Mayo is the last out-station on the River Sepik under the Wewak Diocese. Fr. Peter Wasko was the guest speaker for the three days, and Bishop Tony and I arrived on the Saturday to receive a big welcome. Over sixty locals in traditional dress met us on the river. They had made a floating platform out of two dugout canoes powered by two forty-horsepower motors. We both transferred to the platform and sat down in the two cane chairs like two chiefs decorated with flowers. This part of the trip lasted more than one hour, and by then a large crowd had assembled, singing and dancing on the river bank. Another traditional group took over from here and led the Bishop up the mountain to where the stage was assembled. Banners and flags were tied to trees and bamboo posts. One banner read, "We are church alive in Christ"; they were certainly alive on this day. To the delight of everyone, the Bishop showed a video that night, and the following day ninety-four adults received Confirmation. After Mass and several speeches, everybody took off home while Bishop Tony, Fr. Peter, and I took off for Tongujamb village, where the Bishop had another busy day of Confirmations and meeting people.

When we arrived at Ambunti, there were five hundred children at the station. It was announced on Sunday the Bishop would show a video on Monday night, so the Bishop set up the screen even before he had taken a bath; otherwise the crowd might get out of hand. The movies are still a big crowd puller in outback in PNG. By the way, the Bishop has to use the tractor to transport himself and his cargo over that bad patch of road near Marwi.

At present, Bishop Tony and all the Bishops of PNG are in Rabaul at the General Assembly Meeting. Our three deacons and several priests are there also. The meeting goes on all this week and finishes on Sunday. The assembly is to draw up a plan of action for the Church in PNG for the next ten years. The Catholic Church in the whole country is praying for its success. So, with that, I wish you well and hope you enjoy the summer.

August 10, 2004 Many thanks for your letters and papers. Our first letters crossed somewhere over the East Sepik Province. The photos were lovely, especially the one of the old home, although it looked its age. It brings back memories every time I look at it.

Fr. Geoff Brumm has returned to PNG and I never saw him looking better since he had the liver transplant. We thought Geoff would not make it through the last time, so it is a great surprise to see him walking about on his own again. Geoff wants to die at all costs in PNG, and it's hard to blame him, after the lovely funeral Fr. Henry Sollner had. As they say in Ireland, his funeral was "lovely all-together"—very respectable. That is one of the bonuses if one decides to return here.

Yesterday, I took a stroll around Ambunti town. Before I left the house,

I had three visitors. Simon Ginbe, the one who walks on his hands and feet, was looking for a lift to Wewak. Then Francis, a Communion minister from Mersie had walked in to collect the Blessed Sacrament for his local church, and the third was a local store man who came to exchange his fifty-*kina* note with fifty *kina* coins which he knew I had from the Sunday collection. After seeing to their needs, I headed in the direction of the hospital. On the Sepik side, people were cleaning fish and washing plates and dishes. On the right side, two young men, stripped to the waist, were using grass knives to clean the area around the house. Further on another man was hacking down a forty-foot tree to make way for his new garden. As I came close to the hospital, I met a large group of young people, who were the Bauabaua drama group. They were going around the parish performing two dramas—one on how to look after your health and the second on Aids awareness. By the time I reached the hospital a long line of people were waiting for the clinic to open. Some were already complaining about not having enough staff at the clinic, and they asked me if I had any medicine in my house to help them.

One patient, Cletus Uti, was getting ready to get transferred to Maprik Hospital. He was worried about himself and the trip, so I prayed with him and told him not to worry, as he would be in good hands.

I continued my morning stroll to the end of Ambunti air-strip, where Peter Wanwajai lives. Peter is a teacher He has a daughter, a nurse, and a son, Alfred, an engineer working on the Maprik Highway. His family are all grown up now except Danielle, a late arrival, and she is twelve years old. I had three letters for Peter; however, Peter was gone to Wewak, so I gave them to his wife, Agnes. I stayed twenty minutes. Agnes gave me a block of timber to sit on; she spoke about the family and about people we both knew. Before I left, she went to her earthen stove and took five sago rolls off a hot plate; she wrapped them neatly in a banana leaf and told me "have them for lunch".

My next stop was the town market. It's a double shed surrounded by security wire. The market place was packed at that hour; smoked fish, betel nut and flour buns were the main items for sale. I visit the market a couple of times every week. I buy a few fish and bananas, and the people give a few extra free. They say, "Father likes discount." This particular morning, the Yambuns had come to market, and the wife of Alfons, the pastoral worker, gave me flour, smoked fish, or "rubber nose", as the locals call them. Before I left the market, the basket was full of smoked fish. Luckily, I met the Bauabaua Drama Group again and gave them some fish and the five sago rolls. When I returned to the Father's house again, two young men were waiting for me in the tractor shed. They wanted references as they had applied to Raiha School of Nursing and a good reference would go a long way in being selected. This meant it was back to the office and my morning stroll was ended.

Now, before I forget, Agnes, the wife of Simon Kevin (former manager of Timbunke Farm), gave birth to twin boys four months ago. We were praying for her, as it was ten years since she gave birth before. The christening was on July 4; one is called Francis and the other Paul Simon. Simon has five cowboys now!

Timbunke farm is going very well. However, the road to Timbunke is still out, even now during the dry season. Last year they had no meat for Christmas at Wirui Catholic Mission; I went down with the diesel canoe and took three carcasses to Wewak by Angoram road. This is the only way to get meat to Wewak at present.

Our education system is also going through a rough patch. Our vocational school has only eleven students and none of them have paid the school fees. The high-school used to have 350 students; at present they have 130. Here at St. Joseph's, we have only eight teachers when we should have fifteen. Nobody seems to worry or get too excited about it; everyone has enough to eat, why stretch yourself, and this is PNG. Last week I met some of the family of Philip Baundu[10] who were in Timbunke with me. There are thirteen children in the family. Brian, one of his sons, is working with Air-link as a security man. He is a fine man now, dressed up in his guard-dog uniform. He told me his sister Bridget is also working with Air-link in Madang. They were such a lovely family and it's nice to see them all getting on with their lives.

Sr. Maura keeps me up to date with the GAA results. Her brother e-mails it to her every Monday. It was nice to see Waterford beat Kilkenny and Mayo beat Galway. I feel sorry for Roscommon, as it is nearly seventy

10 A teacher in Timbunke.

years since they won an All-Ireland. Yes, I am going on home leave next year, please God. God Bless you.

January 2, 2005 I hope you are all keeping well and looking forward to a bright New Year. Here on the Sepik River we had another interesting twelve months, although the weather pattern forced us to change our pastoral plans several times during the year; it was neither too wet nor too dry.

During the month of October, Damien Anton and I were on a pastoral visit to Walfain village and well out of sight of the Sepik River when word came to us at night the river had gone down and the lake, which we had crossed by boat, was drying up. The people told us that we should get back to Ambunti as soon as possible or wait until the next rains arrive. We left next morning, and four carriers helped us to take our belongings over the mountain and down into Yaragai village where our fifteen-horsepower motor was waiting for us. The lake had turned into a mud plain, however, and the channel had still a little water for me and Damien to use two oars. The problem was to know where the water was as the channel went from side to side. Hundreds of white egrets gave us some indication, as they were standing knee-deep in the water, watching us with great caution for two hours pulling and shoving our boat. At the mouth of the lake the water was rushing out carrying hundreds of dead and living fish along with it. Several women from the near-by villages were out in their canoes collecting the live ones. One woman pulled her canoe close to our boat and threw live fish with both hands into our boat. Another woman came from the other side and did the same. Luckily the water was about two feet deep at this stage and we could use our motor again to bring our extra cargo of fish out to the main river and back home to Ambunti.

This year the pastoral workers made a nice light canoe for the parish. It is specially designed to get through narrow waterways and it can easily be lifted over logs, which block up the creeks from time to time. I am going to paint the canoe red and white as a reminder of Cork's great win over Kilkenny in the All-Ireland hurling final. I know you are still celebrating by the Banks of the Lee; we are also celebrating by the Banks of the Sepik!

We had a lovely Christmas in the parish this year. Fr. Peter Wasko visited twelve out-Stations in the Black Water area, and I stayed on the main Sepik district. At the main station the youth arranged carol singing on Christmas night. It was very impressive to see a torchlight procession made from palm leaves light up the roadway around the air-strip and back to the church for midnight Mass. I was there with my hurricane lamp, while the district administrator, Paul Gumour, brought along his Coleman lamp. When we arrived back at the church, a large crowd had gathered to witness forty-nine babies and four adults receive the Sacrament of Baptism. It was a beautiful night, and everybody had the full moon to light up his or her journey home on Christmas morning.

For Family Sunday, the Liturgy committee asked the parents to sit down together in church with their children. It took some time, and most co-operated. It was the first time that men and women sat down together in church. It looked very nice and I am sure the experience will have a positive outcome.

One Sunday morning, as I was heading upstream in my speedboat, I met a family coming to church in their pull-canoe. The father was standing up in front and the mother was sitting down behind with a child sitting on her lap. In between were four small children. As I passed by all the children waved to me with great enthusiasm. I thought to myself that they were as happy in that canoe as if it was a Mercedes-Benz.

The mobile phone has arrived in the East Sepik Province, but only as far as Wewak town area.

This year three of our elderly Missionaries died at our retirement home here in Wewak: Fr. Karl Want ,84, Fr. Henry Sollner, 82, and Fr. Hugo Schulz, 94. I happened to be present when Fr. Sollner took ill and I was beside his bed when he passed away. All three had worked on the mission fields for over fifty years. They are all laid to rest in our mission cemetery here in Wewak.

This may be my last Christmas in Ambunti Parish. I prepare for home leave in early May and I am looking forward to seeing you all. God Bless and take care for 2005.

January 3, 2005 Greetings and best wishes from all here on the Sepik River. A few months ago, I blessed a new church in Marwai village. It's a little place back of the Watchkuk Mountains. The church is called after St. Arnold Janssen. The people told me, "We are SVD Catholic and we want St. Arnold to help us grow in faith." The church is just an ordinary bush building—no twin towers or stained-glass windows. Inside the church is a large photo of St. Arnold hanging behind the altar, and at the back is a beautiful picture of Bishop Leo, SVD. Three clans from the Watchkuk Mountains attended the opening of the new church. One clan leader told the gathering, "St. Arnold will look after us now and protect us from the evils of the world." During the meal after the Mass a young mother with four children came to me and asked if Fr. Michael Fiedel was still alive. I told her he was alive and strong. Then she said, "He baptised me when I was a baby and he gave me the name Gesta, the name after his own sister." The young woman is still known as Gesta. It's amazing the things people remember. Marwai village has been taken care of by SVD missionaries since 1948, so it's hard to blame them if they associate themselves with the SVD.

Last year I had a surprise visit from Fr. Jan Szweda, our Provincial, for the occasion of my fifty-seventh birthday. I returned from a Parish Steering Team meeting to find he had cooked my dinner. He had prepared chicken, potatoes, cabbage and carrots. You couldn't get much more Irish than that. We had two wonderful days together and, would you believe it, he travelled by PMV. Unfortunately, he had a nasty accident on the road out to Dagua when he drove at full speed into a riverbed, which he had to cross on the way to reach Dagua. He had forgotten all about the dip in the road. Fr. Jan injured his back, and he needs four months to recover. It means a lot of extra work for Pat Hogan, the assistant Provincial

You know, Pat and I are due home this year and both of us are looking forward to the break. So that's the end of the page. God Bless you and all the confrères.

January 31, 2005 I hope you are keeping well and happy after Christmas. There were just twelve hours left in 2004 and I had another church to bless for the Massanbuk people. Massanbuk is just three minutes' walk up the hill from the parish house. Sr. Alice, Fr. Peter Wasko, and I made the short trip this afternoon to find that many people had already gathered. My first impression was the lovely view from the hilltop. One had a full view of Ambunti town and the surrounding hilly country. I thought it was an inspiring place to meet the Lord and that the Massanbuk have chosen the hilltop for that very reason.

On my arrival, I was briefed on the programme for the day. First, I should bless a statue of St. Michael "locally carved", and then bless the church, followed by Mass. The Liturgy was well prepared, and there were no shortcuts to the procession in and out of the church. It was important every member of the community got involved.

After Mass, everyone gathered around in the shade and the speeches began. One leader was called on to say a few words, but before he began some people told him to keep it short as he had a habit of going on and on. Well it seems he didn't hear them as he went on in his usual style for twenty minutes.

William Kapwan then gave a rundown on the history of the Catholic Church in Ambunti. William is one of the oldest men in the community and the people hold him in high esteem. When he started to talk he looked up to the sky as if he was talking to St. Michael, whom the church was called after, and everyone listened as he tried to recall from his memory the history of the work of early missionaries.

He went on, "In the beginning only a few people came to church, about ten families and most were women. The big change came in 1986 when Fr. Eddie Baur, SVD, gave a 'Life in the Spirit' Seminar. Before that we knew nothing about the Holy Spirit, now we know quite a bit." After the seminar, he said a lot of young people got involved and started prayer groups in their communities. Today four communities attached to the Ambunti main station have their own prayer house. These communities meet on Tuesdays and Thursdays for family prayer. William went on to say, "The Church at the main centre is full up and this is the result of the Charismatic movement."

When I was asked to speak, I told them of an experience I had some years ago in the Lower Sepik. I was at an out-station and visited the prayer house in the village before the sun rose. When I entered, six elderly women were already praying. They had a statue of Our Lady at the front and a hurricane lamp lighting on the table where the statue was standing. Shortly after, the six women got up and left. When I asked them later why they left, they told me, "The first thing we do every morning is we visit the church to say our morning prayers. Then we go to check our fishing nets and baskets." I told the Massanbuk people they could also use their prayer house for private prayer as it was an ideal place to get away from the activities of the village and spend a quiet time with the Lord.

When the speeches concluded two young boys arrived carrying a mobile table; one had the top and the other the legs and they began to assemble it right beside where I was sitting. With some difficulty they tried to put the pieces together and there was no shortage of advisers. The youth continued to ignore all advice and managed eventually to get the pieces right. A white tablecloth was then spread on top, and the food started to arrive straight from the fire, still in cooking pots.

The guests were first to eat; it was self-service, there was plenty rice, bananas, and homegrown vegetables. Everyone had enough and long after I had eaten, some people still had stocks of food on their plates. Most people were sitting on the ground or on logs, which were rolled into position for the occasion. One man was sitting on a four-gallon Shell drum. There was lots of talk and laughter as if we had opened a multimillion supermarket. They were lost in their own world. Then I started talking about the "Asian Wave" that hit the Indian Ocean. Some had already heard, but they wanted more details. When I told them one of our SVD brothers from Aceh lost fourteen members of his family, everyone showed immediate interest. On that sad note it was time to wave the old year goodbye and a prayer meeting was about to start to welcome the New Year. Now the Massanbuk have their own house of prayer to do just that.

On my last trip to Wewak I stayed at our SVD house for ten days. During that time I did my shopping, got the land cruiser repaired, and I also finished writing my Christmas letters. One morning early, I went for a walk along the sea front at The Wind Jammer Hotel.

There wasn't a soul on the beach at that hour, only two dogs sitting on their rear end looking out to sea. If I took a guess, I would say their owners were out in the canoes fishing off Wewak point. I walked on for a mile and met a man walking towards me. We got talking. He said, "I see you saying Mass in Wirui Cathedral." I told him how beautiful the sea was and the sandy beach. He said, "Yes". Then he went on to tell me his story about the sea how it killed three members of his family during the tsunami in Aipate in 1998. At the time of the disaster, he was working with a road construction company and survived. His name is Frances Swano. The tragedy had a profound effect on his life; now he is a regular Mass goer at Wirui Cathedral.

At this time, we are making a collection for the victims of the "Asian Wave". All of PNG is responding well. I think it is the same all over the world. One of our diocesan priests told us the tidal wave went through his parent's home in India. His parents were at Mass at the time and escaped unharmed.

I hope to see you all in May. God bless and take care

February 8, 2005 Here in Ambunti, what can I say? If I take a look out the window, things look just the same as when I arrived here nearly ten years ago. However, on the pastoral scene there is a lot of activity in the parish from the kindergarten school right up to the senior members of the community. Right now, the parish pastoral team is giving a thanksgiving retreat at the out-stations. Fr. Peter Vasko and I returned on Sunday after completing two retreats in different areas of the parish. I think you could say, we have our favourite communities to visit. Fr. Peter can now drive the speedboat, which means he can take off any time he likes; as for myself, I am still doing bush patrol but not as much as before.

Last week when I visited Walfain the people were all in good spirits. They had returned that day after spending two weeks out in the bush digging and panning for gold. I didn't ask any questions, but it unfolded during the week that they had found a rich vein.

We stayed in a large traditional family house, and as is customary we spent the first evening talking about parish matters, hunting stories, and local gossip. The women of the house sat in the firelight next to a bundle of firewood, cooking sago. At the other end of the house where I was sitting, a group of men were sitting around a hurricane lamp in full conversation, while others listened in the dark. One lady couldn't hide her jubilation. She came across the floor and said, "Father, I found a nugget of gold the size of my thumb, I see it as a blessing from God." She moved away from the light and came forward again with the nugget in her hand. I didn't know where she was keeping it, but it was important I should see her precious metal. The other twenty or so occupants in the house were not so jubilant or outspoken about what they had found. However, they all agreed, Father should get some gold as a thanksgiving offering to God, and I should pray strongly that the vein of gold they were now following would not disappear. The community agreed to give me one penicillin bottle of gold but after much shaking and pressing of the bottle the cork wouldn't fit. A second bottle was called for and some late contributors added a few extra grams.

I am sure I would be right in guessing that most of the community are back in the bush today trying to find some more of that valuable metal, while I am wondering if my prayers will help.

The retreat went very well. Simon, the community leader, did his best to keep the retreat team happy. When I first arrived in this village, Simon's son John was crawling on the floor; now he can climb a coconut tree like a bear. Last week he must have climbed the tree four times, because when Simon thought we needed a drink he called on his son to climb the tree and drop one or two coconuts down.

One morning while I was hearing Confessions, an argument went on outside the church as to how long it was since my last visit. I could recognise Simon's voice. Simon said it was three months. The woman said it was only two months. Simon counted out December, January and February, that's three months. Both were strong in their opinion, so I was asked to intervene. Luckily, I knew my last trip was on December 29 and now it was February 5, which made it a little over five weeks. Now the lady could tell me her last Confession was five weeks.

On a lighter note, today there is plenty of activity on the station. The European Union has given our Catholic school a grant to upgrade it. Work has started on two teachers' houses. The parents are providing labour free of charge, in drawing the gravel, levelling the building sites, and mixing the cement. New classrooms and an administration block are also on the agenda. Mersie and Avatip villages, which are in Ambunti parish, are given grants as well. It has taken five years to get this far, and it could take as long to complete the project; nevertheless, the project gives the parish a bit of variety and makes life interesting and challenging.

Yesterday, Monday, a new generator arrived for Ambunti town. We may have power for twelve hours a day once it is installed. I still have the solar power here on the station installed by Fr Jan Czuba in 1987. It's getting older and weaker. If the sun doesn't shine, there is a blackout and the generator must be put on to give the batteries a boost. Solar is actually very good, but it has its limitations.

This year I have an SVD seminarian, Alex Koma, from the Highlands. He is still trying to get used to the Sepik River. On his first trip in the canoe, the driver Pius Balson told him to take off his shoes because if he fell in the river he could swim better without them. Next week Alex will go to the high-school to teach religious instruction and it won't take him too long to adapt to the Sepik way of life.

Next May, I am due on home leave, and I am looking forward to a fine summer and a few games of football and hurling and seeing all the family and friends again. God Bless and take care.

PART III

PORT MORESBY: 2005-2010

Divine Word College, Port Moresby

December 1, 2005 I am back in PNG after a wonderful holiday. The highlight of the holiday was my Silver Jubilee Mass. At that Mass Mrs. Cormac presented me with a stole and my brother John invested me in a chasuble over my alb as a symbol of my ordination. I hope to wear it for another twenty-five years.

Saying goodbye was not easy this time as so many people have gone to their eternal reward. I guess its all part of life, saying hello, saying goodbye, letting go, and beginning again. Here in the college I am doing just that, beginning again as spiritual director to the students in the seminary and also spiritual director to different religious congregations.

When I arrived here at the college, the ground had all the appearance of a desert. It was dry, dusty, and all the grass was burned out, both by the sun and by fires. Yet in the middle of all this there is life, spiritual life. If you take an early walk around the campus you can hear songs of praise coming from the different congregations. There are the Capuchins, Dominicans, Marists, Missionaries of the Sacred Heart, Franciscans, SVD, Mariannhill, Carmelites, and further up the road is the Catholic Theological Institute. All these congregations are within a stone's throw of each other. Outside the main college grounds are the Marianville Sisters, the Canossian Sisters, the Xavier Institute, and the De La Salle high-school. After reading that list, you would be forgiven if you thought I was writing to you from Rome. Further down the road is the Bomana Prison with over 500 inmates, and it is part of our apostolic work to visit the jail.

I have been to the jail a few times since I arrived here. My first visit was on October 30 to say Mass, and only inmates who were low risk were allowed to attend. I was told before my visit that the Catholics were by far the majority, so I was expecting a big crowd. Before Mass I counted sixty-five inmates, and once Mass started another twenty or thirty arrived. I asked if anyone here was from the Sepik, and to put up your hand so I can see you. Five prisoners put up their hand, and I spoke to them in the Sepik language, but there was no response. Then they started with a hymn they all knew, and it was so loud as if they wanted to shout all the week, and could not, but now were getting rid of all their frustration. After Mass one inmate asked me to get him a Bible and another gave me a letter to post to his family. As I walked out towards the main gate one young man walked along with me, so I asked him where he was going. He was going to the juvenile compound which was right in front of us. I was relieved to hear this and asked him when he was due to be let out? He answered without thinking, 2016. I told him that if he wanted to survive, to make it his home, and I wished him good-day.

Another Sunday I was saying Mass at a settlement called Nine Mile (being nine miles from the city centre). Before Mass one of their leaders introduced me. He said, "Now I want to introduce you to an old Sepik missionary priest, Fr. Michael O Donovan, who has been in PNG for years." I thought to myself, it is a reminder that time keeps moving on. I have been to Nine Mile a few times since for Baptism and a Mass for the dead, so I am still doing some pastoral work with the students during the weekends.

As for life in the seminary, you might ask what is it like to be back again after twenty-five years? For years I never wore a watch on the Sepik, but here in the seminary the clock rules the day. The first bell goes at half past five in the morning; it must be the Capuchins who ring it, as it comes from that direction. In the SVD house we start the day at six o'clock with morning prayer and finish the day with night prayer at eight o'clock, followed by silence and study. The students prepare breakfast, and two local women prepare lunch and dinner. During the weekends most of the staff and students are out doing pastoral work, which means each one looks after himself, except on Sunday evening when we all return to base and the students take turns to prepare this meal.

My role in the college is spiritual director, to give conferences to our SVD students and prepare them for pastoral work in the parish. The seminary is a life of theory, ideas, concepts, and information. After they finish their formal training, the students must come face to face with the real world and learn on the job once again. Last month I was busy preparing Steve Menau who will be ordained deacon next month on how to administer the sacraments of Baptism and Marriage. This is my area of work now. It is very interesting and challenging for me, though the Sepik and its people are not far from my mind as I try to settle in here to city life.

Fr. Steven Rex, SVD, one of our PNG missionaries, returned to Brazil three weeks ago after his three months holidays. Here in the college we gave him a big farewell party before he left. On the morning he departed most of the students went to the airport to say goodbye, and they waited there until the plane went out of sight. Some SVDs expressed their feelings, that if they persevere on their journey to the priesthood, one day they also will be saying goodbye to their family and friends.

The students at the college are very helpful. They have shown me several skills, like how to use the computer. They also gave me a few lessons on how to drive in the city of Port Moresby. They told me I was no longer a country driver, and I should get used to traffic lights, roundabouts, and two-lane traffic. At this stage I am finding my way to the airport, the supermarket, and petrol pump. The city has very few signposts as the rascals sell them for scrap iron. This makes it very difficult for a beginner. As I said, I am beginning again, and in more ways than one.

On the social side of life, we play cards a few nights a week; watch TV and visit our SVD confrères in the city. On December 16 I made a visit to Wewak Diocese to help out for Christmas and meet some old friends from the days in the bush. With that, I wish you a happy Christmas and a peaceful New Year. God bless you all and take care.

January 8, 2006 I am just back from Nine Mile after saying Mass there. The people there gave us lots of fruit and vegetables and some scones as an offering. There are nine of us here at the college at the moment, and Fr. Alex Garuai joins us every Sunday evening, so the fruit and vegetables won't last long.

Yesterday the Marianville Sisters asked me to say Mass in the woman's prison. Only six of the seventeen inmates were Catholic, and one of them was from a village on the Sepik. She had two black eyes after a boxing match with another man's wife. She got two weeks in jail for her troubles. The women had their heads shaved, which made them look more like men than woman. After Mass everyone sat down on the cement slab and chatted about Christmas and the death of the former Prime Minister, Sir William ("Bill") Skate. Some found the time boring in prison, and only for the support of the other prisoners they would go crazy. They look forward to newcomers, and they had a few of them over Christmas.

Next Saturday, the Missionary Sisters of Charity have asked me for a day of recollection. They have eighteen sisters here in Port Moresby, and thirteen in Wewak.

When I was in Wewak I called to see Bishop Tony Burgess and he is looking great. He invited all the priests up to his flat for Christmas. We had drinks, crisps, and chocolate, and the conversation was very relaxing. Br. Jack is building a retirement home for the Rosary Sisters. Br. Daniel is after putting on a lot of weight and is slowing down a lot. Fr. Rudy Studden is in bed all together, but he has no notion of dying.

After one week in Wewak, Fr. Jan Skotniczny came to collect me and I stayed with him for one week. Fr. Jan is alone in Kunginjini, and he is very busy building up the station. I was introduced to Kunginjini Parish twenty-four years ago, and I still like going back there. Fr. Jan and I had a busy Christmas. I stayed at the main station, and hundreds of people came for Confession. We just had to give up and give them general absolution. On Christmas night and Morning, the church was packed, with four or five hundred people standing outside. For Holy Communion we emptied five ciboriums for midnight Mass and the same again on Christmas morning Mass.

My last week in Wewak was also a pleasant one. I played cards most evenings in the community room, and Fr. Geoff Brumm joined us on a few occasions. He is in top form, thank God. During the day I went swimming, and I joined in to watch the soccer games at St Mary's Community School. The announcer at the microphone was delighted to see me, and he announced to the people that I came every day to watch the games, and he asked the people give me a round of applause.

Br. Matthew, a former missionary in PNG, has returned to say one last goodbye to all of us. The doctors have given him only six months to live.

He looks in good form but when he speaks you know he is sick man. He got a big welcome at Boram Airport. The Rosary Sisters and the nurses arranged it. He hopes to take a trip to Timbunke and Kanengara, where he worked most of his life. Everyone is delighted to meet him, especially the locals. Br. Matthew told the locals he was ready to let go; he said he had a good life and had given it all he could.

To change the subject from death to life, the Wewak Diocese is very much alive with all the pastoral workers, young priests, and sisters. After Christmas one of the Rosary Sisters made her final vows at an out-station in Passam Parish. Her name is Sr. Loretta, a nurse by profession. Over forty sisters and fifteen priests were present. It was well done, and Fr. Waldi was very pleased; the day was dry, and a big number of people attended.

Maprik has its own radio station now with all the local news and Christmas greetings being relayed. Two local priests are taking over Ambunti Parish, where I was for over ten years. That is a big change for the local church, to have their own priests to cater for their needs, and to support them as well.

Today I received *The Harp*, with all the news from the Irish province. Now that I am in Port Moresby I am much more in contact with the SVD than when I was in the bush. It is good I don't have to worry anymore about outboard motors, canoes, bad roads, and mosquitoes. Now I am going for a jog around the soccer field. The other Fathers play tennis, and the students play all sorts of games. So, on that happy note I will sign off, and wish you every blessing for the New Year. God bless you and take care.

May 8, 2006 I don't feel like writing at all now since I am able to use the internet and the internet phone. However, I had better put a few words on paper before I forget what is happening around the place.

We had a lovely Easter here at the college, and for the Easter Vigil Mass I went to Nine Mile outside Port Moresby. The chairman, Joe Gigmai, had arranged to have the Mass at two o'clock in the morning. When I arrived, there wasn't a soul to be seen, only a light in the church. When I entered most of the congregation, to my surprise, had arrived and were lying on mats sound asleep on the church floor. They already had half a night's sleep behind them. Then they woke up and tidied up and left the children sleep on until the Baptismal water woke them. When the service was over I decided to go home and get a few hours' sleep, but the people told me to wait on as the women were preparing a meal, and it would be ready soon, so I waited. The church leader told me, "Father there is no hurry. We are waiting for the sun to come up, so we can walk home in the light." When I looked into the church again, half the congregation were gone back to sleep. It was daylight when I got home. If the Easter Vigil Mass is at the same time, I think I will go to the church at nine o'clock, have a sleep, and wake up when it's time for Mass.

Yesterday I said Mass in the prison, which is only five minutes' drive from here. I say Mass one Sunday in the month in the male prison and on Saturday on occasions in the female section. The number of females in prison is small; it goes from ten to twenty and only five or six are Catholics. The male prison has over 500 inmates and nearly half of them are Catholics However, the number who come for Mass varies between sixty and a hundred. The prisoners are well organised; they have their own prayer leader, chairman, and secretary. The chairman usually stands up before Mass and welcomes everybody. He gives a special word of welcome to Father, and to the new faces in the congregation. There are always a few new faces every week, and it is easy to pick them out from the rest as they stay in the back and sit down together, looking unsure of themselves. Then after Mass the chairman comes to the front again to say a few words. This time he wants to thank everybody and a special word of thanks to the inmates who have done time and are about to go home during the coming week. The chairman asks them to come to the front and say a few words of advice to those inmates still staying behind. He usually tells them to behave well, that that is the soonest way they will get out, and that is followed by lots of handshakes and goodbyes. The inmates tell me, "It is important to support each other when we are in here otherwise we would go crazy." Some days the prisoners pass by the college here in their mobile cell going to work collecting firewood or cutting grass, or some may be going to a court hearing. Their mobile cell is a wire cage on the back of a lorry. If the prisoners happen to see me on the road or on the grounds they are sure to call out, "Father Michael, hello." You would think they were going to a football match, as they are so cheerful in their wire cage. I also meet one or two prisoners in the city who have been released, and they come talking to me on the street. I didn't recognise them, as they look so different when dressed up, and the hair had grown again.

This week I am in charge of the SVD College, as Fr. Joe, the Rector, and Br. Raj are at a formation board meeting in Mount Hagen. Tomorrow I must go shopping as we are having a celebration on Saturday for Fr. Joe Maciolek and Fr. James Uravil on the occasion of their silver jubilees. We are expecting over 150 guests. Fr. James is president of the Catholic Theological Institute (CTI) and he is here eighteen years, so he has a lot of friends. Fr. Joe is also here a long time and he has many friends as well in the locality

Next week I am giving a retreat to our seminarians who are preparing to renew their vows, and the week after I will give a four-day retreat to the Canossian Sisters. The Canossian sisters are involved in teaching and in health care.

Sometimes you may be wondering what I am doing all day. Well, one Saturday in the month we have a staff meeting to sort out any problems, and one Saturday in the month we have a meeting with the students to give them an opportunity to let us know their worries. They usually have concerns about food: it is too greasy, too cold, or the meat is all gone when the last students arrive. The car is also a concern because everyone wants to drive. We also have one Saturday in the month for our SVD Fraternity meeting. This is where all the SVD in the district come together for Bible sharing and discussions about Society matters. It is usually very good. We have a nice lunch with wine, chocolate, and ice cream.

Then I must be available to the students for spiritual direction when they come to see me. These sessions can be complicated and worrying at times, as some students don't know what they want from life. I have to give them a passage from Scripture to read, like John 1:35-42 where it says, "Jesus asked the disciples who were following him, what do you want?" I ask the students to think about this question during their prayer time and come and see me in one month. I also spend some time on the computer preparing my conferences, which I give to the students every Monday if I am at home.

I think it would be very hard to go back to the bush now after getting used to city life. Here I have TV, daily newspapers, telephone, e-mail, computer, and meals are cooked for me every day, and what's more I have no worries with bad roads or boats. However, city life has its problems with law and order. To avoid such problems, we don't go out at night.

Last Sunday two new Fathers from Indonesia arrived here at the college to learn Pidgin English. We don't know where they will be appointed to yet. They are very young and eager to learn. One of our students, Paul Boi, lost his sight and we sent him to the Philippines to see if they can do anything for him. It doesn't look too good, but we can only try our best for him.

Two months ago, I was appointed Spiritual Animator to CTI. This means I must keep in touch with the other spiritual directors at the college and call a meeting every term to discuss any issues that may be of concern. We have over 170 students, and twenty staff members. Everyone has a part to play in keeping the community alive and active, and above all in looking after the spiritual side. God bless you and take care.

September 9, 2006 On August 21 I flew to Wewak for the ordination of Fr. Stephen Menau. A diocesan priest, Fr. James Huros, was ordained together with Fr. Stephen. Both priests are from the islands off Wewak and that would explain why the crowd was not as big as expected. The island people find it hard to travel in big numbers. There was a great buzz around the cathedral for days leading up to the ordination. The Wirui parishioners were cutting and raking grass, and others were arranging flowers around the altar. Br. Herman was checking the light and amplifier, and the Wirui choir were practicing for two days in the vicinity of the Sound Shell stadium. It was encouraging to see a whole new generation of people in action since I first arrived in Wewak. Bishop Leo and Bishop Ray were no longer centre stage, and Br. Lothar or Fr. Fincutter were no longer controlling the public address system. In their absence was Stella, a local lady who works in the parish office. Bishop Anthony Burgess was the main celebrant, and he performed well; as one says, practice makes perfect. After the ceremony, friend and family members gathered in the Wirui dining room. The local people had prepared all the food, and, would you believe it, a large pig cooked in traditional style was laid out on top of the dining room table. There wasn't a trace of it when we arrived next morning for breakfast. It was really a local celebration, and they were doing it their way. I went to the ordination to represent the rector of the seminary, Fr. Joe, who was on holidays at the time, and besides me was the one who prepared Fr. Stephen to administer the sacrament of Confession, and Fr. Harry Janissen, SVD, who prepared him for his first Mass. Every day for seven days Fr. Harry and I went for a swim at four o'clock. Fr. Harry goes every day for a swim, and he is really looking healthy. Like me, he is also learning how to use the computer.

I had just returned from Wewak and eaten my dinner when I heard all the screaming outside the college gate. When our students went to investigate they discovered Br. Augustine Taiwi had been murdered by a criminal gang. The minibus he was driving at the time continued on for a few hundred yards, and it came to a halt against a tree. Two of the gang were arrested, but the one that threw the iron is still at large. The motive for the killing is not clear though there are several stories going around. One thing for sure the killers knew him, and he knew them. Br. Augustine was only 46. I knew him very well, as I had assisted him one week at the Xavier Institute when one of the bishops to give a course failed to turn up because of ill health, and I was asked to stand in and give a seminar on prayer. We had a lovely goodbye Mass here at CTI chapel for him, and his body was taken back to Aitape Diocese to be buried in the St. John of God cemetery. Paul Boi, who lost his sight last Christmas, has returned from the Philippines and Fr. John O Mahoney was his escort for the trip. I had not met John for twenty-five years. We sent Paul to the Philippines hoping they could do something for him. He has a little bit of sight and can recognise day from night. At present he is learning Braille in Goroka, and we will see how it goes from there. God bless you all and take care.

January 12, 2007 I hope you are all keeping will since I last heard from you. I am keeping well myself, thank God. I am back in PNG over a year already. It was a very enriching year with all kinds of everything which included airport ministry, rector, spiritual director and retreat master.

Brother Anthony, who usually takes care of SVD and other religious congregations travelling overseas for home leave, went on holidays for three months, so I was left to co-ordinate the goings and comings of our confrères from the airport to their place of lodging and back to the airport again to catch their international flight next day. There was more to it than driving people to the airport, as some travellers had to renew their visas, and others wanted to get their tickets changed. It was a learning experience for me, and luckily I had the students and some of the confrères to help out with the early morning flights. It was interesting to observe the people saying farewell to family members, and others just arriving being welcomed with big smiles and hugs from their loved ones. Sometimes I met people from Wewak, and they were equally surprised to see me as they thought I was still in Ambunti. I always kept an eye out for the Wewak flight to see if I could recognise some of the passengers. Once I was told to pick up three people from Poland, two men and one woman. They did not speak English, so all I had was their names on a piece of paper. As I waited outside the arrival area, out came two men and one woman so I showed the man leading the way the paper. He took one look at it and told me to get out of his way. I waited on and out came another two men and a woman. This time I waited just in case I would get it wrong again. When everyone had passed through I approached the three Europeans with my piece of paper, and when they recognised their names they were so delighted and relieved that someone had come to pick them up. I also met several of our SVDs passing through during the year, including John Ryan, John McCarthy, John O'Mahony and Gary Roche. Now that Br. Anthony has returned I don't have to worry any more about the airport ministry.

Our rector of the college, Fr. Joe Maciolek, was also on home leave and I was standing in for him during the three months. My main job was to keep the college running and pay the bills. I went shopping twice a week to the Food World supermarket with some students, and the students made sure I wasn't forgetting the ice cream and honey. The bread was delivered every second day, and the freezer came once a fortnight on order. We managed very well, and I noticed a few students put on weight during this time. Paying the bills was a bit more demanding as I still consider myself new to the city, and it was my first time keeping financial reports on the computer. Fr. Joe is back, and he is now holding the reins again. Last September I returned to the college after giving an eight-day preached retreat to twelve sisters in the Nazareth House of Prayer. I have given four retreats there already this year. The theme of the retreat was "A Call to follow Christ", and the sisters asked for silence all through the eight days. The retreat house is only four miles from here and it has nice grounds to walk around. The sisters told me that it was hard to have any fruit there with all the different birds that inhabit the surrounding area, and that the parrots are the biggest intruders.

I went to Lae city in September also to give a retreat to the priests, brothers, sisters, and pastoral workers. It was my first time in Lae, so one of the priests, Fr. Chris, showed me around the city, which has a population of 190,000. A large number of these people are unemployed, and this is causing a big problem with law and order in the local communities.

This year I had a few surprise visitors from the Sepik. On October 9 a blind man from my former parish, Timbunke, came to visit me at the college. His name is Jerry Hensen. Back in 1987 the Christian Brothers asked all the parish priests if they knew of any blind children in their parish, as they had a school for the blind in Goroka. In the village of Suimbo I knew of a family with three blind children, two girls, and one boy. After some months consulting with their parents and the village leaders it was arranged to let them go to the school for the blind. All travel and other expenses were seen too, and finally the day of departure arrived. The village people had prepared a farewell party for the children and everybody stayed back from their gardens to wish them well. Augustine, the eldest girl, and Jerry had no problem in getting into the Daihatsu car, but Lucy made a run to escape and refused to go. Her mother went to her rescue and brought her back to the car. Then there was a big debate about whether she should go or not. Most of the men said, "Let her stay back as she is too young, and she can go next time." I was still standing by the car and ready to close the door when I told Lucy, "You can go for one week, and if you don't like it you can come back." With that she jumped into the car, and a whole new life began that day for the three blind children. That is all of nineteen years ago now, and Jerry arrives at my door one morning, 500 miles away from home. I asked him how he got here, and he told me he came for a youth meeting to Port Moresby all by himself. Jerry told me when he got off the plane he just listened to the people's footsteps and followed them out of the airport, and when he came outside he called out for a taxi and told the driver to take him to the Christian Brothers, and the rest is history. Jerry stayed four days with us here in the college. I asked him about his two sisters, and he told me Augustine got a scholarship to the States, and came back with a master's degree in English, and Lucy also has a job, and Jerry is working with the National Aids Council. During dinner one night, Jerry gave us an inspiring talk about his physical disability, and it gave us great encouragement, especially as one of our students, Paul Boi, lost his sight last Christmas. Paul is now learning Braille in the same school as Jerry attended.

My former Bishop, Tony, made a surprise visit one morning to see me. He was also attending a meeting in Port Moresby at the time, and he has seven seminarians here at the college that he wished to see.

Last year we had over 170 seminarians at the college and twenty-five graduated on November 18. Most of the students are on holidays at present, and we start again in February. On December 18 I went to visit Fr. John McCarthy who is stationed up in the highlands of PNG, and I had a lovely holiday with him and the community for the most of three weeks. God bless and take care.

January 26, 2007 I hope you are keeping well after Christmas and the New Year Celebrations. By the time you receive this letter the days will be much longer, and spring will be in the air again. It's a beautiful morning here in Port Moresby. We had some rain last night and it makes the place look so fresh looking and green. It will soon be time to bring the lawnmower out again.

We are still on holidays here at the college. Next week the students come back, and the week after we start classes. Our numbers are down this year by all accounts, but we don't know for sure how many will turn up until the day arrives.

Last week I was out in the Bereina Diocese giving a workshop on vocations. Seven girls and five boys attended. As a group I was not able to get much out of them, but as I spoke to them one by one the real picture began to emerge. One girl wanted to join, but her father was against it, so the sisters could not accept her. Others were only 16 and had dropped out of school because of school fees. One boy came because his parents would like him to be a priest. Now I hear two boys are joining the Missionaries of the Sacred Heart (MSC) next week, which is good news. I stayed in a little house next to the sister's convent which is in the middle of the village surrounded by pigs and poultry. It was like living back on the farm before Ireland joined the European Union.

This Christmas I did not visit Wewak, as I had promised Fr. John McCarthy I would call to see him in Par, his parish in the Enga province. It was my first time to visit this part of PNG. I flew to Mount Hagen on December 18, and the car Fr. John sent to pick me up broke down so there was nobody there to meet me when I arrived. I was a bit worried about being robbed as I was carrying passports, air tickets, and computer spares for the provincial office in Hagen. After waiting half an hour, a young man approached me and asked, "Are you waiting for someone?" I told him I was waiting for Fr. John McCarthy. He said, "I know him. He is the vocation director for the SVD." Without further delay we took a bus into Hagen city. The following day, Fr. Romel, SVD, drove me to Par. It's about a two-hour journey on a tarred road. On the way we met a group of young men all armed with bush knives. They were leading a bull by a rope and judging by the length of its horns he must have been five or six years old. Fr. Romel presumed the bull was part of a bride price in transition.

I stayed in Par for eighteen days, and I met most of the SVD Fathers working in the diocese. I was surprised to see so many young priests, and the few older ones are still extremely active for their age. I helped out in the parish over Christmas with Confessions and Masses. On Christmas Day I had Mass for the Poor Clare Sisters. On December 27, most of the priests came to the parish centre for a meeting and Christmas dinner.

I was surprised to see most of a hundred people coming every day to Mass at Par. Bishop Herman told me it is the same all over the Diocese. On Christmas night at Par the church was packed, at least 1,000 people. All the children gathered around the altar, and I had some difficulties reaching the lectern to read the Gospel. Fr. John had prepared the Liturgy very well, and he spent some hours the day before rehearsing with the disabled people who were taking a key part in the Liturgy on Christmas night. After Mass, Fr. John handed out over fifty presents to the disabled peopled who attended

Mass. I believe a few extra callers came to see Fr. John the following days to avail of his generosity during the Christmas festivities. The word had got around that he was giving presents to the disabled.

This week I received several phone calls from my friends in Wewak. They were looking for money to pay for their children's school fees. George Balson, one of my canoe drivers from Ambunti, told me he got robbed in Wewak town and he had no money to go home. I asked Fr. Joe, SVD, to give him a hundred *kina* and I would repay him later. Damian Anton, another helper from the Sepik, asked for 500 *kina* for school fees. I gave him 200, and so the list goes on. They were very disappointed I did not go to Wewak to see them, and they said, "We came to Wewak specially to meet you." I was able to support them all a little as I had received a lot of donations in the Christmas mail. All the best for now and take care.

April 27, 2007 Since I last wrote to you, I have received an extra assignment to look after our SVD parish at Kuriva and at the same time remain spiritual director at our SVD College. It means I will not be available to give retreats, days of recollection or conferences on the same scale as last year. I still have over thirty sisters and as many more seminarians for spiritual direction on a regular basis. The Handmaids of the Lord Sisters were looking for an elderly priest for their junior sisters, and they had no doubt in their minds that I was in that age bracket now. They asked me to accompany their seven junior sisters on their spiritual journey for 2007. At Xavier Institute there are sixteen sisters preparing for the vowed life, and I am also involved in their spiritual formation. There are also the Missionary Sisters of Charity (MSC) which average about eight through the year; I give spiritual input to them every month, and, mind you, the sisters don't let me forget. The new appointment means I spend about four days a week in the parish and three days a week at the college. To make my dual lifestyle more convenient and to avoid taking cargo from place to place, I have bought an extra tooth brush, Bible, dictionary, towels, glasses, and those utensils which are essential to my everyday needs.

Before Fr. Alex Garuai, SVD, left the parish to take on further studies, he introduced me to the different communities in the parish, and in Port Moresby city we went from one office to another to get familiar with the running of the diocese. When I asked at the registry office for marriage forms, the clerk asked me, "Did you bring you partner along"? After that we went to a hardware shop to buy some utensils for the parish house. In the store Fr. Alex sat down on a beautiful office chair to attend to his shoe. When one of the assistants saw him, he told him to get off, and added, "That is a white man's chair." Fr. Alex is from Buka Island and he is as black as charcoal. A few days later, Fr. Alex got sick, and I happened to be in the house when a little girl was standing outside. She told her mother, "Father is sick." "Black or White?" asked the mother. "Black," answered the child. I was telling Fr. Alex afterwards, and we thought it a good idea if we should stay around a bit longer to see what other amusing incidents would surface. We had a good laugh at the whole thing.

The following Sunday, Fr. Alex and I went to an out-station called Badiroho for Mass. It happened there was only one chair for the priest to sit on. Some people in the congregation saw the need for a second chair, but it wasn't in the village. One got a bright idea and got two bags of cement lying at the side of the church and put one on top of the other next to the altar and a green banana leaf to cover them. Just before Mass another village man thought he had a better idea; he went to his house, came back, removed the cement chair and replaced it with a five-gallon oil-drum. The drum served its purpose, but I would not recommend it for watching television or reading the daily newspaper. Its owner did not have that worry.

From there we went to meet the parish chairman, Willy Denis, who worked for four years as a civil aviation officer in Port Moresby. As we sat down on the veranda of his house, he expressed his opinion that life was much better back in the village. He stared out at the river and said, "We have water all the year around, and the gardens are our bulk stores. We have all we need as regards food and water, and there are no worries like paying water bills and buying store goods." He was comparing life now to his life in the city some years ago. Fr. Alex went on to tell me that Willy Denis was a good driver, and I might need him to drive the parish car in times of emergency. True enough, last week I had my first emergency call, a mother in labour who was not able to deliver. When I arrived in the village the mother had already given birth to a still-born baby girl. The people told me there was no need to take the mother to hospital but to wait and baptise the baby. After a short delay the village midwife brought the still-born baby wrapped in a blanked and placed it on a bench outside the house. All the village children came to see the little infant, and I was surprised this custom was allowed, as it was forbidden in other parts of PNG to introduce the children to the hard facts of life at such an early age. When the people were ready, I started a prayer service and baptised the baby Mary Magdalene. After the burial all the children put flowers on the grave, which was only a short distance from the house. Willy Denis told me that every year there are between ten to fifteen emergency runs to Port Moresby General Hospital with mothers in labour, but the majority are people bitten by poisonous snakes.

Our next visit was to a village called Akuku. When we arrived there most of the village people were still sleeping, having been up all night at a "wake" as one of their elders had died. After a long wait a few adults came and a big group of children, the ones that slept the night through, and they made a big contribution to the singing during the Mass. After Mass I was taken to bless the corpse and say prayers for the dead while a group of young men were gone to Moresby to find a coffin. It was almost midday at this stage, and John Alua the church leader and his family invited us for some refreshments. John was not feeling well, and his daughter was taking care of him. His daughter told me all the places in PNG she has been too, and I asked her how she managed to visit them. "Oh," she said, "my husband was a bus driver, and I was the conductor." By PNG standards she was a well-travelled woman. While we talked, the kettle boiled, and eight cups of tea and a plate of homemade scones were placed on the floor of her semi-permanent house. Two of our seminarians, Clement Daimas and David Bakio, were also present as this is part of their pastoral programme. At present there are three seminarians and one brother gaining pastoral experience in Kuriva Parish. Bonaventure Imbosi is here because his passport is not in order, and his trip to the Philippines is on hold, and Francis Gende is teaching at the Catholic school next door.

The parish consists of the main centre and six extended communities. Most of these communities can be reached by car, so I can say two Masses every Sunday and drive back afterwards to the college in less than forty minutes. So far, the work is very enjoyable, and it is nice to be back with the grassroots people. Last Sunday I got ten ropes of bananas which would be well over 1,000 bananas. I took them back to the college where they will have bananas enough for two weeks. In some villages, the people cook the bananas and feed them to the pigs instead of meal. Fr. Alex Garuai had a very good garden. He had planted corn, peanuts, and pumpkin and pawpaw trees. The local priests don't have the same support as we missionaries have, so they must generate some income themselves, and having a good garden is one of the best means.

Here in Kuriva we eat a lot of home-grown food, and the seminarians and I take turns in cooking. Tonight, we will have chicken, pumpkin and bananas, followed by pawpaw for desert. The Coleman lamp will be hissing away on the side table as we share household jokes about our own daily experiences. I want to wish you the joys of Easter, and may the risen Lord be a light for your life. God bless you and take care.

May 2, 2007 I am back in Kuriva Parish for the weekend after attending a retreat on SVD spirituality. Fr. Michael Somers was the retreat master. During the third day of the retreat one of our elderly priests, Fr. George Miozga from Poland, had a heart attack and died a few hours later. Fr George was 74 and had spent forty of those years in PNG. He had a lovely funeral, and over forty priests and twenty sisters at the retreat were able to attend. The Lord had timed his departure very well. Madang is a beautiful place to make a retreat as it is beside the sea, and several Fathers from the Highlands who only see the sea once a year took advantage to have a swim once or twice a day. It was nice for me to meet some of the confrères from Wewak Diocese and catch up with the latest developments there.

My first Easter at Kuriva was very well attended. We had all the celebrations at the main centre, which made it easier for me to prepare the Liturgy, and most people from the out- stations were able to cover the distance from their out-stations in one hour. We also had thirty-nine Baptisms, all beautiful babies younger than two years, except three adults who had missed out on the sacraments somewhere along the line. Just now as I write this letter a local woman has brought me twenty-four bananas. I will pause for a moment to test one out.

At this time of year, I don't get much correspondence from overseas, but when I returned from Madang last week I had four letters from parishioners from Timbunke and Ambunti. One letter went like this: "Dear Father Michael, I know you are a very good Father, and I know you will never change. Do you remember when you gave me a pair of trousers and a towel two years ago? Well, the trousers are worn out, but the towel I am still using. The Bible says ask and you will receive, and I believe you will solve my problem, because you are still the same, a very good Father." After all that excessive praise I sent him the price of a trousers.

Kuriva Parish house is right beside the Catholic school, and an old convent and a sub-health centre. Some days when it rains the children come knocking on the door looking for plastic bags to keep their schoolbooks dry while they walk home from school. These children seem to love the rain, as it cools them down from the heat of the day. The old convent, which was abandoned by the sisters some years ago because there was no priest there to celebrate Mass, has one occupant. She is an elderly woman who never married, and the story is that she had to leave her village because the people accused her of making sorcery and witchcraft. She was there when I arrived, and her name is Onie. Fr. Alex used to give her something to eat every evening, and I have continued the same practice. She is a lovely old lady who is completely innocent. She doesn't speak my language, and I don't speak hers. When we meet we just nod our heads like monks in strict silence, and when she is hungry she shows me her empty plate and we bow again, and the message is understood. The parish board asked me to get her removed from the station, but I told them, "How I can do something like that when every time I meet her she has a Rosary beads in her hand, and she comes to Mass whenever I am here." After Mass I see her sitting out on the veranda warming her bones in the morning sun, and again fingering the beads. I must now try to learn a few words of her language as I don't expect her to learn mine.

The school grounds and the mission station have a six-foot security fence erected around its property. The first thing I do as dawn breaks is to unlock the security gate and give three bangs to an empty gas container to alert the residents there is morning Mass. Just beside the security gate, Eugene Amaia, the officer in charge for the health centre lives with his family. Each morning I hear the family reciting their morning prayers and singing hymns. A stranger would be forgiven if he thought this house was the real convent, though one of their daughters, Agnes, has just joined the religious life.

A day has passed since I started this letter, and all is quiet here after two hours of a down-pour yesterday. I looked out the window to see the station covered in water. The Kuriva Bridge got jammed with dead wood and debris, and the spill-over came our way. I thought at first it did not do much damage, but when I went out to the bridge this morning, people were telling me their gardens were destroyed. Fr. Alex had planted fifty pawpaw trees six month ago and they too are resting in peace, all dead.

Kuriva Bridge is usually a meeting place, a bus stop, and a market place for the local people. I go there to meet the people, and to buy fruits. One man has his market under a large rain tree, and he sells noodles and betel-nut, a strange combination. He loves talking and meeting his costumers. Today there were about fifty people sitting under the tree, and they all seemed to be taking the day off or on holidays.

Fr. Alex, the former parish priest, is settling into Par with Fr John McCarthy. Before Fr. Alex left Kuriva Parish, we had a week of celebrations in the first week of Lent. To cope with the farewell dinners, we had to postpone the Lenten observations for some days. Fr. Alex had trained altar boys and girls to assist him during Mass. Some of them are very young and they feel very important in their gypsy shawls. One morning I was standing at the wrong side when approaching the altar and the server told me I was at the wrong side, so I moved over, and he was very pleased that I was doing things Fr. Alex's way. There is another little girl too—Vickie—and she knocks on the door every so often, with a plate of food in her hand, and says, "My mother is worried about you, it's no good if you are hungry" and she skips off after doing her good deed. Once a week, the station children come to watch a DVD in our meeting room. This was something started by Br. Rudi when he was here two years ago, and the tradition is still in practice.

The mobile phone is making fast progress in PNG. It is like a culture shock for the rural people. They find it amazing to think something the size of a bar of soap can help you to speak to your friends at the other side of the world. That is development. Ten years ago, when the women started wearing long trousers some men did not like it, and I over-heard one man saying, "That's development, Aye!"

This week the country goes to the polls to elect a new government. Prime Minister Sir Michael Somare is still going strong. He was in Lae city last week and gave the people a gift of fifty million *kina* to repair the roads in the province. A politician told the people in Lae he had a pain in his back after going through the city. The day after, there was a letter in the *Post-Courier*[1] saying, "You drove once through the city, and your back is paining. What about the people who live here and have to travel these roads every day?" The wit and the sarcasm are starting to roll out, and how the people are enjoying it.

Last Monday I went to the police station to get my fingerprints taken. It is part of the process to obtain a permanent visa. Does this mean I am going to stay the rest of my life in PNG and become part of its soil, or is it more for convenience sake? Time will tell. So, it's time once again to sign off and I hope this letter finds you enjoying life. God Bless and take care.

October 1, 2007 Much thanks for your many e-mails and newsletters received through the year. I am sure you are in good health and keeping up to date with all the latest in PNG. I had one bad day myself—it was the day our neighbours Kerry hammered us in the All-Ireland football final. I am sure I wasn't the only one from Cork to feel the same way. "Only a game of football?"

Yesterday I returned from Yule Island after giving a six-day retreat to twenty-four OLSH Sisters[2]. It was school holiday time, so quite a lot of this group were teachers. Yule Island is a lovely place for a retreat. You could talk out loud to yourself there, and no one would hear you.

The national elections in PNG passed off generally well without much hassle. Fr. Paul Kanda, our first SVD from PNG, stood for the regional seat in Enga against Peter Ipatas, the sitting governor. Paul came fourth place with 29,000 votes, and Peter Ipatas got over 120,000. Most people felt Paul did better than expected, but he was still a long way off the mark.

1 The *Papua New Guinea Post-Courier* is the country's main newspaper.
2 Daughters of Our Lady of the Sacred Heart.

Seven priests stood for the election, and only one got elected, and that was Fr. John Garia from the Kundiawa Diocese.

Digicel, the mobile phone company from Ireland, is still under threat of a shutdown from the government. The company is erecting steel towers at an alarming rate in several provinces and dishing out mobile phones to customers at a reduced price; buy one, and you get two for just 100 *kina*. I drove into the village of Akuka one morning to be told that some men went out hunting last night with their mobile phone, and they just called us to say they shot two deer, and they asked for help to bring the meat back to the village. To a certain extent the mobile phone has energised the communities, knowing they can speak to their family members who live away from home at the press of a few buttons. Like Ireland, I know of families here in Port Moresby where father, mother son and daughter have one each. People here are getting to know more about Ireland every day because this Irish company has opened up a whole new way of life for them. I think the Irish will put the old *garamut* on the Sepik into liquidation.

I must say the parish work is going very well. The people are very good to me, and I am getting to know them, and they are getting to know me. On the first Sunday of September while Limerick and Kilkenny were preparing for the All-Ireland hurling final, I was in Kuriva preparing to administer the sacrament of Baptism. We had sixteen lovely babies, some were pink skin, others were chocolate colour, and a few were nearly as white skinned as me. They were all dressed in lovely bright clothes and their parents were also dressed well for the occasion. I thought to myself that PNG is really finding its way—if only the government could look after the roads, schools, and healthcare. This year I have baptised over fifty babies and I would say by the looks of things I could have at least twenty more to baptise before the year is out. What a difference it makes to have all these kids playing, screaming, and running about the village. One weekday I went on a sick call to visit two old men who were close to death. As I prepared to administer the sacraments over twenty children circled around me and watched every move I made. I tried to get them to say the "Our Father" in Pidgin, but they did not know it. The second man was sitting on a piece of cardboard box outside his house. He sat with his legs bent up, and his jaw was resting on his kneecaps. The same group of children circled again, and I noticed two of them had their hand on the old man's shoulders, as to say, "We are looking after him." This time I said the "Our Father" in English, and to my surprise they were able to follow me. One of these old men has since gone to see St. Peter, and the other one with the bended knees is still waiting.

As I drove outside the village that morning, the Legion of Mary were holding their praesidium, and they were delighted I saw them in action. I joined them in prayer and gave them the final blessing. I thought how proud Frank Duff would be if he saw them, fourteen women dressed in blue and white, and two men in white shirts and black trousers. Afterwards one of the ladies invited me to her house for lunch. She has one son in grade twelve, and when I asked her what her son has in mind for the future, she replied, "That is something for God to decide." I thought he might be interested in the priesthood since his mother is such a devout Catholic. Then she changed the subject and asked about the puppy dogs she had asked me to give her. When I told her that we had seven pups at the college, she gave me two clusters of bananas as a deposit to keep two for her.

There are some fine stately women here in the parish. They drive to Mass in their four-wheel drive Land Cruisers or in company cars out for the weekend. This was not something I had experienced at Timbunke or Ambunti, but this is Port Moresby, and the lifestyle is quite different.

Sr. Eliane Chariot from the Carmelite convent came to our spiritual directors' meeting one day and gave us a talk about her own experiences as a spiritual director. Her talk was very enriching and encouraging. Sr. Eliane is 82 and she still walks like a young lady. I hope to get Pat Hogan to give a talk to all the students at CTI when he is available. You may not know I am the spiritual animator for CTI, and it involves a lot of extra work besides having several meetings during the year.

Two weeks ago, I was out at Kuriva, and two schoolboys were having a heated argument at the water tank. One boy was washing his feet with tank water, and the other boy told him that the water was for drinking and not for washing feet. He told him a second and third time, but the boy kept washing his feet. Then he said, "Will you not listen to me?" Then the boy washing his feet replied, "Do you think you are Michael Somare that I must do what you tell me?" At least he knew who the prime minister was.

December 11, 2007 Since I last wrote to you I have been to Wewak for eleven days. I arrived there on October 22 for a four-day workshop on a "Listening Skills and Community Building Workshop" given by Patrick Rasmussen. At one point I watched a video of Br. Daniel's funeral taken by Fr. Janusz Skotnizny. "It was a lovely funeral altogether"—a big line of clergy and sisters, and a big gathering of lay people. Br. Daniel had built up a good relationship with the families around Wewak by repairing their sewing machines, a skill he picked up from his shoe-maker's trade. He also had a good contact with the wider community when he worked in Wirui Store, and later in the hardware store. Br. Daniel sold a large variety of nails at a cheap rate, and that was the magnet which pulled the customers. When a customer from the bush would ask for nails, he would call out the different varieties, and the customer wouldn't have a clue what he was talking about. Then the man from the bush would put his hand into his *bilum* and take out a nail and show it to Br. Daniel and say, "That kind", and immediately the message was clear. Br. Daniel was also the cathedral bell-ringer every morning at 6am. He would wait by the pull rope for several minutes to get the exact time, so in many ways he made his presence felt, especially to those who lived in the Wirui settlement and used the cathedral's bell as their alarm clock.

On my fifth day in Wewak we had family feast. Fr. Joe Roszynsk celebrated his silver jubilee in vows and Fr. John Vegvari celebrated seventy years in vowed life. A barbeque was held at the lower house, and the presence of the SVD friends made the atmosphere extra special.

The following day it was off to Mambe for the ordination of Denis Nyaura, SVD. Fr. Rudi Stodden, the former parish priest of Mambe was unable to attend, but when his best wishes were announced he got a big ovation from all present. Fr. Rudie is more or less confined to bed, and he was so pleased to live to see Denis ordained. I called to see him, and he was very proud to have two SVD priests ordained from his parish, and one more seminarian studying in Mariannhill Seminary.

The great day we were all waiting for was Fr. Otto Separi's consecration on October 30 as the new bishop for the Aitape Diocese. There was a great buzz in the days leading up to this event, and the main concern was transport—how to arrange vehicles for all who wished to attend. We

SVDs took two double-cab four-wheel drives and set out at four o'clock in the morning and arrived at St. Ignatius High School four and a half hours later. The Poor Clare and the Presentation sisters made us all welcome, treating us to coffee and sandwiches. When the Prime Minister Michael Somare arrived by helicopter at 10.15am the celebrations got underway. The celebrations were well prepared, and several *singsing* groups took part in the Liturgy. Fr. Peter Artekain and Fr. Lawrence Tanu led Fr. Otto up to the altar and handed him over to Bishop Austin who was the main celebrant that day. His own clan wore traditional dress, and also accompanied Fr. Otto to the altar. This was probably the most touching moment of the whole celebration.

As the service progressed, black clouds were gathering overhead, and everyone from the Wewak side were getting anxious about the return trip. The Wewak-Aitape road is known for its flooded rivers and streams, over one hundred in all, and it sure did live up to its name. Those who left early and those who left after the main meal all found themselves together lined up at the River Swine. The river, which is no more than two hundred metres from the sea, was rushing down from the hills, and it was too dangerous to drive through. Five bishops, the Nuncio, and Fr. Jan Szweda, our Provincial, were among the crowd who had to give way to the brown monster that sparkled and roared in the night light. The Nuncio came to the river and said he had to go as he had a meeting the following day in Port Moresby. Fr. Casper Talmai, an elderly diocesan priest, turned his back to the river and told all present, "Be patient, and respect the forces of nature." And that's what we just did. Most people were pacing up and down the road to pass the time away. It reminded me of the prisoners in Bomana jail walking back and forth inside the compound to pass the time. The Missionaries Sisters of Charity kept themselves occupied saying the Rosary. At one stage a drunkard came along and told us all what to do. However, he then fell into the river, and only for a sago tree he could have been in serious trouble. We were happy when he left the scene. We waited six hours before it was safe to cross. After that we drove on for two more hours, counting our blessings after every river until we all lined up again at another creek. The flood waters had washed out a culvert, leaving a large gap in the road. When we arrived, the youth from the area were already gathering stones to bridge the gap so vehicles could cross over, and they were demanding 100 *kina* from each car. Bishop Tony and Fr. Waldi came on the scene, and eventually the youth settled to let us through for twenty *kina* each. There were at least twenty-five cars on the road that night. I can tell you we were all happy to arrive back in Wirui at two o'clock in the morning.

The Wirui community has changed quite a lot over the last few years. There are only a few SVDs in the house now, but it is wonderful to see all the young local priests taking part in the celebrations, and our task now is to support and encourage them to stay the course. Change was inevitable, and tomorrow will never be the same as today.

In the meantime, I have given a six-day retreat to the Dominican students at the Xavier Institute, and a day of recollection to the priests and bishops of the Archdiocese of Port Moresby. I am still taking care of Kuriva Parish with the help of three SVD students. There are always little things of interest happening in the parish. One day I was down at the market, and an elderly man came to shake hands with me when he found out I was from Ireland. He said with a feeling of gratitude, "I was taught in school by an Irish sister, Margaret Sweeney"—so their work is much appreciated long after they have left the scene. Another day in the parish, I was officiating at a little girl's burial, and when the grave was complete her playmate put seven marbles on the grave so she could play marbles in heaven with the angels.

Last week, two Rosary Sisters from Ambunti Parish, where I spent over ten years made, their final profession at Mersie sub-station. Their names are Sr. Odilia Kuias and Sr. Geraldine Impanponj. Fr. Alphonse Nogoru, a local priest, is now looking after Ambunti Parish, and I hear he is well liked by the people. All the seminarians are on holidays, so the place is very quiet at present at the college. I will be going to Kuriva Parish for Christmas, and after that a new priest will take over, and I will be full-time Spiritual Director at the college. I will also be giving retreats and workshops to religious here in Port Moresby. With that, I wish you all a Happy Christmas and good health for 2008. God bless you.

January 31, 2008 I hope this letter finds you well as the days are stretching and the year is moving along. Thank you very much for your support for the missions. This year I can support five students with school fees. I had a normal Christmas at Kuriva, and most of our activities centred on the main station. Everyone was lending a hand to clean the station and decorate the church. I took out the lawnmower hoping to get a bit of exercise while cutting the grass, but when the youth saw me in action they felt it was their job to push the mower. A score of young children came too and raked up the grass, and the station was spotless that same evening. In the Parish of Kuriva the station children didn't have any expensive toys for Christmas; instead, they were happy to go to the parish dump, collect the empty tin cans, and play with them on the parish lawn. I don't know the rules, but they were having lots of fun when playing with the cans. One evening as they played a dispute rose among the children, and suddenly their laughter and amusement turned into shouting and tears. Some children cried on the spot where they played, and others cried all the way to their homes. The game was abandoned, and the tin cans were left scattered on the lawn. I thought to myself, it will be some time before these children play together again. To my surprise, they were back again the next evening playing and enjoying the game as if nothing had happened the day before. Maybe that's what Jesus meant when he said, "We should become like little children."

The women decorated the church with sago branches. One lady contributed balloons and decorative paper, and it all helped to create a Christmas atmosphere. For mid-night Mass I had only two babies for Baptism and when I asked the catechist why there were so few, he told me, "They are not ready." A little girl was standing beside me heard our conversation and said, "Mammy has a baby in her tummy." I smiled at her, and thought, was she telling me Mammy's baby is also not ready?

In the week leading up to Christmas there was a lot of drink consumed in and around Kuriva Parish. The people had received royalties from the logging company in the area, and easy-come, easy-go. A lot of that money went down the hatch for Christmas. Now I am writing reference letters for the parents to the timber company, looking for help to pay their school fees. I told them they should collect the empty bottles and make a little contribution themselves. One evening I took a stroll out to Kuriva Bridge and met a young man with a string bag full of bottles hanging from his shoulder. I asked him if he was collecting the empty bottles. He smiled at me and said, "These ones are full to the neck."

Vanapa is another village in Kuriva Parish. I said Mass there on Christmas Eve. The people had decorated the decking on a bailey bridge that runs through the village with balloons and home-made candle-lights made from bamboos, kerosene, and a piece of cloth used as a wick. They had placed over fifty of them along the route to the church. It was most impressive in the night, and I know now why they told me not to come before nightfall. That same day, the Vanapa people decorated every truck and car that passed through their village with flowers and sago branches as a sign of friendship, and at the same time wishing the travellers a happy Christmas.

It wasn't such a happy Christmas for the Sisters of the Sacred Heart. They were going to Port Moresby to do their Christmas shopping when they were held up by an armed gang who ordered them out of their car and drove off, leaving the sisters standing on the road. I had passed by just before the hold-up, but I am sure the rascals knew that the amount of food Father had in his car was not worth robbing.

I visited another village before Christmas and I noticed all the trees that provided shade in front of the church were cut down. When I asked the church leader what happened, he told me he got very angry when he saw the village elders drinking in front of the church and taking advantage of his hard work in cutting the grass and keeping the place clean. He had cut the shade trees down.

On New Year's night the family of Eugene Amaia, the officer in charge at the Kuriva health centre, prepared a nice meal and came to the parish house to share it with me. Eugene's wife told me she had cooked a duck to ring out the old year and welcome the new one. The family has a flock of ducks, but their family dog was stealing the eggs from the duck house. Their son Norbert had to teach the dog a lesson.

During the month of January, I was going back and forth to Kuriva introducing Fr. Justin Nenat, SVD, from Indonesia, and I also was attending a two-week workshop called, "Journey towards Inner Freedom" for priests given by Bishop Gilles SMM [3] and Sr. Desneiges. On Sunday, February

---

3 Society of the Montfort Missionaries.

3, Fr. Justin was installed as the new parish priest of Kuriva by Bishop John Ribat, MSC [4]. Bishop John asked me to attend the installation and thanked me for helping out part-time in the parish, and that was the final handover to Fr. Justin.

Last Monday a group of us went to see Kevin O Sullivan, the manager of the Digicel mobile phone company in PNG. Kevin is from Cork, and there are thirteen others from Ireland on the staff, and one of those is from Ballineen. You can guess I will have some Irish visitors during the year. Before we left we had a cup of Barry's Tea, and Kevin gave us mobile phones, and wind-up chargers to take with us. He also gave us two boxes of t-shirts with Digicel printed in large letters on the back. I gave them all away to my friends. I sent one to Simon Kevin from Timbunke, the farm manager, as Digicel will soon be linking up that province with the rest of PNG.

I will close off now by wishing you a happy St Patrick's Day and happy Easter, and once again thanks for your generous donation. I will be keeping you in my prayers, and all going well I will see you in September. God bless and take care.

March 24, 2008 Many thanks for your St. Patrick's Day greetings and Easter Greetings. I hope you are keeping well, and I am sure you are looking forward to the long fine days of summer. The following is my Easter letter, which you will give you an idea about life at this end.

I am back at Bomana today after helping Fr. Justin out for Holy Week at Kuriva. The Easter services were very well attended, and the rains stayed off, which was a great blessing for the people who had to walk long distances to the parish centre. Fr. Justin did all the hard work preparing the readers and drama groups, and I just followed the program drawn up by the parish council.

While I was at Kuriva, four high-school girls came to greet me with all smiles, and gave me a hug saying, "How happy we are because you helped pay the school fees for our best friend." They told me they were very worried, and their friend was worried too because he could not continue his education due to school fees while his class mates could continue theirs. His

---

4 Missionaries of the Sacred Heart.

father died when he was a child, and his mother returned to her village and married again. The young boy was left behind with the extended family to look after him. He walked over one hour to Kuriva primary school each morning for eight years as did the rest of the village children, and now these girls were so glad that he is now with them in high-school.

On February 3, Fr. Justin Nenat, SVD, was installed as parish priest of Kuriva Parish. Bishop John Ribat, MSC, Fr. Joe Maciolek, rector of Bomana, and I as the former parish priest were present to officiate at the ceremony. The parish was well informed about the coming event through the school children, and each community took part in the Liturgy, which made it a special day for all present. Bishop John called on me to ask Fr. Justin to come forward after the Gospel, and the installation took place followed by applause from all present. Bishop John told Fr. Justin, "You will find it hard in the beginning, but given time you will learn, and understand the people you are called to serve." In my address to the Kuriva people I told them to look after Fr. Justin the way they took care of me. Fr Joe gave a brief history of the SVD involvement in the parish, and the parish chairman, Will Denis, expressed his thanks to Bishop John and all present for participating in this special occasion. This was followed by a pleasant meal prepared by the parishioners in the parish meeting room.

Fr. Matt Lunzer, SVD, one of our Sepik missionaries has gone to his eternal reward at the age of 92. We were sharing some stories about his life here in the seminary last night. Fr. Matt went on home leave to the States some thirty-three years ago, and he asked his people to help him buy a Land Cruiser. The people told him it would be much better if he built a church with the money. Fr. Matt said, "If I build a church in the bush, and cannot get there the people will have no Mass, but if I have a Land Cruiser I can get there to say Mass, and that's much better." Fr. Matt bought the Land Cruiser and for several years he told us missionaries he had the best car in the diocese for the bush roads. I happened to inherit Fr. Matt`s Land Cruiser for almost ten years when I took over Ambunti Parish. I believe it is still going, and if so, it is thirty-three years old. It was money well spent.

On March 18 we had the Chrism Mass at St Mary's Cathedral. There were over fifty priests concelebrating, and the SVD was well represented, with ten priests taking part. Bishop Brian Barnes was the main celebrant, and he is handing over the reins to Bishop John Ribat on April 5. Bishop Brian celebrated his seventy-fifth birthday on Easter Sunday and the congregation sang "Happy Birthday" for him before he left the altar.

Fr. James Uravil, the former president of CTI, is returning to India on April. Next Sunday he is saying his last Mass in the jail for the prisoners. The youth group from St Joseph's Parish are going to provide the music and Radio Maria is going to broadcast the Mass. Fr. James has been saying Mass for the prisoners for ten years, and we priests at the college helped him out when needed.

Two weeks ago, the sisters from Marianville asked me to say Mass in the women's prison. A big group of forty plus catholic women from different parishes also attended. The women brought along bread, rice, meat, and different types of fruits, and after Mass the nineteen female prisoners had a different menu for lunch that day. I like going to the prison as it gives a bit of variety to life.

I was also at the Xavier Institute for five days giving a renewal course to five sisters, five brothers, and two priests. One priest had an interesting story about his first day at school. He told us he had no trousers to go to school, but when all the village children left that morning for school, he followed them. The teacher sent him home to find trousers and he returned the next day fully clothed. That's how things were forty years ago.

I was writing this letter when one of the seminarians called out to me, "A Calcutta sister is here to see you." It was Sr. Frances Donoghue, MC. She was here for a meeting, and she called to say happy Easter to John and myself. Their congregation is doing very well here in PNG. They have eleven houses in the country. They have almost sixty sisters from PNG, half of whom are overseas, and they have seventeen junior sisters.

Geoff Brumm from Australia passed through Port Moresby the week before Easter. I called to see him, and he was not well. He took all his personal belongings with him, and the feeling is he will not be returning. Geoff loved life, and he says that ever since his liver transplant every extra day of his life is a bonus, so let us keep him in our prayers.

I am keeping very well, thank God, and so are all our students and staff. With that I will sign off by wishing you God's blessing and take care.

April 27, 2008 For almost three months now we had a very nice wet season, with no downpours, but just enough to keep every place green. The hills around Port Moresby are all growing peanuts, corn, yam, and pumpkin. Our students have made some good gardens at the back of the college, and we should have fresh vegetables in a few weeks' time.

On Tuesday morning, the first of April, I went to the airport to pick up two of our elderly missionaries who were returning from overseas. The 80-year-old Fr. George Schubbe was the first through the customs. He arrived in a lovely black suit, and when I admired it, he told me it was the suit he wore for his diaconate. He must have looked after it very well because that's over fifty-five years ago. Fr. Harry Janissen, who is 79, arrived in a wheelchair, and his first complaint was that he didn't get a cup of coffee on the plane. Otherwise, Harry was in good form, and he can walk with the help of a crutch. While in Port Moresby, he visited some of his friends, and one day he went out to Kuriva Parish with Fr. Justin. Harry is now back at Wirui and enjoying his retirement.

The same week we had a formation team meeting for three days at the SVD college. It meant we had four extra priests to celebrate our foundation day at CTI on Wednesday evening. Every year we celebrate foundation day on March 25, but this year it was transferred to April 2. Each college has a foundation day, so we SVD had fifteen priests concelebrating; our students decorated the church, and Fr. John McCarthy was the main celebrant. On Friday evening we had a social connected with foundation day. We invited representatives from the other colleges, and we had an enjoyable evening with plenty to eat and a few drinks as well. It reminded me of our get-togethers in Donamon back in the seventies, songs and stories from the students and staff. Each college contributed some food, cakes and soft drinks. Afterwards, we had to sort out which plate and dish belonged to which college.

On Saturday, April 5, we had made plans to have a picnic as a farewell for Fr. Joe Maciolek and Fr. James Uravil, but the rains came down, and instead a busload of us went to St. Mary's Cathedral to witness the handover by Bishop Brian Barnes to Bishop John Ribat. It was a beautiful community celebration with government dignitaries, bishops, priests, sisters, and laity all taking part. Bishop Brian was well known in PNG for his outspoken views on corruption, and for his weekly programme on Radio Maria.

Fr. Joe left us on the following Monday after ten years as rector of Divine Word College. Fr. Joe was a very good community man; he kept the college running smoothly, and he always made SVD members and visitors feel at home when they called to see us at the seminary. He will also be missed for his expertise on computers and his willingness to repair and install computer programmes. Fr. Joe is expected to return to PNG after a year's sabbatical in Europe, and his appointment has not been announced to date.

Fr James Uravil also returned to India after eighteen years here in the campus. He had various roles, as rector, lecturer, and five years as president of CTI. He also spent some years in the Highlands doing pastoral work when he arrived as a young missionary. Now he returns for good to his home country with a white beard.

Both confrères made a big contribution to the formation of our future priests. We will miss their presence, but life goes on, and the challenge will be taken up by the new teachers to keep up the standard set by their predecessors.

Fr John's McCarthy's first major job as rector was to get the library in order, and catalogued, and it will take him a few more months before this is complete. In the meantime, he is taking nine students for homiletics two days a week. The new president, Fr. David Willis, OP, has taken up his posting already, but he has only a tourist visa, so he is not completely settled in as yet.

On Holy Thursday, Sr. Maria Sura, SSpS, left for her first mission appointment to Ghana. I was told her luggage was not at the airport on her arrival, but Fr. Francis and Fr. Martin from PNG were there to meet her. I met two OLSH sisters in the Food World supermarket before Easter, and they are going to Africa when their passports and visa are approved, and one Sister of Charity said goodbye to me last month, as she is going to Kenya in two weeks' time. Fr. Denis Nyaura, SVD, will shortly take off to Bolivia. It's really encouraging and uplifting to see these young missionaries leaving their own country to share the Gospel with other nations.

On Sunday, April 13, I took Archbishop Douglas Young to Bomana Jail to say Mass for the inmates. Bishop Douglas was staying here in the college overnight after attending the bishops' conference in Port Moresby. Three of the prisoners knew the bishop, and they were delighted with his visit. One Sunday at the jail I was in the middle of Mass when a strong argument flared up outside the building. Suddenly every neck was stretched like a crane to see what was going on outside. I thought for a moment I would be the only one left in the building. When I asked their church leader after Mass what was the matter, he said, "Just a little scuffle between cellmates."

On April 25 I returned from Madang after my annual retreat given by Bishop Francesco Sarego. There were forty-four SVD, and seven SSpS sisters, consisting of thirteen different nationalities. Half the priests were young Indonesians, Filipinos, Indians, and Polish. Four of the regular confrères could not make it because of a landslide along the Okuk Highway near Gera village. It will take three months to open a bypass there, as it is one of the biggest landslides to occur in that region. Before leaving Madang, Bishop William Kurtz blessed our new SVD mother house. It's a large monastic-style building with twenty-seven rooms. This house will be our new headquarters, with meeting rooms and offices, and it also has four rooms designed for wheelchairs and rooms for those who need full-time care. The house is dedicated to St. Michael the Archangel, and his statue is now placed inside the main entrance door. Our Provincial, Fr. Pat Hogan, gave us a nice story about the carved statue which came from Steyl, and how it survived the Second World War.

Our students have a two-week break from studies right now, and some are staying with families and friends in the locality. Next Sunday I will give them a six-day retreat at the Nazareth House of Prayer. With that I will sign off. I will be taking my home leave in July or August and I hope to see you then. God bless you and take care.

May 15, 2008 I hope you are enjoying life and the summer days in Ireland. I plan to be home around the last week of July. In the meantime, life goes on here as usual.

I am just back from giving a retreat to our students at the Nazareth House of Prayer, and the week before that I was in Madang for my annual retreat given by Bishop Francesco Sarego. While I was there Fr. Alex Garuai, SVD, told us an amazing story about his brother and six others, how they were lost at sea for twenty-nine days, and survived. They began their journey in a twenty-three-foot fibreglass boat powered by two forty-horsepower motors. The seas were rough, but they continued to ignore the warning signs. Somewhere along the journey they capsized, and for three days six men and one girl hung on to the overturned boat. After three days in the water, the sea calmed, and they managed to turn the boat in the water and see-saw the water out of it. The two motors had dropped into the ocean when the boat turned which was lucky for then as that gave the boat more buoyancy, but a knife and a sail remained in the boat. After turning the boat, they remained at sea for twenty-six more days, presumed drowned. A rescue team was dispatched but found no trace of survivors and called off the search. It rained most nights at sea, so they were able to catch fresh water with the sail, and that's how they survived their ordeal until they ended up on a small uninhabited island. There they were able to make a fire using their traditional method, and they captured a large turtle which came out of the water to lay its eggs, and they also managed to get some coconuts which grew on the island. On seeing the smoke on the island an elderly couple who were out fishing went to investigate and discovered it was the missing boat and its crew from Bougainville, who had been missing for twenty-nine days.

Fr. Alex is now in Bogia Parish in the Madang Diocese, and from there he is doing business studies at the Divine Word University. Before Fr. Alex entered the SVD he was a bank official. I said to him, "Before you were counting other people's money, now you will be counting SVD money." He hopes to graduate in 2009. Fr. Alex was telling me how he and Fr. Peter Kim went to the doctor for a check-up. The doctor told Alex he should lose weight and he told Peter to eat more and put on some weight. You know, Alex used to take a spoon with him to Moresby and buy a litre of ice cream and eat it all in one go. It was no wonder he was oversize, but since he went to Bogia he is back to normal size again.

We have made some minor changes at the Divine Word College since Fr. John took over as Rector. We bought a larger fridge for our staff room. It could have a knock-on effect for our staff—that is, if we visit the fridge too often between meals, and we could also become a bit larger and rounder. We also have new ice-cream cup and spoons. It means it takes longer to eat less ice cream. Our chapel too is looking different since Fr. John arrived, and he is still working to get our library in order. Yes, life is quite different here from the Sepik River; we even get the two daily newspapers delivered to the door every morning during breakfast time.

On April 25, Mariannville High-School held their culture day. The show had sixteen provinces taking part, and all the *singsing* groups were dressed to perfection in traditional attire, as there were prizes for the best dressed. It was a wonderful show of culture and tradition. Fifty of the students are going to the World Youth Day in Sydney in July, and this show helped to raise funds for their trip. At the moment over 900 youth from all over PNG are making plans to attend World Youth Day. Five of our seminarians are also going.

Marianville High School is an all-girl school with 525 students, and for the past two weeks Fr. Victor D'Sa and Fr. Valerian are giving retreats to the students there. We SVD also have weekday Mass there when it is our turn. The OLSH Sisters are in charge there, but most of the staff are lay teachers.

Since Fr. James Uravil returned to India I am going more frequently to the prison every Sunday. I have noticed with the last two Sundays my congregation was less than fifty inmates. I later discovered the Salvation Army gave a radio and a solar panel to each cell, and the inmates were listening to a live-broadcast religious program. When I told my confrères here at the college, they told me I must improve my homilies, or put more life into the Liturgy. You may be surprised to hear the *Word* magazine is being read in the prison. The Carmelite Sisters get it every month, and they pass it on to the inmates. The story carried in the April issue about the bishop in Paraguay who could become president was very interesting. We were all talking about it at the retreat in Madang, when he was elected president the same month.

Fr. Pat Hogan is coping well in his new task as Provincial. He is getting used to the travelling that goes with the job, and he has a lot of senior advisors. Fr. Pat will be going to Rome in June, and afterwards to Ireland for a short holiday, and the following month, on July 21, I go for home leave.

This time on home leave we will have a wedding in the family. My nephew is getting married to a Kerry girl on September 6, and I am to bless the wedding. The Diocese of Kerry has sent me on an application form to fill in, and I must also get a reference letter from my Provincial stating that I am a priest in good standing. You know the first three times I went on home leave I went for funerals in the family, and in between I missed out on five of my nieces' and nephews' weddings. God Bless and take care.

January 27, 2009 I hope you are all keeping well after Christmas and the New Year. You must be looking forward to the long days once again, and hopefully a fine summer.

Well, 2008 saw the end of the *Word* magazine and most of us SVD feel we have lost a friend that we knew all our lives. It was such a wonderful magazine with a great variety of interests. However, life moves on and change is inevitable. After saying all that, I want to say thank you for being a promoter of the *Word* for many years and also a big thank you for sending the *Word* on to me every month. You know where the *Word* magazine used to end up after we were finished with it here in the seminary—in the top security prison in PNG.

I was on home leave last year and though the weather was not good, I enjoyed the time with my family and friends. The farewell party was also very good, and it is nice to have the support of the local community when one heads back to the mission fields. Now I am back again in the seminary as spiritual director, and it's the same as if I had never been away. We have seventeen SVD students in our college this year, and nine other students doing their novitiate in the Philippines. Our three newly ordained priests are assigned, one each to Argentina, Philippines, and Bolivia. They are now in the process of getting their passports, visas, and work permits in order.

Since I returned to PNG, I say Mass in the prison every Sunday. Their day begins with a roll-call, and over 200 low-risk inmates stand in line dressed in their blue and red uniforms. When their number and name are called, they step forward, the Catholics going to their place of worship, the other dominations having a combined service in a covered shed at the opposite side of the enclosed yard. Those who have no interest in the Lord's day go back into their cells. Over Christmas the Catholics increased in number from around sixty to eighty, mostly juveniles caught up in petty crime. I have to welcome the new faces every Sunday; they are not tourists or visitors but young men in trouble with the law. After Mass, there are several requests to post letters or make phone calls to their families to come and bail them out or visit them. These requests are easily met. It's when inmates are looking for a character reference after committing murder or armed robbery that puts me to the test. One inmate was delighted to tell me he got remission from seventeen years down to eleven years. One Sunday after Mass, one inmate was walking along with me when his number was called out and he should go immediately to the visitors' shed. Well, his two eyes sparkled like a hound spotting a hare and he made a direct line to greet his visitor. I thought what a difference it can make for a prisoner just to have someone to come to see them. Usually the visitors bring a saucepan of cooked food, which is a change from the rice and tin fish they have every day. The prisoners say it is a taste of freedom, as it is the food they eat in the real world. I also get letters addressed to me looking for Bibles, Rosary beads, and reading material, and they sign off their letters saying, "Your faithful friend from behind bars". I used to take them the old copies of the *Word*, but that has come to an end. Last month I gave them a Roscommon calendar instead.

All the schools in PNG reopen on February 2, and the seminary starts with an orientation week for all students, and then it is down to the study once again. We have 135 seminarians enrolled to date, and there are at least five or six we are not sure of as yet. The Xavier Institute, which is also here beside the seminary, has twenty junior sisters and seventeen junior brothers doing a six-month course preparing them for their vowed life. I am looking forward to working with them all at some level either in giving days of recollection, retreats, or spiritual direction. There is a great variety of students here from all over PNG and we have two students from Ghana studying theology as part of their overseas training program.

Here in Bomana, the students grow tomatoes, lettuce, pumpkins, and greens. During the dry season the garden must be watered every evening with paid water from the city water board. When the students were gone on holidays I did the watering every evening. One evening I went to the garden to find a woman and two young boys helping her to fill her *bilum* with our garden products. When they saw me coming the woman ran away, but one of the boys put up his hand making a friendly salute and he greeted me in a most polite manner saying, "Hello, Father Michael." He was convinced I was a real gentleman, and I didn't say anything to him that would change his mind.

Another little story for you: a young seminarian, now a priest in Ghana, was studying for the priesthood. As he studied, he prayed that his mother would become a Catholic before his ordination. At the same time, the mother was praying that her son would leave the seminary. The years passed by, and the seminarian was in his final year of study and preparing for his ordination. When the mother realised the son wasn't going to change his mind, she decided to become a Catholic—which goes to show, a mother's prayers are not always answered.

I will sign off now by saying thank you once again. I will keep you in my prayers and wish you good health and may God grant you many blessings. Take care.

June 22, 2009 Today the nation celebrates the Queen's birthday, which means it is a free day for the students and all public servants. It also rained a little this morning, enough to keep the place looking green.

Fr. Pat Hogan, our Provincial is returning to Ireland today, as his health has not improved since he returned to PNG three months ago. Fr Pat has been in PNG for the past twenty-five years, and he may not be returning if his arthritis does not respond to the medication he is taking. Fr Pat was in charge of our retreat house in Goroka for seven years, and now I am being asked to take it over in 2011. The priest there, Fr. Alois Blasl, is 71 and he feels it`s time to retire. To take on this ministry I must go for further training either in Australia, Rome, or Ireland. I have decided to return to Ireland next year and do the studies in Dublin. It may take one year, so I could be home for Verona and David`s wedding, please God.

This year I celebrated Easter in the Diocese of Kiunga-Daru. Bishop Giles Cote invited Fr. Victor D`Sa and me to help out in the Tabubil Parish with retreats and to stay over for Holy Week. Tabubil is a mining town attached to the Ok Tedi gold mine. The town has a population of 15,000 people living on the mining lease area, and it is estimated there is another 10,000 settlers camped around its borders. The mining company has not provided enough schools, health care, and other facilities for all these extra settlers, and now the whole system is under fierce pressure to cope with the unexpected influx of people. The mine is due to close in four years' time, and then the whole place well be deserted, as it is situated in one of the remote places in PNG

I arrived at Tabubil after a two-hour flight on March 23 to give a retreat to the Legion of Mary, and Fr. Victor joined me on April 3, and we both helped out with Confessions, and parish retreat as a preparation for the Holy Week. After that I stayed at the main station, and Fr. Victor visited three local communities. Large crowds attended the celebrations, and I met several people from the Sepik area, including one married couple who had named their son after me. The people were very generous with food and donations, and the three OND[5] sisters were also most helpful to both of us in organizing the retreats, workshop for the youth, and drawing up the Holy Week programme. One week later, I met Bishop Giles at Port Moresby airport and we were sharing our Easter experiences when a young girl who was sitting a few seats away from us came and asked me was I from Cork? When I told her I was, she said," I knew by your accent." She was from Adare, and we were able to talk about people we both knew. Her name is Aoife Sexton, now working in Australia and doing some research work here in PNG in one of the gas and oil fields.

At present, the Chinese are developing a new mine for nickel and cobalt in the Madang Province, and they are encountering numerous problems with the local people. The language is causing the biggest challenge, and last month there was a boxing match where thirty of the Chinese had to be hospitalised. One of the problems is that over a thousand Chinese are doing work that the local people can do, and this is causing a lot of tension among the locals.

After saying goodbye to the Limerick lady, I flew that day to Madang where Fr. Alios Blasl and I gave a retreat to our SVD priests and brothers and SSpS sisters. Madang is a beautiful place for a retreat. It is right beside the sea, and most of our confrères went for a swim every day, including myself. The theme of the retreat was, "Faith, Hope, and Love, and the greatest of these is Love". A week later we gave the same retreat in Goroka to a younger group of our SVDs and SSpS sisters. Most of our younger priests and brothers are now from Indonesia, the Philippines, Poland,

---

5 Oblates of Notre Dame

India and PNG. Both retreats went very well, and in September, I go to the Diocese of Wewak to give a retreat to the local priests.

On a sadder note, last month two local priests from Wewak Diocese died. One priest who was only ordained in 2007 died when his car crashed into a tree, and the other priest, who was only 45, died from a stroke. The diocese is still trying to come to terms with the deaths of the two young men. Last Saturday week, PNG had one of its worst road crashes to date. Two trucks overloaded with passengers crashed on the highway about three hours' drive from Port Moresby. Fifteen people died at the scene, and the number now dead stands at twenty-two. The number of injured passengers is believed to be over forty. The world is still in a state of shock after the Air France disaster. It can happen at any time, and so many people travelling nowadays by air. I heard there were some Irish people among those who died. It must be very hard on their families to come to grips with the loss of their loved ones.

On May 18, some prisoners escaped from Bomana Jail. On that day we had a very heavy downpour here in Port Moresby, and while the prison officers were taking cover from the rain someone cut the wire, and fifteen inmates dashed to freedom. Since then, no one has been allowed to visit the jail, and all the prisoners are locked up in their cells. I went to say Mass there the following Sunday, but there was no Mass because of the breakout. The commander gave me a briefing on the situation inside the jail and said things had not settled down yet, and he gave me his phone number, so I can contact him about saying Mass again. In the meantime, I have received a lot of Divine Mercy Novena and Rosary beads from a sister to hand out to the faithful ones behind bars.

On the first Monday of each month the priests of the Archdiocese of Port Moresby meet for a social gathering and rotate their get-together to a different parish each month. Last Monday it was Fr. Justin Nenat who is in charge of Kuriva Parish, which is fifty minutes' drive outside Port Moresby. Over twenty priests and two bishops, were treated to a sit-down meal which the people of the parish had prepared. The Catholic youth, the Legion of Mary, and the Catholic Women combined to do the cooking. They cooked enough food for the whole parish, which included two pigs, home-grown vegetables, and local fruits. It was a real social occasion where everyone mixed, and some shared their day-to-day experiences. Before we left, the guests were given fresh fruit and a plate of cooked food wrapped in a plastic bag to take home. The parishioners said it was the first time to have a priests' gathering in their parish, and they were very happy to be part of it. This is all for the moment and I will keep in touch by phone and e-mail in the meantime. God bless you and take care, and I will keep you in my prayers.

August 6, 2009 I hope you are keeping well. I have not heard from you for some time. I blame myself for that as I did not write. The summer is not too good back home by all accounts with all the rain. We seldom talk about the weather here, but we had no rain with the last five weeks, and the dry weather is starting to bite. The trees are losing their leaves, and most of the dry grass is burned off just by anyone who sees anything that will burn.

Right now, our students are having a two-week break from study, so everyone is in a relaxed mood, and the students are planning to have a picnic one of these days. They usually have a few chosen places to go, like Ela beach or the botanical gardens in Port Moresby. One of our students decided to leave us two months ago, and at the moment we have sixteen SVD students studying in the college. Two weeks ago, the Blood Bank came to the college, and over sixty students donated blood, and I gave them a pint myself. I thought it might help to keep down the weight. The food at the college is very good, and it is hard to keep fit as a result.

I was busy for the month of July between spiritual direction and teaching Tok Pisin to Fr. Frederick Obeng from Ghana. Fr. Frederick is a teacher himself, and he is picking up the language fairly quickly. In May, I had another priest from Vietnam for two weeks for Tok Pisin lessons, and that proved to be a bit more difficult. On the side of spiritual direction, there are always a few new ones seeking direction, and a few old ones coming less often. At this time of the year, when the students are under pressure from exams, they tend to put off their appointments, so they can focus more on their studies.

On a lighter note, I have a prison guitar here in the workshop for repair. I need some wood glue, varnish, and guitar strings, and the guitar needed a good cleaning, as it was black from years of human sweat. This is one of the many jobs I am asked to do from prisoners once Mass is finished. Playing the guitar in their spare time is one way to help ease the pressure.

Joyce Meyer, a famous evangelist from the States, visited the prison last month when she was here in Port Moresby for a brief visit. All the inmates dressed up nicely for the occasion, and Joyce Meyer gave them an encouraging talk to pray to God for the grace to change and get back to normal life once again. Before she left she gave them all a little plastic box which contained soup and toiletries. Radio Maria is coming to the jail one of these Sundays to record the Mass and broadcast it to the nation. The prisoners are very good at singing and playing musical instruments, but they will have to improve in their response to the Mass.

Our oldest priest, Fr. John Vegvari, died two weeks ago. He was 95 and spent most of his priestly life in the Wewak Diocese. Fr John came from the wine-making area of Hungary, and it came as no surprise to anybody when he became an expert in wine-making here. He also had other hobbies like repairing clocks and watches and planting fruit trees. At the age of 90, he was still able to use a chain-saw, and he kept the Wirui kitchen supplied with firewood for several years. He said it was his way to keep fit, and at the same time he was making a contribution to the community. Fr. John was a soldier in the Second World War, and he claimed his survival was due to Our Lady as he had several narrow escapes with death, and one brush with death was when he stepped over a land mine. In his later years, he used to have long chats on the phone with his brother at home. Of course, nobody knew what they were saying as they spoke in Hungarian. They were probably encouraging each other in their old age to keep going to the finishing line.

Just over a month ago, we had a very sad case here in PNG, when a young mother took her four young children to the river and drowned them. The mother then went to the police station and gave herself up. Since then several mothers have expressed their opinions how they feel when their husbands leave them for a second wife and leave them all by themselves to cater for the children. This never happened in PNG before, and people are asking questions. Where was the community? Could they not see the woman was in trouble, and needed support? Most people are blaming the husband for this sad affair, and it also shows the traditional values that supported the community in the past are no longer practiced today.

It may be of interest to you to know the Prime Minister, Sir Michael Somare, and his son, Arthur Somare, the State and Enterprise Minister, have launched a new transport system for the River Sepik. It will travel from Wewak to Ambunti twice a month delivering health supplies and transporting people, and their produce to and from Wewak up the Sepik River. This service was long overdue, and it will make life for the Sepik people much easier, especially in the wet season when the roads are in bad condition.

The football and hurling seasons are in full flight. Cork are doing well in the football, and they lost to Galway in the hurling. With that I will sign off and wish you a nice day and take care.

November 14, 2009 I hope this letter finds you in good form. Our school year has come to an end and there is the usual tidying up to be done before everyone takes off.

Today, Saturday, we had our eleventh graduation at the Catholic Theological Institute. Archbishop William Kurtz, SVD, was the main celebrant. Twenty-seven students graduated and will move on to the next step to the priesthood. This year also, five members of the formation team will move on to new pastures, including myself. I have been asked by the Provincial Council in PNG to take over our retreat house in Goroka in 2011. To take on this ministry, I must go for further training. After looking at all the options, it was decided St. Beuno's[6] in Wales was the best choice. Their first course on spiritual direction runs from January 16 to April 1 and the second course, on guided retreats, runs from May 4 to July 13. This means I will be passing through Ireland after Christmas on my way to St Beuno's and returning to PNG later in 2010, please God (it's not finalised yet).

I was back in Wewak last month giving a retreat to the local priests. It was a nice experience being with the young priests, most of whom I have known as seminarians. While I was there I met some old parishioners from Timbunke and Ambunti; one was Bernard Bowie, who was my helper on the Sepik. I had received a box of mobile phones from Digicel

---

6 The Jesuit Spirituality Centre in North Wales

(an Irish connection) and I had given one to Bernard. He was delighted with the mobile phone, and his children were more so. The children told their father, "If you meet Fr. Michael, tell him we will look after his grave when he dies!"

Since I last wrote to you, two of our priests who worked in the Wewak Diocese have died. Fr Ruddi Stodden died on November 5. He was 81. He spent most of his life working in bush parishes building churches and classrooms. Fr Rudi was very proud to have two local SVD missionary priests from his parish, and he also has one more student in the seminary that he baptised in one of his former parishes. He had spent the last five years in the retirement house in Wirui, where Br. Michael Kulimbao took care of him.

Four days later, Fr. Geoff Brumm died in Australia at the age of 63. Fr. Geoff had worked in Wewak Diocese for thirty-six years. He suffered from arthritis for several years, and one of the side-effects from the medication he was taking to control his sickness caused liver failure. He got the option ten years ago of a liver transplant, and after some consideration he told his doctors, "If you think it will help give it a try." Fr Geoff lived almost ten years with his new liver, and from that day on he saw every day of his life as an extra bonus. He did suffer quite a lot in the last few years, so he was transferred to Australia where he could receive better treatment. Both priests served the Lord faithfully for many years.

I am still going to the jail for Mass. However, this year there were a lot of disturbances in the jail. There were two major escapes one in July, and another in September, and no visitors were allowed. Church services were also cancelled. At the moment, everything is back to normal, but one never knows when the next dash for freedom will take place. Last Sunday I was back again at the prison for Mass, and we started off the Mass on a high note, singing, "Together again, praising the Lord."

The prisoners had lots of stories as to what went on in the meantime. One prisoner to whom I had given a nice shirt, so he could look well in court, had this to say to me: "Father, the day before the court I was transferred back to my district for the hearing. We had to take a boat and the sea was very rough. The waves were huge and turned the boat over. I and two inmates had to rescue the police who were wearing shoes and in danger of drowning." He felt good telling me about this life saving act, and he feels this will go a long way in reducing his sentence. He has already written a letter to the governor of the prison looking for a concession for saving the lives of the policemen.

Here at the Divine Word College, the year was quite a challenging one for both the teachers and the students. Our two SVD students from Ghana settled in very well to the system, and they intend to stay two years more in PNG. Next year we will have nine new candidates, but we have to wait to see how many will turn up on the day. In the meantime, all the students are preparing for their long holiday at home with their families and friends.

As regards me, it was another interesting year. I gave several retreats, and there was the prison ministry and spiritual direction to seminarians and junior sisters, so there was a lot of travelling and variety. My new ministry at the retreat house in 2011 will be much along the same lines, and everyone is telling me I am the right person for the job, so I will leave it in God's hands and see how it works out. My four and a half years here at the seminary as spiritual director were very enriching, and it was a great challenge to work with young people who want to give their life to the Lord.

This year we had a long dry season, almost four months without rain. Our mango trees must like the sun because they are laden down with fruit. We have mangoes every day, and any time of day. The flying bats come at night and knock quite a lot of mangoes off the trees. Then the students gather the best ones in the morning. One old lady comes around during the day to collect spoiled ones and feed them to her piglets. There is no doubt she doesn't forget herself, so we can thank those who planted the mango trees.

A few disappointments along the way: one of our good students asked for time out, Cork lost the All-Ireland, and the request for a new tractor for Timbunke was not approved due to other pressing needs. However, the Catholic Mission located on the Ramu River had more luck. Their tractor arrived three months ago.

ST. BEUNO'S, NORTH WALES

March 20, 2010 As you can see, I am writing to you from St Beuno's, and you may be wondering what I am doing here. Well, I am "getting in touch with myself" and preparing myself for my new ministry to take over the House of Prayer in Goroka come 2011.

St. Beuno's is a Jesuit spirituality centre which runs several courses during the year, mainly on Ignatian spirituality. There is something here for everyone. I am doing the three-month programme right now. I met a very interesting lady here, who had come to prepare herself to meet the Lord. I presume we are all here to meet the Lord, but this lady was diagnosed with cancer and feels her encounter with the Lord will be pretty soon.

I must confess everyone I have met so far has been really nice; it's just that a few stand out for different reasons. Fr. Tom has a unique sense of humour and he gives us a laugh when things get a bit serious. Fr. Brian is the only Jesuit I see smoking. I see the smoke two stories up drifting past my window when he foes outside to have a puff.

The thirty-day retreat was something special; but you would have to experience it to know what it is all about. The silence was something else, but the place itself is ideal for such an exercise, and each one supported the other by observing it. A few of the participants spent some time solving jigsaw puzzles as a way of helping them to relax.

I go out for a short walk every day up to the terraces behind the house, which are beautifully laid out with evergreen hedges, lawns, and flower-beds. Garden seats are also available if you want to sit and look across the valley towards the sea and watch twenty-five or more windmills along the coast rotating to the forces of nature. Just about half a mile away is a little prayer house built on top of a hill, called the Rock Chapel. Several people go there every day to meet the Lord in prayer. After the thirty-day retreat, I spent three mornings trimming the pathway to the Rock Chapel, as I found the briars were scratching my ears on the pathway leading to it.

Wild-life is also in abundance here. I have seen foxes, badgers, pheasants, squirrels, and birds too many to name. I hope these names don't make you homesick. These creatures must find St. Beuno's a holy and safe place to live.

The weather is cold but dry most days. We had a beautiful fall of snow one night and it lasted over a week. The snow is still visible along the hilltops in the region. Some of our participants made snowmen and took photos to show to friends when they return home.

There are people here from all over the world, and it is most enriching to listen to their stories and about how they happened to end up in St. Beuno's. I had no difficulty in finding the place myself. When I got off the train in Rhyl, I saw another chap with a big suitcase going in the same direction as myself. I asked him where he was heading, and it turned out, of course, to be St. Beuno's, and we both shared a taxi.

I will finish now as it is almost eleven o'clock and I am sure most people here have already got their first hour of sleep. One night before retiring, I opened my window to get a breath of fresh air, and I could hear a fox barking up near the graveyard, a bit scary in that place. At that hour of the night, he was probably going socialising.

Many thanks for you St. Patrick's Day greetings and letter. It was the only one I got, as it's all e-mail now. It's still nice to get the hand-written letter. Until we meet again, God bless and take care.

Divine Word Missionaries, Maynooth, Ireland

June 2, 2010 Br. Nicholas and I arrived safe at Maynooth on April 1. It is very quiet here at present as all the third-level students have left for the summer break. I am still studying the art of spiritual guidance and retreat-giving. I will be finished in three weeks' time. Most of the material I have covered before, so it is not too difficult. I found the time at Beuno's very helpful and enriching and, come next year, please God, I will be able to guide the seminarians and the junior sisters through their thirty-day retreat. I will let you know when the time comes how it went.

I have received some nice letters from the directees in PNG, telling me they are praying for me and they are looking forward to my return.

On June 20, Dominic Campbell from Moate is getting ordained. His brother is married to my niece and living in West Cork. My niece is expecting her second child during that time, and all the family are hoping she will make it for the ordination. I have met Dominic here in Maynooth. He is a nice young man and says he is well aware of the challenges facing him in this day and age. Keep him in your prayers, as it not easy to be a priest or religious in Ireland today.

We had Confirmation in my parish last month, and I met a lot of priests from West Cork, and they were wondering where do we go from here? I tried to cheer them up and told them to go to St. Beuno's and make the thirty-day retreat and they will recover new energy and strength to keep going by the grace of God.

The Missionaries of the Sacred Heart are starting their annual Novena this week.[7] They are expecting over a thousand people to attend each day. They have three sessions to accommodate the crowd. It's mainly elderly people from all over West Cork who attend it. My brother John never misses it and says it's his annual retreat.

I have a family Baptism and marriage coming up in July and August. I see this as a bonus before I return to PNG in October. God bless and take care. *Lukim yu behain.*

---

7 Based in their house at Myross Wood in Leap, near Union Hall.

Above, Fr. Michael is taken shoulder-high through the village before blessing the new permanent church at Yindkum out-station in Timbunke Parish. The church was directly built by the community and supervised by Fr. |Michael.

Left: altar girls in Ambunti.

Cosmos Bunan (left) with Simon Kevin, who is holding a bridle donated by an Irish farmer.

A prayer meeting at an out-station in the parish of Ambunti.

The parish church in Timbunke is designed in the shape of a traditional Spirit House.

Saying Mass in Ambunti.

Above, a Spirit House in the making in Kanengara Parish.

Right, a Christmas crib designed by a local artist in Ambunti.

The garbage men in Ambunti who collect the toilet buckets with their tractor and trailer.

Simon Kevin, the farm manager in Timbunke, with his family and Fr. Michael.

Crossing the Sepik in Timbunke.

The primary school in Ambunti succumbs to flood water.

Jimmy Bau and his family outside their motor repair shop in Ambunti.

Left, Simon Gimbai, who walks on his hands and legs as a result of the polio he contracted as a young man.

Grace before a community meal in Ambunti.

Fr Michael with catechist Paul Kambu and church leader Alex during a retreat in Tambunam, Timbunke Parish, in 1989.

Young boys navigating the Sepik.

Paper money, which will serve as a bride price, being displayed in a village in the parish of Ambunti.

Above, Fr Michael with priests who participated in a retreat at the House of Prayer in Goroka.
retreat

Right, with Monica Makuaka and her friends returning from the garden.

Inspecting the pawpaw garden with Fr. Yosep Messa.

Inmates at Bomana Corrective Institute practice before Mass.

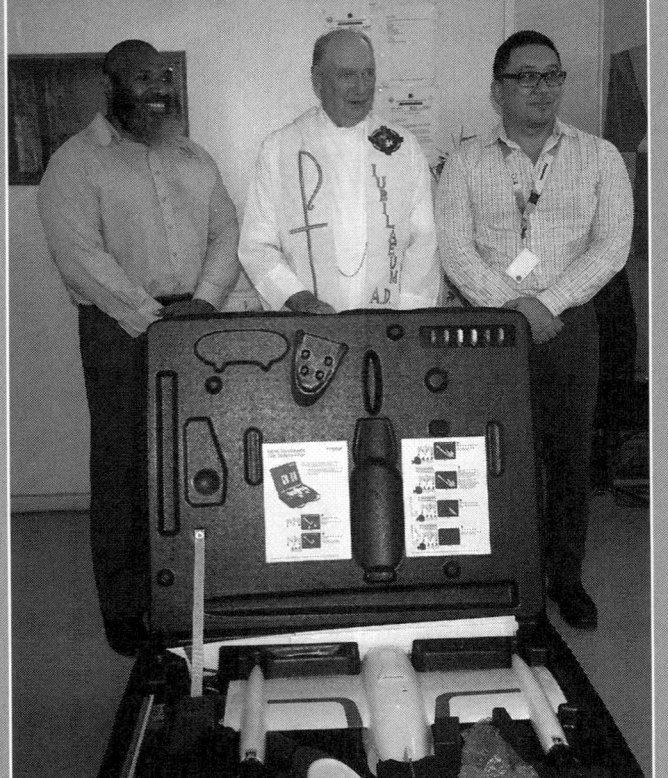

Above, seminarians at the Divine Word College in 2020.

Left, at the blessing of the first commercial drone to arrive in PNG.

The participants at a a retreat given by Fr. Michael to Cardinal John Ribat and twenty-nine priests in the Archdiocese of Port Moresby.

PART IV

GOROKA: 2011-2018
PORT MORESBY: 2018-2021

House of Prayer, Goroka

January 1, 2011 I am back again in PNG, making it my tenth departure from Ireland. It's just twelve months since I arrived in Cork to be greeted with frost and snow and I believe the weather is even colder this year. Well, I cannot complain here in Goroka; the weather is just like the fine summer days we had in Ireland last June. The climate is perfect, not too hot and not too cold, and it's the same all the year round. I also notice on the head stones in the graveyard that most of our missionaries here lived well into their eighties and nineties, so it must be a good place to live.

Goroka is a small country town with one roundabout and one set of traffic lights not functioning for some time. Its main feature is a large country market and the Highlands highway passes through the outskirts of the town, taking all the traffic from the seaport in Lae city right up to Enga province to the Porgura gold mine. The town market is alive with activities all day, every day. Most of the trading is in fresh food from the gardens. It consists of cabbage, carrots, potatoes, lettuce, tomatoes, rhubarb, coffee beans, and a host of native fruits and vegetables. It's all produced by hand, and it is the main cash-flow for the people who live in the locality. The highway is something else. There is a constant flow of articulated trucks hauling supplies up to the Highland regions. I can hear the trucks revving up for the mountain climb here in the House of Prayer. Lucky, we are 200 metres in off the highway.

I have now taken over from Fr. Alois Blasl, SVD, as director in the House of Prayer, or the "Burning Bush" as it is known to others, but that is a Biblical expression which has different meanings for the locals, so we use both names. Fr Alois is returning to Austria after forty-three years in PNG. Sr. Ignatiele has been here in the House of Prayer for seventeen years and she is also thinking of moving on when a replacement can be found. She just celebrated her seventieth birthday on December 20.

Last month Sr. Dorothy from Timbunke Parish was here on retreat. I knew her as a schoolgirl when I was parish priest there twenty-eight years ago. Dorothy and her friend used to knock on the door of the parish house on their way to school and ask, "What time is it?" Another time, they would ask for pictures books and a few days later return with a smoked fish wrapped in bananas leaves. Sr. Dorothy told me her school pal got married at the age of 16 and all her children have outgrown the mother. Sr. Dorothy is a social worker in Madang Town and is helping people fight against AIDS.

I had a look at the Directory of the Catholic Church in PNG last week to discover we have almost 1,000 sisters, 600 priests, and 100 brothers, nineteen dioceses, and twenty-two bishops in PNG. On a further note, the Divine Word University and Marienville Secondary School are recognised as being among the best in the country.

My first job when I returned from home leave was to visit Bomana Prison. I had promised the prisoners during my last Mass I would come back to visit them, then I added sure most of you will be gone home when I come back. One inmate put up his hand. "Father, I will be here for fourteen more years" Sure enough, he was there sitting in the front seat of the church, but he looked tense and drawn. I told him you have to make yourself a home if you want to see your time out. I wonder what present the prisoners got this year for Christmas in Bomana. Last year each one got two sandwiches and a tin of coke.

This Christmas morning Fr. John Ryan asked me to have Mass at St Mary's Parish in Goroka town while Fr. John went to the extended communities in the parish. The Mass was really nice. It was like saying Mass at home in Ireland. The congregation knew all the Christmas hymns and the altar servers played "Silent Night" on tin whistles. After Mass, the Sunday school teacher brought all the children around the crib and sang "Happy Birthday, Baby Jesus". I am not really involved in parish work, but I go out at the weekends to meet the locals and to add a bit of variety to life. I must spend two days cutting the grass before the retreatants start returning. I don't like pushing the lawnmower around when everyone is supposed to be in silence and I am the one disturbing the peace.

2010 was a remarkable year: it had variety and challenges, and on the sporting field it had plenty of excitement too. I met some wonderful people at St. Beuno's, including one elderly lady who told me she had come to St Beuno's to prepare herself to meet the Lord. She wasn't expecting to live long and may have encountered the Lord at this stage. My sister Nan died after a long illness last September, and I thank God I was present to be with the family on that sad occasion. On a happier note, I had a family wedding and a family christening, so the Lord timed my homecoming very well. Cork winning the All-Ireland football final after twenty years was a special moment to remember, and Tipperary did us all a favour by beating Kilkenny in the All-Ireland hurling final. On the local scene it was a Castlehaven victory in the under-21 county football final, which was a moment to remember in the parish. I have to mention the farewell party organised by James O Neill and Paddy O Donovan prior to my departure for PNG. The party is a moment to treasure and it is also encouraging to know I have the support of the local community back home.

My new home here in Goroka is quite interesting so far. I am meeting lots of new people, mainly religious. I had three former students from Bomana seminary preparing for ordination to diaconate and the priesthood and two more have booked in for this month. It's encouraging to see these students returning to their former spiritual director and to see them making decisions and getting on with their lives.

Having that said, we move into another new year, and I wish you good luck, good health, and happiness for 2011. God bless you and take care and I will keep you in my thoughts and prayers.

January 6, 2012 It's that time of year again to send you my Christmas Greetings and best wishes for 2012. It was another interesting year here in PNG, especially on the political front throughout the year. Last May Prime Minister Michael Somare went to Singapore for major surgery on his heart and remained there for over three months. In the meantime, the members of parliament elected a new prime minister on August 2. His name is Peter O Neill. I was told his father comes from Northern Ireland. He emigrated to Australia and from there he went to PNG as a patrol officer and fell in love with a local girl. Their son Peter was educated and became a leader in his community and he is now one of the prime ministers we have at this time of writing. Michael Somare has now returned to PNG and the Supreme Court has declared him as the rightful prime minister. The power struggle is still going on; we just hope a peaceful solution will solve this issue.

While the political struggle continues the country is enjoying a mining boom. A large deposit of gas and oil has been discovered in the Highland region and the project is making steady progress despite the remoteness of the oil and gas fields. There are 13,000 people employed in the project. At present the oil refinery is being constructed in India and it will be flown directly to the project sight and assembled there. An oversea company has that contract, and it will take 128 flights to deliver the refinery, each flight carrying seventy tons. There is a Kilkenny man here, David Freyne, employed with the World Bank and he is involved with the landowners to acquire the land for the airstrip which is five kilometres long and one kilometre wide. The deal is that the land goes back to the landowners once the oil refinery is delivered. David Freyne invited Fr John Ryan and me out for dinner one evening as he wanted to celebrate Kilkenny victory in the All-Ireland hurling final. I told him I will repay the complement next year, meaning of course Cork could win then. David was not too hopeful about that for a few years more.

On September 13 Papua New Guinea had one of its worst air crashes in its history. The plane was travelling to Madang when the engines failed and the pilot had to make a forced landing ten miles from the airport. Twenty-eight people died, while the pilot and three others survived. Most of the passengers were on their way to the Divine Word University for a thanksgiving Mass for the graduation students.

Two months ago, I was out saying Mass at St Mary's Church in Goroka and the theme of the readings was on wisdom. I told the congregation that my father used to tell me to drive easy and avoid having an accident, as we were never so happy, and it would be a pity if something should happen to us now. I still kept driving fast because I thought I knew better and now after all these years of driving I now know my father was right. He had learned over the years that speed kills, and I was still learning. That's wisdom, I told the congregation; you learn through experience and sometimes the hard way. Mass was not finished when a bad accident took place a mile outside the town. A bus went speeding down a hill, hit a bridge, and bounced off the railing to the other side, killing two people. Some people on the bridge jumped the railing and died also. Many more were injured. The following Sunday, the parishioners told me I should give that sermon to the drivers in PNG before they killed a lot more people.

Fr. John Ryan is in the process of starting up a new musical band in Goroka town. Boys and girls are practicing most days in the parish house. The band is progressing well, and it should be ready for public viewing in a few months' time. Fr. John is in Goroka now over sixteen years and he is well known in this area. Last week he invited me to his parish, as a friend had given him a plum pudding for Christmas and he said, " I won't feel good if I eat it all myself!"

The year passed by without too many difficulties. We had lots of rain but that did not cause us too many problems at the House of Prayer, except our bananas took an extra month to ripen and the grass never stopped growing. I was out two days every week for an hour pushing the lawn-mower; it was good exercise.

We had a moderately busy year at the House of Prayer: Some months were very busy and other times were slack. Our retreatants were mainly religious, the majority being local sisters. We had over twenty seminarians preparing for the diaconate and ordination to the priesthood. Last month I had a deacon, Ludwig Teika from the Lae Diocese, who was ordained on December 8. He is the first local priest to join the Mariannhill Congregations after fifty-two years of missionary work in PNG. He has been appointed to Bolivia. The Diocese of Kundawai had three deacons ordained this year and the Diocese of Rabaul had five ordained to the priesthood and five more seminarians ordained to the diaconate. Our own SVD deacon, Cosmas Komble, has postponed his ordination as his clan did not agree to his ordination being held in the Highlands, a two-day walk from their home place.

We have quite a number of local priests ordained already in PNG, but some are finding the commitment very difficult and are struggling to find their place in the community. This is one of our priorities at the House of Prayer—to help these young men make adjustments and find fulfilment in their priestly calling.

I also gave two priests' retreats this past year, one in the Diocese of Aitape and another in the Goroka Conference Centre to priests from all over PNG. This was organised by Bishop Gill Cote from Daru-Kiunga Diocese. Next May, I am going to Port Moresby to give two retreats to the seminarians in Bomana.

Last year we had two new bishops appointed, both teachers at Bomana seminary: they are Bishop Rolando Santos from the Philippines and Donald Lippert, a Capuchin from Pittsburgh. We are still waiting for the announcement of a new bishop for Wewak Diocese. The rector of Bomana seminary, Peter Artiken, is high on the list for this vacancy.

This Christmas I was out helping Fr. John Ryan in St Mary's Parish. I went to two extended communities outside the main town called Faniufa and Lopi. I had two Baptisms at Lopi, and the church was packed. After Mass all the people were hugging each other and wishing each other a happy Christmas as if they had not met for years. They were really into the spirit of Christmas. For the Mass offering the people filled the boot of my car with bananas, pineapples, oranges, and sweet corn. I shared the offering with the sisters, where we had a lovely Christmas dinner, and Bishop Francesco Sarego was also present. It was a nice family gathering for Christmas Day.

I hope you had a blessed and holy Christmas also, and I wish you good health and many blessings for 2012. God bless you and take care.

December 28, 2012 It's time again to wish you all a very happy Christmas and many blessings for the coming year. I hope you had a peaceful Christmas and that 2012 had some good memories for you also.

Here in Papua New Guinea we had some surprises and some sad calamities. The most tragic event was the sinking of the ferry boat the *Rabaul Queen* on February 2. No one knows the exact number of people on board, but it is believed it was close to 400; most of the passengers were students returning to college to begin their academic year. One mother was accompanying her twin daughters to college when she was thrown overboard, and she could not swim. Her two daughters tried to keep her afloat until help arrived, but a big wave pushed them apart. The mother disappeared, and the two daughters survived. Lucky it was day break when the accident happened, and a number of fishing boats were in the vicinity and rescued over 246 passengers from the sea. Those inside the *Rabaul Queen*, over 140 passengers, could not get out and lost their lives. Seven survivors enrolled here at the Goroka University, but their hearts are still with their dead classmates lying in peace in 1,600 metres of water in the bottom of the Bismarck Sea.

We had a national election this year, and the big surprise was that three women were elected to the house of parliament, which is an indication the women are making themselves heard. Peter O Neill, whose father comes from Northern Ireland, was elected the rightful prime minister. He may drop in one day to see where his ancestors came from. We had Prince Charles and his wife Camilla visiting here last November and the people are saying he should come more often as Port Moresby city got a badly needed facelift before they arrived. All the potholes around the city were filled in, the waterways were cleaned out, the grass and hedges trimmed, and all the city rubbish was put out of sight. From here Prince Charles and his wife went to Australia to watch the Melbourne Cup, and I read in the newspaper the following day that the first seven horses across the line were all bred in Ireland.

I was in Port Moresby for the month of May and gave three retreats in the Nazareth House of Prayer and I observed the explosion of second-hand cars from Japan in the city. The country has gone up a gear since the discovery of the gas and oil fields. Even the Irish are picking up some of the spoils. Denis O'Brien's mobile phone company Digicel has reached the four corners of PNG. Last year he donated eleven ambulances to different health centres in the country. I was happy to hear Timbunke Parish, where I was stationed for over twelve years, also received one.

Maybe I could do with one of those second-hand cars myself after an experience I could have done without. When I returned from Port Moresby my car was standing idle for one month. I took it out on the highway to go to the bank and the horn went off. I could not stop it. I kept going and

I noticed everyone running out of my way. They must have thought it was a police chase. I had a clear drive to the bank and when I arrived I kept my composure, came out of the car, opened the bonnet and disconnected the battery, and finally the horn stopped. At that stage I noticed over 200 heads looking in my direction wondering what it was all about. It was a rat that was to blame for all the excitement, having exposed the wires when nesting near the engine block.

I also gave a retreat to the Rosary Sisters in Wewak this year. They are in the process of becoming self-reliant as most of their younger sisters are either teaching or nursing. They are praying that their founder, Archbishop Leo Arkfeld, will be canonised one day. While I was there, 319 women from the Wewak Dioceses had their convention at Tangugo pastoral centre. Thirty-seven of whom were from Ambunti in the Upper Sepik where I was parish priest for ten years. We hadn't seen each other for eight years and they welcomed me in their traditional style with bundles of hugs and Sepik baskets. After that they filled me in on how life had treated them since we last met. Rita Pious who lives on the mission station told me only two of her ten children were at home now, and one of her daughters, Ingrid, who I showed how to cut grass with a lawnmower, is now hired as a forklift driver in a gold mine. Rita Markus who also has ten children has only one attending school, and one for her daughters, Monica, whom I wrote a reference letter for some years ago, is working here in Goroka. We met in the bank one day. These are little opportunities of grace when we meet old friends and share some of our peak moments. Most of these women are now grandmothers, and they told me they did not have to wait too long.

Back here at the House of Prayer we have at least 100 bananas trees. One of the problems is that most of them are producing together. I give them to Fr. John Ryan who passes them on to the prison and the hospital. One day I was out in the garden and a little girl, Rose Badue, came to see me. She told me she was getting her First Holy Communion at Christmas and asked would I buy her a pair of shoes. She has a small sister who is just starting to talk. She came as far as the fence and started calling out "Fr. Mick Fr. Mick." She kept calling until she got my attention and then ran back along the furrow between the ridges to her mother, delighted that I had taken notice of her. I went to the fence to say hallo to the mother and

I noticed several people all down on their hocks attending to their crops. It took me some time to identify them, as the colour of their skin blended in so well with the soil they were tilling. It was only when they moved that I realised they were people. Then I noticed a cardboard box under a banana tree moving, it was an eight-month child letting us know "I am here too." I thought to myself, what a fine healthy outdoor life these people have. They eat what they grow and grow what they eat, and it's all done by the work of their hands. I did buy the shoes and socks for the little girl a week later, and she showed great delight when receiving them as she skipped back to her parent's bush house just beside their garden.

To sum up the past year, it was another grace filled year at the House of Prayer. I prepared five sisters for the consecrated life and nine deacons for the priesthood. I gave six preached retreats to religious including the national priests retreat again this year organised be Bishop Gilles Cote. I gave my first thirty-day retreat in June, and several priests and sisters including bishops came for directed retreats through the year. Sr. Ignatiele also helped with these directed retreats. Students also came from the Goroka University for spiritual direction to discuss some sensitive issues. Over all it was very enriching to accompany these people on their journey of faith and I give God all the glory for whatever peace and grace people encounter during these retreats. For Christmas I went to St Mary's Parish to help Fr. John Ryan for three days. With that I will sigh off, and Please God I will see you all next July.

January 18, 2013 I am back again in PNG after another wonderful holiday. This holiday was an exception as the summer was like one I experienced in my childhood days. It was a joy to walk through the summer fields which hold so many memories for me. There were several peak moments, reconnecting with people I had not met for over forty years; though time has moved on, the memories have remained the same. Being present to witness Castlehaven win the football county final and several under-age games were all an extra bonus. Finally, it was the farewell party arranged by the local community that brought the holiday to a closure. It came as no surprise to me that the break from home this time was that bit more of a struggle.

The first job I had to do when I returned from my home leave was to make a rush to cut the grass, as five Missionary Sisters of Charity were arriving; they wear a sari down to the ankles and the grass seeds get stuck in their clothes. This is not an issue with the other congregations. One afternoon one of the five sisters was coming from the clothesline with a handful of clothes pegs and heading towards her room. I told her there was a tray in the laundry to put them into. She smiled as me, and said, "Father, we always bring our own clothes pegs with us."

Six sisters have been here already to prepare themselves for final vows. One sister is a Servant of Jesus, two are from the Sisters Servants of the Holy Spirit, and three are Sisters of the Sacred Heart. The Sacred Heart Sisters are three qualified teachers and they made their final vows on December 17. Four deacons have completed or booked their retreat in preparation for their ordination in January 2014. On a less joyful note, Bishop Anton Ball informed me that his three seminarians who were close to the finishing line have pulled out and will no longer continue studying for the priesthood.

Now I move on to a different topic. The main event that took place here in Goroka since I returned was Fr. John Ryan's farewell celebrations during the first week of November. The main events were spread out over two days. The first day was an outdoor meal for well over a thousand people, and still there was food left over for the following day. The second day was confined to the Liturgy, Bible drama and action songs. Some prisoners were let out to join the celebrations. They put on a sketch reliving the actions and voice of Fr. John when he made pastoral calls there. That drama was followed by an elderly group known as the Catholic Fathers. As they were singing, I said to Fr. John, "You would never get a group like that to sing in Ireland." He was quick to say, "You would get it in a pub!" One of the distinguished guests was the Governor of the Eastern Highland Providence. Julie So-so. She sat on a mat like hundreds of other parishioners. When she got up to speak there were tears in her eyes as she spoke very highly of Fr. John and the many organizations they were both involved in over the sixteen years he was in St Mary's Parish.

Fr. John always tells a story about one Christmas night when he was about to celebrate Mass. He had arranged with one mother to put her baby into the crib, but she never turned up. Fr. John looked around and spotted a young mother holding a baby, and after some hesitation she agreed to put her baby into the crib.

Sometime later, Fr. John asked the mother why she was so reluctant to put her baby into the crib on Christmas night. The mother replied, "Jesus was a baby boy, and my baby is a girl." Speaking about babies, St. Vincent de Paul used to send me cartons of clothes with some baby kits when I was in Ambunti. I met one of the mothers recently and she pointed to her 15-year-old daughter as one of her daughters who had used the kit. I used to give them to the catholic mothers to distribute them as they knew best who was due to deliver and who needed them most.

Right now, Bishop Francesco is building a new school here in Goroka. Four classrooms and a large workshop are complete. Three teacher's houses are still under construction. The school will be called St. Joseph Technical College. One such college in a remote area in PNG is known as a barefoot college as the students walk to school in their bare feet, something I did myself over half a century ago. Several people have told me in casual conversation their grandparents never wore shoes and the soles of their feet were quite hard.

Denis O'Brien is still building classrooms in PNG. The latest one is at an old Church-run primary school in the Wewak Diocese. These classrooms come complete with an office, solar lights, two water tanks, two toilets and showers, desks and chalk boards. The latest report on the *National* newspaper says that since the establishment of the Digicel Foundation[1] in 2008 it has delivered classrooms to eighty-two elementary schools and eighty-seven primary schools. This will give you an indication as to how well Digicel has progressed here in PNG—and also the growing number of children now going to school.

Here in PNG we have two Fr. Johns from Ireland. The second is Fr. John McCarthy who was our Provincial for the last three years and has now returned to Ireland for medical reasons after thirty-four years of missionary service. Before Fr. McCarthy left, he gave me all his PNG stamps, so when you see all the different stamps on the envelopes you know where they came from.

---

1 A charity set up by the Digicel mobile phone company, founded and owned by Irish businessman Denis O'Brien.

Br. Andrew Simpson, a Christian Brother who worked at the Divine Word University, died last June. He was the vice-president of student affairs. He loved chocolate, and his students put two bars of cholate into his coffin before they laid him to rest.

It has been raining here with the last three weeks. The mountains that ring around Goroka are covered with cloud and mist most days. On a clear morning you can see smoke going up from the little huts dotted around the hillsides. Early morning smoke from gardens also signals people at work. The heavy rain has contributed to several land-slips along the Highlands highway. One land-slip closed the road for six days; it is the only lifeline to the Highland region.

I celebrated Mass at St Mary's Parish on Christmas Day, and the church was packed. Fr John's musical band played lovely Christmas hymns and they received a round of applause at the end of Mass. This also brings me to the end of the page, and now I can wish you a belated happy Christmas and many blessings for 2014. God bless you.

December 24, 2014 I hope you are well as another year has passed by. It has been a year of many blessings here at the retreat house. Retreatants came from ten different dioceses; most were nationals and the majority were sisters. Several deacons came to prepare themselves for ordination and all are ordained to the priesthood at this stage. One deacon, Patrick Posani from the Diocese of Aitape, was once a married man who lost his wife and two children during the 1998 tidal wave and after that tragedy he decided to become a priest. A sister also from that same village lost her whole family and she survived because she went to visit her aunt who was in hospital. After finishing high-school she wrote to the sisters of Our Lady of the Sacred Heart and they bought her a ticket to experience their "Come and See" program. When her relatives discover she was entering the convent they were very angry with her as they hoped she would get married and have lots of children who would take ownership of her land as she was the only survivor in the family.

Another vocation story I thought worth mentioning concerns Fr. Gerard Mulholland, SVD, who died last November. In his young days he was an ambulance officer and he was called out one Christmas night to a terrible accident in South Maryborough in Australia. Everyone was killed except for one lady trapped inside the car whom he couldn't get to her. He asked, "Is there anything I can do to help you?" She replied that she would like to see a priest. It was five minutes to midnight on Christmas Eve and he wondered to himself where he could get a priest at this hour, as they were probably all saying Midnight Mass. Just then a car pulled up and a man got out of the car, walked over to him and said, "I am a Catholic priest. Is there anything I can do to help here?" That incident brought Fr. Jerry back to the Church and to eventually becoming a Divine Word Missionary. He once told this story at a priest's meeting and one old priest stood up and said, "I was that priest." After three years in PNG, Fr. Jerry returned to Melbourne as his health was showing early signs of motor neurone disease. He said two weeks before he died, "I am looking forward to Heaven as they tell me it is a pretty good place." This story is from *The Catholic Leader*.

In June I was back in Wewak Dioceses for two weeks giving a directed retreat to the Franciscans sisters. That same week a local contractor was repairing the road up to Boys' Town[2], close to the retreat house where Japanese soldiers camped for two years during the Second World War. Four heavy machine guns are still there pointing out to the sea, and a tunnel that you could drive a bus through was also cleared up. One evening I made an inspection as several people from the town were doing the same, to discover one woman was collecting what she thought were Japanese bones, and some youth were gathering helmets and empty mortar shells left behind after the battle of Wewak Hill. The clean-up was to prepare the way for the Prime Minister of Japan, who was coming to PNG, and laying wreaths in memory to the soldiers who died there. Grand Chief Sir Michael Somare asked the people of East Sepik Province to come to Wewak in their tradition dress to welcome the prime minister and let him see our culture, as the world media will be focused on the visit. Thousands came and lined up along the road from the airport to the historical sights he was to visit, waving PNG flags as he passed by.

Our Bishop of Goroka, Francesco Sarego, was made Grand Chief by the government of PNG this year. It's a title to show how much the government appreciated his efforts in the development of the country. Bishop

2 A centre for young offenders.

Francesco has reached the retirement age of 75, and the process has begun already to appoint a replacement to take over from him.

In June also, there were great celebrations in the country to mark the first shipment of 80,000 tons of natural gas to Japan. Since then several shipments of gas has been sold to the Asian market. It has set the country on a roll. There were engineers and all kinds of professional people from overseas, including Ireland, working on this project for six years. I was surprised one day when I got a letter in the post from a Michael O'Donovan, who was working on the gas fields. I thought first it was a mistake until Michael explained his parents were Frankie and Margaret O'Donovan from Skibbereen, and his father Frankie comes from Carrigillihy, Union Hall. It was a nice surprise.

The Chinese are also coming into PNG in their thousands, and there is quite a bit of resistance to their presence. This past year the local landowners stormed the Ramu nickel and cobalt mine in Madang as they were not engaging the natives in the project. Now I have seen in the *Wantok* newspaper pictures of locals employed by the company and pushing wheelbarrows. The Papua New Guinea women are also complaining to the government in the media how the Chinese have flooded the home market with cheap clothes and the women cannot sell their home-made products. It was one of the success stories in PNG where women were trained to make their own clothes. When they had completed vocational school, they were given a free sewing machine and rolls of cloth to go home and start their own business. I remember when I was in Ambunti Parish I used take out twenty or more sewing machines every year to the vocation school; they were graduation gifts given by the school to the girls who had completed their training. The Chinese now have made carbon copies of the popular clothing women wear in this country for half the price, and the small woman business groups are up in arms.

Last Easter I had another surprise waiting for me. I went out to celebrate Mass at one of the communities in Goroka. On Easter Sunday morning it was the turn of the elderly woman to take the Liturgy. They were to perform a traditional dance welcoming the bride to meet her future husband. Now they were adopting this traditional dance to celebrate Christ's resurrection. They made a procession to the church one hand up and one hand down like birds changing direction in mid-air and at the same time singing a song in their mother tongue. I hadn't a clue what they were singing except the last word was Alleluia. They were expressing the joys of the resurrection and Angels flying from the tomb with the good news "Christ has risen!" The people here are very creative when it comes to Bible drama and action song. When it comes to dramatizing the Devil, it's a real comedy.

In the world of sport, PNG made history this year when it won two gold medals for weight-lifting at the Commonwealth games in Scotland. The athletes got a rousing reception when they returned to Port Moresby. Prime Minister Peter O'Neill gave the two gold medallists 100,000 *kina* each (about €30,000 Euro) and he encouraged the others to aim for gold.

This year also, two of my predecessors, Fr. Alois Klijn, 91, and Fr Alois Blasl, 76, passed on to their eternal reward. Both worked here at the retreat house for a number of years. Fr Alois Blasi was better known to me, as he introduced me here to the running of the house before he left and told me to stay ten years. I thought he was asking a bit too much at the time, but you know I am nearly half way there.

Fr. John Ryan has just returned from his Sabbatical year. He would be happy to know that the band he established here in Goroke is playing every Saturday in the town. I asked them one day to play "Danny Boy", and it was no trouble to them. I will miss Fr. John as he is now appointed as Chaplain to the Divine Word University in Madang. With that, I wish you and all the community a blessed Christmas and good luck and good health for 2015. God bless and take car.

January 1, 2016 I hope you are all keeping well after another year has come and gone. Its six weeks now since I left home, and life is getting back to normal once again. The morning I left home, I got a bit worried at Cork Airport as the plane was delayed for over forty minutes due to gale force winds. At 8.30 the pilot got the all clear to take off and I was to get a connecting flight to Singapore at 10.55. I was already thinking of plan B, to get a return ticket to Cork or book into a hotel and reschedule my ticket. As it turned out, there was an escort waiting for me when I arrived, and he told me, "We will have to take a short-cut and go straight to the check-in counter and on to the Airbus before the door is closed." Things picked up from here on. I got four seats for the price of one at the back of the plane and I was able to lift up the arm-rests and have a good sleep when I felt like it. It really shortened the journey. After the plane took off, soft drinks and peanuts were given out, and dinner and breakfast were served as we continued on our twelve and three quarter's hour journey to Singapore. It was Thursday morning local time when we arrived there. There was no rush now as I had twelve hours stop over to get the connecting flight to PNG. It was morning again when we touched down in Port Moresby. Brother Raj, SVD, picked me up from there and the following day I flew to Goroka.

I got a pleasant welcome when I arrived, with lots of bear hugs and mother hugs, whatever you call them; it all helped to soften the home feelings which surfaced on departure day. Twelve retreatants had booked in for retreats before Christmas, so it was back to life as usual. Three of the retreatants were deacons coming for the last phase of their spiritual formation before ordination day. Three were young girls thinking about joining religious life, and the rest were sisters in religious life for years. Everything went very well in my absence, except for one thing. One Father put petrol in the car by mistake instead of diesel, and I was left with a disabled car. However, I made it back to the house. I thought first it that the dirty fuel was the problem, but the mechanic found twenty-five litres of petrol in the tank and the car is on the road once again. Problem solved.

A number of major events have taken place during the past year. The ordination of Bishop Joe Roszynski, SVD, for the dioceses of Wewak was one of them. He is fondly known as "Big Joe" as he is 152 kilos. He had booked a retreat here before his ordination, but he could not come as the road was closed and the airlines were booked out as a result. People came from all over the diocese in their traditional attire of grass skirts, leaves, feathers, and painted faces for his ordination. The people of the diocese had to wait two years before "Big Joe" was appointed to fill the vacancy left by the death of Bishop Tony Burgess.

Papua New Guinea celebrated forty years independence from Australia on September 16. There were great celebrations all over the country. Some people complained, "We are forty years in the desert and have not yet reached the Promised Land."

On May 31, Fr. Andreas Warmut Neansugel, SVD, a local priest was asked to bless the first fly-over in PNG. It was built by a New Zealand company at the cost of 60 million US Dollars. The city of Port Moresby is experiencing an influx of second-hand cars from Japan and new roads are been built to cater for the extra traffic.

Denis O'Brien's Irish-based company, Digicel, is also expanding in PNG. He has already 800 towers erected in the country and he has another 360 to roll out this year, and that will give Digicel one hundred per cent coverage. One of my former prayer leaders on the Sepik told me that the village people had to make a bamboo ladder and climb up to the top of the tree where a platform was built, and only there could they receive a signal for their mobile phone in the beginning. Now with a new dish in his village he can receive and make calls from inside his house.

While parts of the country are developing fast, other areas are experiencing a lot of new challenges with law and order. Last year the provincial governments banned liquor sales in their province over Christmas to control the situation. Some people thought they could smuggle beer into the province by using an oil tanker. The driver had passed one checkpoint and at the second checkpoint was asked where he was delivering the fuel to at one o clock in the night. The driver became nervous and the police checked the oil tank to discover 700 cartons of beer inside. Your guess is as good as mine as to who drank the beer.

This year many parts of the country have experience a long dry spell with no rain for four months. The government has helped out a few provinces most in need with rice and tin-fish. Most people still depend on their garden food to survive, and the price of home-grown food has trebled at the market place. The rains have come with the last few weeks and people are out planting in the gardens again, including myself.

Next year, Sr. Jaroslava from Slovakia will help out at the retreat centre. She was here two weeks ago to meet me. It will give the retreatants a choice about who they want to direct them in the coming year.

On December 13 we had a special Mass in Goroka to start the "Holy Year of Mercy". Over a thousand people attended and afterwards we marched through the town to open the "Door of Mercy" at north Goroka

Church. Bishop Francesco was the main celebrant and we are still waiting for a new bishop to replace him.

One surprise this year: the Divine Word University has a new lady president. She takes over from Fr. Jan Czuba who held the post for twenty years. This is the way the country is going, letting go and handing over to the local people.

People are now celebrating Christmas and the New Year with fire crackers imported from Indonesia, and they seem fascinated by the atmosphere it creates. With that note I hope you had a holy and happy Christmas with your family. Happy New Year. God bless you.

December 1, 2016 It was good to hear from you during the year, and to know that all is well at your side of the world. It was another interesting year here in PNG, full of surprises and a few disappointments also. The ordination of Bishop Dariusz was the main event that took place in Goroka on August 20. Our new bishop is from Poland and he is a member of the Holy Family Congregation. He spent nineteen years as priest working in the Mendi Diocese, so it was no surprise when the people from Mendi came in bus-loads to his ordination.

There was a great buzz in the diocese in the days leading up to his ordination. Everyone was asked to give a hand wherever needed. I volunteered to erect the grand stand, only to discover a team of men already working with bamboos, bush rope, and homemade blinds. I didn't feel part of that trade and left them to it. I ended up blowing balloons and pinning them up on the veranda. Every parish was asked to contribute a pig and fruit and vegetables. This was to provide a meal for 2,000 people that were expected to turn up for the two days' celebrations. Among the congregation was the bishop's 70-year-old mother and ten members of the family. The people of Mendi diocese dressed up in full traditional attire. Their head dress was glittering in the morning sun as they sang and danced all the way to the altar followed by seventy priests and fourteen bishops. The weather was kind to us, and both days went off without a hitch.

The Diocese of Rabaul also had good reason to celebrate this year. They have six deacons ready for ordination and last June four MSC sisters made their first vows. One of the four was Sr. Geraldine from the Sepik, where I spent my younger days. Last month, Bishop John Ribat, a native of Rabaul and a member of the MSC congregation was made a cardinal by Pope Frances. It is a historic milestone for PNG. There was great rejoicing in the country when the announcement was made, and the national papers gave it full coverage the following day. Prime Minister Peter O'Neill was one of the first to congratulate Bishop John. Over a thousand people gathered at Jacksons Airport at four o clock in the morning to welcome the new cardinal when he arrived back from Rome. The red carpet was rolled out and four traditional groups sang and danced as he made his way to the arrivals' area. As an extra bonus the national airline paid the air fares for those who went to Rome to witness the occasion. Our new cardinal is the seventh child of a family of nine. His father died when he was a young boy and his mother had to take care of the family. When he told his mother that he wanted to become a priest, she told him, "You can go, but only if you will be a faithful priest."

The Diocese of Madang had four ordinations to the priesthood this year, and Wabeg Diocese had three. They all came to the House of Prayer for the last stage of their formation. Brother Stan, SVD, from Poland who worked here in PNG for many years and had a strong desire to become a priest was ordained this year. Bishop Anton Bal was willing to accept him at the age of 65, and the process for his ordination began. He came for his retreat here in June and was ordained deacon the following week. In the meantime, he got very sick and he returned to Poland. It was diagnosed there he had advanced cancer and could not return to PNG. It was thought first Bishop Anton would go to Poland to ordain him; instead, a bishop who was a classmate of Br. Stan's in the seminary ordained him on October 11 in a wheelchair. As I am writing this letter, Fr. Stan's condition is not good, and he is only waiting to meet the Lord. He is at peace with himself that his lifelong desire to be a priest has been fulfilled. He died a few weeks later.

Last September we had a workshop for the welfare of priests. This idea came from the Bishops' Conference that something should be done for priests in crises. Bishop Bill Fay came to launch the programme and he hopes this program will continue again next year.

During the year one bishop came to me, feeling really down. His deacon, who was due to be ordained in a few weeks, was not going forward, and this was the second time it had happened. After listening to the reason why he was not getting ordained, I said to the bishop, "The forces of nature are always a challenge on the road to the priesthood." He just bowed his head in agreement.

On a lighter note, every Sunday I help out at St Mary's Parish. For Holy Week I went to Faniufa, an out-station of St. Mary's. When I had finished the Easter Vigil Mass the choir started playing the tune "He is alive" and the whole congratulation got up and started dancing in Charismatic style. Such a surge of joy I haven't seen since Castlehaven won the county final back in 2013. I joined them and said to myself that I must make the most of life, as the most of mine is gone.

The "Year of Mercy" made a big impact here in PNG. It seems to have touched everyone's lives. For the closing Masses, thousands gathered at the main centres in every diocese. Hagen Diocese had over 15,000 for the closing Jubilee Mass and it was estimated 5,000 were packed into the new cathedral for the first Mass that was celebrated there. The new cathedral is far from finished, but it is useable at this stage.

Right now, PNG is hosting the under-20 Ladies' World Cup soccer games in Port Moresby. The host country was allowed to participate. Our ladies lost the three opening games but got one long-range goal to the delight of everyone present at the game.

Prime Minister Peter O Neill was under a lot of pressure during the year to step aside and face allegation issues, which the university students demanded. He refused their demands and survived to live another day. His picture was on the paper one day with his son, and his name is Patrick. You cannot get more Irish than that. He still remembers his roots. Since the Cardinal's appointment he has invited the Pope to visit PNG but not before 2019, as next year there is a general election and the following year there is an Asia Pacific Economic Cooperation meeting in Port Moresby and around the country. Preparations are already taking place for these two important events.

On November 27 we had a farewell dinner for Bishop Francesco. He was known for his patience, kindness, and humility, and got on well with his priests and co-workers. Some said he was like the father of the prodigal son. Now at the age of 77 he is returning to Italy to retire. Our new bishop is also a fine person. He is moving around to the parishes to get acquainted with the people and with the running of the diocese.

Now I can wish you a happy Christmas and best wishes for the New Year and I will keep you in my prayers and thoughts and hope for the best as the New Year unfolds. I am keeping well myself and I hope this letter finds you also in good form.

December 1, 2017 I hope you are all keeping well after another year has come and gone. What's another year? For me it means I have now moved into another decade and my health is normal for my age, thank God.

It was a year dominated by the wet season and the general election. The heavy rain caused land-slips on the Highlands highway, leaving truck drivers stranded for several days. Mechanical diggers were working by moonlight to keep the road open to carry up supplies to the three million people that depend on fuel and other basic goods. The limited supply of goods led to panic buying. A truck load of cattle was among the long line of articulated lorries that spent six days at a road block while the locals gave them grass and water to keep them alive. A number of priests and sisters had to cancel their retreats as they too could not travel due to the condition of the road.

Here in Goroka I was about to celebrate Mass one Sunday at Lopi when I observed some ladies coming to Mass with a pair of shoes in one hand and a bottle of water in the other. When they reached the church, they washed their feet and put on their shoes, which were designed more for city life than for the mud lanes between the houses in the settlements. Now we are experiencing a long dry season and it's the dust we are complaining about now.

The general election is over but still there are several disputed results. The campaign went on for six weeks and it was a change from the street preachers that kept reminding us of the end times and hell fire. There were 3,332 candidates standing for 111 seats. That included 135 women and eight priests. One priest, Fr. Simon Dumarino, a Marist from Bougainville, was elected but none of the women made the quota. Peter O Neill is back again as prime minister and Michael Somare, the founding father of PNG, has retired after forty-nine years in politics.

This year I helped out Fr. Jose, SVD, with three retreats for the students at Goroka University. Fr. Jose is the chaplain there and he also asks me from time to time to say Mass for the students. I happened to celebrate Mass there on Pentecost Sunday. I was surprised when I saw the church beautifully prepared for the occasion. They had red ribbons hanging from the ceiling as symbols of tongues of fire coming down on the Apostles, and above the altar were the seven gifts and the seven fruits of the Holy Spirit in full display. For the Prayers of the Faithful, seven students came forward and prayed in seven different languages and I added another in Irish. There were no Irish people in the congregation but there were a number of lecturers from overseas sitting in front of me with a big smile on their faces. It was encouraging to see so many young people full of life and energy chatting around after Mass, and the variety of style the young ladies were displaying from head to toe goes to show how fast they have adopted to the fashions of the western world.

Another Sunday I got another surprise when my former headmaster, Joshua Kuara, was waiting for me outside the church door. We were both together in Ambunti Parish for ten years. We had a great chat about the people we both knew, and we spoke about the dead as if they were still alive. A few of them had passed away peacefully during the year. Our chief motor mechanic, Dieter from Germany, was one of those. He used to get angry with us priests when we would put our cars into his workshop covered with mud. He used to say there was enough mud on the car to grow sweet potatoes, and you know it was nearly half true. Another man who died here at the mission station during the year was out main gardener, Rudy Auguwa, from attack of asthma. The first thing Rudy used to do every morning was to get his spade and remove the dog soil from around the grounds. Rudy and I often had a good chat and a laugh in the middle of the day when the sun got too hot for us to work in the garden. He was from the Sepik, so we had more than gardening in common. He is buried here in Goroka, many miles from his boyhood home. Now it is memories of the years gone by that bind us together and make them so special in our lives.

I was back in Wewak for the ordination of Andrew Masi, SVD, on

October 31 and I met lots of my former parishioners. One lady, Donna Laki, now in her thirties was only a schoolgirl when I left Timbunke twenty-two years ago, and she amazed me when she recalled her childhood memories about my time in her parish.

It was Bishop Joe's fourth ordination in just over two years as bishop. He has another ordination on December 8. Bishop Joe is as big and as round as ever. The people have a saying here when they see a well-fed man, "His wife must be a good cook." Well, this saying does not apply to Bishop Joe.

Here in Goroka at our Liturgical Catechetical Institute (LCI) we got a new manager, Fr. Adam Samsel, and he informed me that he sells statues, crucifies, and rosary beads all made in China as they are cheaper and stronger than the ones that come from the Philippines. I was sharing this with Sr. Dominic, SSpS, and she told me the Chinese are also selling Communion breads. It's just a business, anything to make money. We have an SVD student here from Russia. He is the first SVD from that country to come to PNG.

There was great excitement here on November 5 when Ireland were playing PNG in the World League Rugby cup. It was played in Port Moresby and PNG overcame the Irish in a score of 14 to 6

I had a very nice celebration for my seventieth birthday. We had the usual ice-cream, cake, soft drinks and beer, and a delicious meal. Most of the priests attended. Some sisters and the kitchen staff were also present. A few weeks later, Bishop Dariusz celebrated his fiftieth birthday and it was the same again, only this time we had a full roasted pig. Again, I want to thank you for your letters, prayers and donations during the year and I hope to see you all in 2018. God bless for now and I wish you happy Christmas and every blessing for the coming year.

January 1, 2018 Christmas has passed by, and you could say it was a wet Christmas with all the rain. Our five water tanks are overflowing. They were really put to the test last year as we got three and a half months without a shower of rain. Christmas was very quiet here at the Mission compound. It was the children from our employees that kept the place alive. One evening I was walking through the grounds when two children jumped out of the fish pond and ran after me. They had a toy motor car the size of the full-grown rabbit they got for Christmas and they wanted me to see it. Now I see them pulling it around after them with a string. We have a special needs child here also. Her name is Jennifer. When I came here in 2010 the children used to take her out for a walk every evening, each child holding her by the hand as they slowly moved round the ground. Now Jennifer can walk on her own, but she finds it difficult to keep her balance. The bigger children spend most evenings playing volleyball and a few others were deeply engrossed in learning how to ride a new bicycle. The place had all the sounds of cheerful, happy children. Schools reopen on January 29, and the place will be back to normal once again. Gregory and his wife here at the mission station adopted a three-month-old baby girl just before Christmas. The mother of the baby is still going to school and wants to finish her education and give up her child for adoption. One day, Gregory's daughter Jasmin brought the baby around for me to see her. She has beautiful brown eyes and Gregory's 3-year-old son Jan says, "Mom has bought a new baby."

I went out to help Fr. Carlos in the parish for Christmas. I heard some very good Confessions, ones that makes me think what a privilege it is to be a priest. Fr. Carlos was very busy during this time. He came here looking for a Christmas tree. I had a forty-foot tree here hanging over the graveyard and I gave him the top half. The parish youth came to collect it and they stood it up in front of the Father's house facing the road. The tree was beautifully decorated, with the Morning Star pinned up on the top. Fr. Carlos went around during Christmas week asking the business people in Goroka for a contribution as he was going to give a gift to 200-plus prisoners in Goroka. He ended up with a lorry-load of food which included rice, soft drinks, biscuits, and home-grown food that the parishioners provided from their gardens. He made the delivery on New Year's Day and this was followed by speeches and words of thanks. It was something Fr. John Ryan started some years ago, and Fr. Carlos wants to keep up the tradition.

On November 15 one of our parishioners, Kaminiel Tovue, died. He was a retired policeman who spent many years in Wewak. We knew each other to see, and when I came here to Goroka we happened to meet again. He had a bad knee, so I used to take him to Mass when he was standing outside his house One Sunday he asked me what I was doing these times.

I told him I had a local contractor, Brian Kuglame, milling fourteen trees around the House of Prayer and I was now cleaning up the place after them. Word got around that I had three trailer-loads of sawdust to be removed, and many people came to collect it for bedding for their poultry farms Fr. Carlos, Deacon Thomas, and I attended the funeral Mass, and there was a large turn-out from the police force.

Our vocation school across the way from here is making steady progress. Last year a new mechanic shop was built, and now the rails are standing for a large multi-purpose building just next to the fence. Lots of students want to enrol in vocation schools now as there is a big demand for qualified tradesmen, and this is the first step in that direction. It is hopeful that the intake of students will grow to four or five hundred within the next five years.

We started off the New Year with seven sisters for a full week's retreat. Four were from Kerema Diocese, two from Daru and one from Kundiawa. January and February are usually our peak month. Next Monday, January 15, our Provincial Chapter is starting in Madang, and a big number of our SVDs are attending it. I could not attend as I had already committed myself here to the House of Prayer to give the retreats.

Our big German shepherd dog Jubilee is ageing. He got the name Jubilee because he was born in 2000. He was a very good security dog and he made a big contribution to the dog population, not just inside the Mission compound but in the surrounding villages as well. Sr. Mary Linda, SSpS, bred German Sheperds for several years, and these dogs were highly sought after by business companies. She is over 80, and it looks like this enterprise of hers will soon come to a closure. I gather some sisters are not too upset about that.

I had a number of phone calls from my former parish, Ambunti, over Christmas and they gave me an update on what's happening there. Some good news and some not so good. The Frieda River Gold and Copper mine which is just up river from Ambunti is about to start operations next year. That will bring big changes to that region. The big fear that local people have is that it will pollute the Sepik River and the surrounding waterways, which are their main source of their income. One of my good friends, Jemmy Bau, died some time ago. Jimmy was a qualified mechanic and he went back to his village to start his own private business repairing outboard engines. Once he found me drifting down the river after I had run out of petrol about two hours from home. After he had given me enough petrol to reach Ambunti, I told him I would repay him double when he came down to the station. He said, "There is no need, Father. Just say a prayer for me." I told him one prayer would not be enough. His wife who was sitting in the canoe with a child on her lap also said there was no need to give it back. When people die it is often the good deeds they do for you that come to mind. The people always have stories to tell when they ring. The young schoolboys and girls have grown into responsible young men and women and a few married couples I blessed have gone their separate ways. I guess it is all part of the human journey.

Just before Christmas two young sisters were here preparing themselves for first vows when Sr. Crista, SMMI[3], got word her mother and her aunt lost their lives at sea. They were on their way to be present for her profession when the accident happened. The boat was over loaded with twenty-one people, plus cargo and fuel in rough seas. Five other passengers also lost their lives. Sr.Crista was here again at the House of Prayer as she is trying to come to terms with the whole situation.

I said it was a quiet Christmas. I think it was the rain that made the difference. Usually I would have free music for two nights when the local villages hold a disco in the open air and the loud music can be heard a mile away. This year that was missing, which was a blessing to those living nearby.

At present I am alone in the House of prayer and I am in the mood for writing letters and answering some of my Christmas mail, so I am taking the opportunity to keep you up to date from PNG. Well, now it's time to stop and I wish you peace and joy for 2018.

January 23, 2018 Many thanks for your emails with all the news from the homeland. I enjoyed reading it very much. There is nothing new happening around here. Life is back to normal after the turn of the year and life seems to move easily through the day without much effort, though one never knows what the day will bring, or the night. Some days we get unexpected visitors, who are very welcome, and it's almost two years

---

3 Salesian Sisters of Mary Immaculate.

now since we had night intruders at two o'clock in the morning. They made a quick exit when the alarm was set off.

This week I had one of our SVD seminarians, Terence Bassi, for three days cutting the lawn, and the grounds are really looking splendid today. There are seven boys in Terence's family and one girl, Lorena. All the boys are in the six-foot range and Lorena is nearly as tall as them. Lorena graduated from the Divine Word. All the family are getting on well in life and their mother says it was her prayers to the Blessed Mother that contributed to their success. I gave Terence some pocket money, most of which is spent in keeping in touch with his mobile phone friends.

The air of the dawn brings the House of Prayer alive here in the morning with all the unseen creatures welcoming the new day. There must be thousands of grasshoppers and crickets hiding in the bushes and flowers while the birds prefer to sing from the tree tops. The frogs have taken over our fish pond; they accompany us every evening with frog songs during holy hour from seven o'clock to eight o'clock. You get used to all these different sounds; it's the newcomers that bring it to our attention when we take it for granted as part of the place.

I often see our retreatants sitting by the fish pond in deep meditation as if they were waiting for some inspiration from the water lilies or from a higher source. Some retreatants prefer to sit in front of the grotto of Our Lady at the other end of the grounds to do their reflections. Just beside the grotto is a fully-grown orange tree. Last year it produced eleven buckets of oranges and that has inspired me to plant a number of orange trees here in our grounds. So far nine trees are growing well and hopefully one day they will bear fruit. I don't know who planted this tree by the grotto, but we are now enjoying the fruits of their labour. As I look out from the veranda chair here, there is another tree that I admire. It is a native tree that always throws a dark shadow on the ground no matter what angle the sun is at. Retreatants are also attracted to this area. It is close to the graveyard where eighteen of our missionaries are buried. One of the sisters buried there in 1985 is Sr. Sigline Maria Poboss, SSpS, who was held prisoner by the Japanese during World War Two. She wrote her experiences in her book called *My Captive Memoirs*. It is well worth reading—that is, if you are not Japanese.

Our SSpS sisters usually look after the graveyard but they are moving on in years and I don't see them coming around now. I cleaned it up last October and it looks like it needs my attention again before Easter. Once I was cleaning the graves when a group of children came to assist me. One of them asked me, "Where do the dead go when they die?" I told him, pointing to the graves, that their bodies go underground, and their spirits to a better world

. He made no response, and I was thinking that he was thinking about Rudy our gardener who had died two months previous. Rudy was not married, and all the children here were like his own and they missed him very much. When Rudy died I saw some children putting flowers on his coffin. Now the diocese is putting a headstone to mark his grave.

A week has gone by since I started this letter. Today I had three visitors from the Melanesian Institute[4]. At the moment there is a three-week workshop in progress there for new arrivals in PNG. There are twenty-one participants made up of twelve different nationalities from India, Indonesia, Poland, Ghana, Russia, Australia, Tanzania, Tonga Philippines's PNG, Uganda, and South Korea. What a marvellous combination, all drawn together by God's divine love. This workshop is held every year to help the new arrivals to understand the culture and people of PNG. It can take a lifetime to know and grasp the culture of the people you work with, and this is a step in the right direction.

The retired Bishop Hank Maarssen also calls for a friendly visit once in a while. He is my confessor and I am his. Though his hearing is fading with the last few years, he is still very active. This past Christmas he went to help in one of his former parishes. He had to return a week earlier than planned as there was a landslide blocking off the road and the distance to reach the out-station was too much for him to walk at the age of 84. I do see him taking his evening walk here at Kefamo most evenings. Bishop Hank spends most of his time now reading, watching television, and browsing the internet for oversea news. I gather from his conversations he is not in love with President Donald Trump. Bishop Henk spent three years translating the Roman Missal from English into Tok Pisin. Sometimes we had a very interesting conversations during meal-time when he asked us to help

---

4 A body dedicated to researching the history and culture of Papua New Guinea.

him translate difficult words like "transubstantiation" from English to Tok Pisin. We somehow never agreed on the one translation.

During the last three months some of our co-workers have moved on to different ministers. Sr. Cathy has moved out of Kefamo. Sr. Teresa is gone down to Australia for a renewal course, Sr. Palladia has moved to Port Moresby to do office work, and Sr. Anna, FMI, has gone to Daru Kiunga Diocese to do pastoral work. Fr. Geovanne, SVD who worked at Melanesian Institute has moved to the Divine Word University to lecture, and Fr. Michaele who was parish priest at Kefamo Parish has moved to Rabaul Diocese. These were all very active and committed people, and we wish them well in their new ministries.

Fr. Carlos Alberto, who has been here only a short time in St Mary's Parish, has built a new permanent church at Bitute. It is on the left-hand side of the road between the Mercy Convent and Goroka Prison. Fr. Carlos was anxious to take me to see it last Sunday. Bishop Dariusz had bought linoleum to put over the cement floor so the people can sit down on it. I also had some timber here sitting under the house and Fr. Carlos made good use of it. I told Fr. Carlos it was soft timber, so he would have to keep an eye out for the white ants. The village people were all there when we arrived, and they are delighted with their new church. Now the community is discussing what name they should give the church and I told Fr.Carlos it was best they selected the name themselves.

Every Sunday Bishop Hank and I go to visit the SSpS sisters for a cup of coffee, a piece of homemade cake, and a chat. Bishop Darious, Fr. Carlos, Fr. Jos, and Br. Morris are also regular visitors. Only a few elderly sisters from overseas are there now. They don't go out much, so they like to see a few callers. They employ some girls to make Communion breads to supply the whole diocese and beyond. Sr. Mary Linda has her regular customers. They are elderly people looking for a meal and Sr. is always on hand to provide it. One Sunday, she asked me to bless three of her callers, and I willing obliged.

The House of Prayer can be very quiet here at times, especially after a busy week, and when I return from delivering the retreatants at the airport and find the place empty, that's a good time to answer my Christmas mail; now with half of them on email, it much easier. I will stop here and retire as another day is coming to an end and so is this page. God bless for now and take care.

January 26, 2018 I hope you are all keeping well since I last heard from you. I am still getting a few Christmas cards. They were posted to my old addresses at Wewak and Port Moresby. Some people don't update their address book. When I look at my own address book half the people I used to write to thirty years ago are gone to meet the Lord and the new contacts are all on email. A few times I went to the post box to collect the mail and the box was empty. The security guard observed my reaction and said, "Father, you write, and you will get letters." I just nodded back and agreed with him.

Still lots of rain every night and it looks like our flower garden is enjoying every drop of it. It is in full bloom to the delight of our kitchen girl Monica. She takes care of the flowers and I help in growing some vegetables. We have a variety of flowers here, ones for every season thanks to Fr. Alois Blasi, SVD, and Sr. Ignatius, SSpS, my predecessors.

Our new second-hand car Toyota RAV4 is in its second year at the House of Prayer, and so far it's going very well. Our old car had been bought by Fr. Pat Hogan in 2007 and was still going reasonably well. I sold it to a local man, or should I say gave it away for 2,000 *kina*, which is about €700. The car had one problem: it was too close to the ground and with all the potholes it was difficult keep the floor from touching the ground. When I had three passengers in the back and luggage in the boot it got even closer.

One Sunday I was out saying Mass and I was preaching about God's plan is better than the one you have for yourself and you should pray to know his plan for you. When we came to the Prayers of the Faithful, one woman started praying that God's plan should come to her village because the Devil's plan was taking over. We all knew what she meant—that home brew and drugs were causing a lot of problems in the village. A lot of young people are drifting to the cities and towns, and when they fail to find work they turn to crime. Law and order is one of the biggest problems the country is facing. There are two million children attending school and when the school days are over they find is hard to go back to village life.

Most of all the gardens in PNG are cultivated by spade, and that's hard work and they want to get on the payroll at all costs. They believe money is the key to a better life.

What I notice here in St. Mary's Parish is that the women are as good as the men at playing the guitar. What took my attention one Sunday was one woman well on in years playing the guitar like a teenage girl. She was sitting cross-legged on the stool, and her loose leg was swaying to the rhythm of the music. When I looked at her inquiringly if she was going to sing the Glory, she gave the guitar one strum and off she went. All the groups that take the Liturgy here on different Sundays have a great command of the guitar, and I think it was Fr. John Ryan's sixteen years here that have contributed to this ministry. One of our top musicians, Emmuel Eman, this year graduated from Goroka University and has been appointed to St. Ignatius Catholic School in Aitape Diocese, a long way from here. We will miss him as he is a top musician and very helpful in church activities.

Last June I told the people of St. Mary's I had a pile of sawdust at the House of Prayer, and if they wanted some for their poultry farms, to come and collect it free of charge. Some people wanted to pay. I told them, "You can give me one of your chickens when they are ready for the oven." Last Sunday I received the first one and I expect a few more. These day-old chickens are hatched out in Lae and they come up to Goroka on order. It's amazing how this project has taken on, where other projects were tried out and failed.

What's making the news here these times is the death of Kato Ottio at the age of 23 from what appears to have been heatstroke. He was a rugby star and he was due to sign up to play for a club in England. The other news is the volcano that has erupted on Kovadar Island off Wewak town, and some 500 people have to take residence on the mainland.

One day I was in Goroka shopping when I saw a stooped old man coming towards me holding an ice-cream cone in one hand and taking a lick as he walked along the footpath. He was really enjoying his ice-cream as if he was back in his childhood once again. It's no surprise to see people walking around holding a whole pineapple by the stem and, having removed the skin, eating the whole thing themselves. There is no shortage of pineapples these times at Goroka market. The people are still waiting for the government to improve the town market. Hundreds of people meet here every day to sell and buy their goods. The women sit and chat with their friends and neighbours while waiting for customers to come and buy their produces. Pineapples are always good to sell and if they don't sell the first day the women can bring them back for four or five days more. If it's bananas or tomatoes, and the sales are not good, the price is usually reduced towards evening. The market is a necessary part of their lives. It is also a place where people meet up with friends and cousins they haven't seen for some time.

Coffee is also a big business here in Goroka. Nearly every day trucks bring bags of coffee into the town to sell to coffee buyers. There is a lot of work in producing one bag of coffee. The coffee trees must be kept clean, pruned, and the berries picked before they fall to the ground. After picking, the berries have the outer skin removed before being dried in the sun. However, all the family can lend a hand, including children and grandmother, and when the price is good it is all worth the effort.

This week a young girl came to see me, asking for my advice as she was going out with a young man from Africa who had a business in Lae city. Then she told me he is a Muslim. I told her if she was my sister I would say no, forget about him and that there were plenty men in PNG she could marry. Then again, it is her choice, and if she wanted to marry him no one can stop her. Finally, I told her don't rush into this marriage and hold on for two years to find out more what he is really like. She is to come again, but no date is set. Before these young girls were happy to marry a man on a pay roll; now they want a man with a car and a business.

One Sunday I was saying Mass for the Lopi community and I took four seminarians along. The people were delighted to meet them and gave them a great welcome. Five days letter who should arrive at the House of Prayer but a truck load of parishioners from Lopi with a big ice-cake to share with the seminarians and all present in the house. We gave them all tea or coffee and we all had a share of the cake. Only the base-board remained. It was a lovely social gathering and it took the seminarians totally by surprise. Before the visitors left they put 100 *kina* on the table to pay the seminarians' bus-fare home.

At Lopi there is a very good sacristan. His name is Leo and he does his best to have everything in order before the priest arrives. One Sunday I was to wear green vestments and I could not find them, so I put on white vestments instead. When Leo saw it, he went immediately to check the calendar to see had he got it wrong. Then I spotted the green one behind the door and I changed to Leo's delight. Both of us often had a good chat while waiting for the faithful to arrive for Mass. He told me about all the priests he knew in his young days and how they all knew him. Then he named them out, and I only knew a few of them. While we chatted, a young girl was combing through her mother's hair and picking out lice and killing them with her thumb nails. This is a common exercise when people meet and have time on their hands. With that, I will sign off and I hope this letter finds you in good form. I will keep you in my thoughts and prayers and Masses.

February 1, 2018 Back to you again, and I am glad you survived the spell of cold weather. It's the rain we are complaining about at this end of the world. Last week we had a downpour and half the bridge between here and Goroka fell into the river. I just got through to do some shopping as four retreatants are coming this week. The police are there directing traffic and only small vehicles can get through. The roads at the moment are in a bad shape, especially the Highlands highway, where all the mountain hauliers are up and down every day.

On January 28 we had a beautiful outdoor thanksgiving Mass for Fr. Andrew Masi, who was at St Mary's for one year as deacon, getting pastoral experience under three different directors. Fr. Szmidt was the first but after a few months he had to go home to recover from a bad car accident. Bishop Hank took over from there until Fr. Carlos was appointed parish priest. Fr. Andrew was back to thank the people of Goroka before he leaves for his mission appointment in East Timor. After Mass, Fr. Andrew told the people why he became a priest. He was an aid post orderly working in Kaugia Parish in the Diocese of Wewak, when one morning he was attending to a sick elderly patient who asked him to get a priest as he felt his time was up. Andrew came back some time latter to tell his patient that Fr. Jannus had gone to an out-station. The patient looked at Andrew and said, "Why you don't become a priest?" These few words never went away. That is only half the story and it is not the biggest half. "The dying advice of a person is considered most precious"—a quotation from *Daily Reflections*, 2018)

When Mass was over, Fr. Carlos, who is a bit of an entertainer, told the people he spent the day yesterday looking for an elephant but only found mosquitoes. He was using coded language to tell the people he could not find a pig to feed all the people; instead he had to settle for chickens at the market. It turned out most people brought their own food. While all this was going on, a sixty-foot crane was in action on a building site just outside the parish boundary and when the jib turned our way its shadow passed over half the people present. This company works every day and does not know of the Sabbath or Sunday. This celebration lasted well into the afternoon with first blessings, actions songs and personal gifts for the new priest.

By the time you get this letter, Fr. Andrew will have left his own land and home and there is something to be said when you see young men and women leaving their friends behind for the Lord. I have seen them take off myself and I think it is a response to love already received. It reminds me of myself going back to that morning after so many years when I left home the first time for PNG. It was like dying, leaving not just the family but all that seem so familiar to me. Then after two days' journey I arrived in Port Moresby to be met by a familiar face, Fr. Vincent Twomey; it was like a foreshadow of the resurrection back to life again. When I recall sitting back on the plane on my first departure to PNG, and when I looked out of the aircraft window and watched the thick clouds pass beneath, I knew the road ahead would not be easy either.

Fr. Carlos comes here to Kefamo Conference Centre for his evening meal and we often have a good laugh when he shares his experiences with us. He told us there is a mentally ill woman who comes and sleeps in his garden house from time to time. One day Fr. Carlos was out walking when she ran after him and put her hands around him. Some onlookers told her let him go, he is a priest. The lady replied, "I know he is a priest. We sleep together at the mission station." To avoid this lady now, Fr. Carlos is taking a different walking track. One day I was shopping in Goroka when the same lady held on to me, and I noticed how all the people stopped to watch the live drama. I gave her the price of a packet of biscuits and she let go. There are several drug addicts in the town and they all have street names. One is called "Red Skin" because he skin is red, another is called "The Dancer", and he loves dancing in front of the stores when they are playing music. The crowd get fits of laughter when his actions get too expressive. At night I am told people play cards under the street lights and this has led to gambling and the townspeople want to put a stop to it. So, you see it takes all kinds of people to make up the world we live in.

I suppose one cannot live in PNG without your own view of life being in some way influenced by theirs. People never seem to be in a hurry except bus drivers. People love to sit and chat for hours. Last week I asked two women who were sitting on the concrete step at the back door for at least one hour what they were talking about. One lady replied, "We are talking about men and women and children." I thought that was a good answer. Once again, thanks for your long, newsy letter. You know letters from home are read more than once. God bless and take care.

February 14, 2018 You may find these stories that I picked up along the way at the House of Prayer interesting. First there is the story of the PNG national flag. It was designed by an OLSH sister and she gave the drawing to one of her 15-year-old students to enter the competition for a new flag. Her design was chosen as the most suitable national flag of Papa New Guinea. Sister gave all the credit to her student, Susan Karike, who died last year and was given a state funeral.

Last year a sister was sharing her life story with me and how she found out who her real mother was. One evening she went to clean the graves near the village with some of her friends. When they came to one grave her friends told her, "That is your mother's grave." She told them, "My mother is alive, she is not dead." Her friends insisted her mother died when she was a child and that was her grave.

The young girl went home and told her mother what her friends had said. The mother was taken by surprise and told the child, "I am your mother. Don't mind what those children tell you." But then, after the mother got over the shock she took the child aside and told her, "Your mother died when you were two years old and I am your mother's sister and I took care of you, and now I am your real mother."

I had a priest here last year who told me when he was a small child he used to dramatize the Mass with his playmates in the village. He was the priest and the other children were the congregation. They chopped up a banana to make Communion breads and were imitating the priest saying the Mass when his mother came along and put a stop to it. At his first Mass he told all present, "Today I am celebrating my first real Mass" and went on to tell them how he and the village children used to play at Mass until it was stopped. It just goes to show what goes on in their little heads when they are that age.

One sister last week shared her experience of travelling on a PMV bus when a youth threw a stone at the bus and broke a window. The driver went to report it to the police. The sister was asked to make a statement and the policeman said to her, "You are a woman from God you cannot lie."

A few days have passed since I started this letter. In the meantime, I have had two visitors from Ambunti. One was Dallin Stephen who was one of twenty altar girls and boys in the parish. They were a very active group of young children, and whenever I made a mistake saying Mass they reminded me afterwards. Once I put the chasuble on back to front and they told me that was a big mistake. Now Dallin is enrolled at Goroka School of Nursing to the delight of her parents. To get in there you need money and blood relations, and Dallin had both. Another girl from Ambunti was on her way to join the Salesian Missionaries of Mary Immaculate (SMMI) when she called here to Goroka. It was her first time in the Highlands and she was worried about her new adventure. Our kitchen staff took care of her, put her on the right bus for Kundiwai, and told the sisters to pick her up at the bus stop. The women are very good that way, especially when they see young girls away from home who need directions to find their destination. Once I was late to collect two young sisters and when I arrived at the bus stop two women were already keeping them company as they were looking anxious and worried in a strange town.

Another morning I went to pick up three retreatants at the airport. The airport was crowded with people and the plane had just arrived. I waited for my three passengers, but I could not identify them and thought they may be on the next flight due to land in half an hour. The three retreatants had arrived and when there was nobody to pick them up they phoned their bishop to contact me on my mobile phone. The bishop rang me and told me the retreatants were waiting for me at the airport go and pick them up. I told the bishop I was at the airport a half an hour and I haven't seen them. Then I asked him what do they look like? He told me they were medium in size. I went to look for them and saw three men standing together and I approached them, I asked them in Pisin, "Did you see some people here from Kerema Diocese? I am trying to find them." There was a huge laugh, as they were the right men. They looked like ordinary country men, and I was surprised that they didn't pick me out from the crowed. This has happened before when sisters arrive without a veil and I was not sure whether they are nationals or Asians. Now I ask them on the phone how I will recognise them when they come off the plane.

This was another beautiful day here in Goroka. A good day to dry the laundry and a good day to be alive. The bridge is repaired after almost two weeks on the mend, and the traffic is moving day and night for four days. I must now go and feed the dogs as they are getting restless outside and they don't know it's Ash Wednesday. God bless for now and take care.

February 15, 2018 Many thanks for your quick response to my last letter. February is moving on, and we had a good variety of retreatants passing through the last month. We had a sister here from Tonga, the fifth from that country since 2010. She is a fine stately women and dresses in her traditional clothes like Solomon in all his glory. She was not just interested in her spiritual well-being, but she got in her daily exercises every day while here, as if she was preparing herself for a mine marathon.

Then we had a Capuchin brother from Goroka Diocese preparing for final vows. He told me over twenty local brothers have joined the order. They all wear the brown habit down to the ground. Maybe that's why they get so many vocations when we SVD have only two local brothers, and we are in PNG over 100 years. After that we had two more seminarians from the same order preparing to be ordained deacons on February 12. The Missionary Sisters of the Society of Mary had three sisters here as they too were taking their final vows on February 22. They are in Mendi Diocese. One of them told me she is a "product" of Fr. Joe Bisson, SVD.

Fr. Joe was in her parish for thirty years and has now returned to the States. He came back for a short visit to collect a gold medal for his fifty years of missionary work in PNG.

That will give you an idea of the variety of retreatants that pass through the house in the course of a few weeks.

Our main concern now is the collapse of a bridge between here and Goroka town. The local people have made a temporary footbridge and are collecting money from every person that passes over it to be picked up by waiting cars at the other side. The locals don't mind the long delay in getting the bridge repaired as long as they are benefiting by it.

We are in the middle of the wet season, and the people keep telling me it is the best time of the year, as we all have enough to eat. Recently my neighbour John brought me a large head of cabbage. I asked him if he used fertilizer to make it grow so big. "Oh no, Father!" I asked him if it was organic, and again he assured me it was pure organic. Then he said, speaking two languages, "*Em save bilong mi*. I know how to grow it." It's true the men and women here in the Highlands all have a diploma in growing local food. They need to, because their survival depends on their garden crops. It's different in the coast where people have plenty sago and fish. Last month, one of our retreatants, Sr. Cecilia from Kungi, brought along two kilo of sago. When I was on the Sepik I developed a taste for it and ever since retreatants bring some with them.

On Sunday February 11 we had a lovely Mass here in the House of Prayer for Sr. Davida, SSpS. She was staying here in the House of Prayer when she got sick and then returned to Poland to discover she had advanced cancer. She is now receiving treatment and will not return to PNG. She is in her early fifties and was working with the national family team in PNG. She was a happy sister who found joy in her ministry. She was known for making beautiful cheesecakes. We all miss her, especially her office girl Julie, who is now employed at the Conference Centre. Yes, nobody knows how life unfolds, and it's just as well we don't. Health is wealth, so take care of yourself.

February 16, 2018 You may find it interesting to know that PNG made history this past week by producing fresh milk from its new dairy herd fourteen miles outside Port Moresby. It cost forty-two million US Dollars to get it started. 740 cows were imported from New Zealand last year. The cows are stall-fed day and night with sorghum, guinea grass, and maize, all of which are locally grown. Can you image the fine tank of slurry you have from that number of cows? The bad news is there is an outbreak of anthrax among the village pigs in Madang Province. More than 600 pigs have died already from this sickness, and the people got strict warning not to eat them. A cruise ship caring over a thousand tourists was not allowed to offload its passengers due to the outbreak, to the disappointment of busloads of people waiting to welcome them on shore to sell their artefacts. Such are the ups and downs of life.

I had to change my own agenda today due to the rain. I had intended to spend a few hours in the garden to put in a few crops and now I find myself back in my room again. Only one retreatant this week, so I have plenty time on my hands. I am booked to give a thirty-day retreat for March and April, and that will tie me down a bit.

It seems it is taking two months for my letters to reach you, and vice a versa. I don't know where the delay is, and this is the first time I have experienced it. I received a letter which was a long time on the way from the AIB bank, and they expected a reply within a month. We must count our blessings now for email.

It's hard to explain how PNG has changed so much in the last twenty years. The number of lorries, cars, and buses now passing through Goroka is an eye-opener, and the amount of people lining up at the BSP bank every day tells its own story. The mobile phone would also have made a big contribution to these changes.

I was in Goroka one day doing my shopping when I saw this sudden surge of excitement. People were running from all directions to see two women involved in a boxing match. These things happen more than once a month, and there is nothing better to attract a large crowd than a public fight or a police chase. Thomas, one of our seminarians, was listening one day to a street preacher saying all kinds of rubbish against the Catholic Church. Thomas challenged the preacher. No sooner had he said anything when a crowd of the preacher's supporters went to beat him up. Only for the police standing nearby he would have been in trouble. Thomas is now a deacon and he in getting ordained on June 9 for the Diocese of Goroka.

This year we have twenty-two seminarians in Bomana seminary and eight candidates interested in joining also. This is very encouraging for us SVD, though we are well aware that of those who come through the door the first day, only one third or less will make it to the finishing line. It goes to show the desire to become a priest or a religious is not enough. One has to have a call that is at the very centre of your soul and is more powerful than any of the forces around you. Bishop Dariusz has asked us all to pray for vocations during this time of Lent, as we have no seminarians for the diocese at this time.

A young boy came to see me last week from the neighbourhood and he asked me to give him some work as he needed to buy rugby boots. I took him on to cut some grass and told him I would give him the price of the shoes. The following two days he came with three other boys and cut the grass which I marked out for him. I am thinking they will have to take turns to wear these rugby boots. Rugby League is becoming very popular now in the country and all the youth are taking it on.

I heard a story recently of a woman who was sentenced to jail for five years and while there gave birth to a baby boy. The child was left with the mother during her time. The other women doing time were like a mother to him. When the mother went home to her village the child started to cry and asked his mother to take him back to the jail. This story came from an inmate who was a friend of the mother of the child.

God bless you and take care.

DIVINE WORD COLLEGE, PORT MORESBY

December 27, 2018 I hope you are all keeping well since I left for PNG last November. It was my thirteenth departure from Ireland, and I am thinking it could be my last one. At Cork Airport I met Sean O'Neill (a neighbour) and we exchanged a few words about our favourite football team, (Castlehaven). I haven't seen an Irish man since. After getting to Heathrow, I boarded a Singapore Airlines flight and landed in Shanghai airport fourteen hours later. I had only a three-hour stop-over there before boarding Air New Guinea flight to Port Moresby. Who should I meet at the door of the plane but one of my former parishioners, Carlos Baras, who was one of the cabin crew? When all the passengers had taken their seats, he tapped me on the shoulder and said, "Come and I will give you a decent seat." After the first refreshments were served to the passengers Carlos sat down beside me and we had a long chat about the folks we both knew. He named several who had moved on from this life, all faithful church goers.

When I arrived in Port Moresby I was wearing my good suit, and one of the officials asked me was I a member of the Asia-Pacific Economic Cooperation (APEC) as some of the delegates were arriving on that same flight. When I said no, he told me pass through.

I am now back in PNG after a wonderful holiday. The summer was excellent. I watched some exciting games of hurling and football. I met many old friends I had not met for years, mostly at funerals. I have to mention my farewell party organised by James O'Neill and Paddy O'Donovan and all the people who helped in so many ways. It was the high point of the vacation. It really shows how alive and active the community is. I will keep you in my prayers as I continue in my ministry here in PNG.

The following Sunday morning I made my first visit to Bomana prison. Only two of the inmates I visited nine years ago were still there. One of them gave me a hug and in doing so I suspect he emptied my pocket, since there was nothing in it when I went to buy fruit at the market. On December 24, Cardinal John Ribat was the main celebrant at Bomana Prison. We had the Mass in the sports field and all the prisoners and visitors were present. The Sisters of Charity provided 700 pack lunches, and several parishes were asked to contribute to the meal. Over forty female prisoners also attended. After Mass, the prisoners entertained the crowd with action songs and Bible drama for two hours, and the meal was distributed after this.

For Christmas I was helping out Fr. Yustinus Nenat, SVD, at Hanuabada Parish in Port Moresby. There I met some Sepik people and a student from Goroka University to whom I gave a retreat a few years ago. On Christmas Day we had a combined dinner with the SSpS sisters here at Bomana where we shared our Christmas stories and sang some Christmas songs.

There is a group of men doing maintenance work here at Divine Word College and another company is upgrading and tarring the road from the main gate right up to the different religious houses here in the compound. We hope all this will be complete before the school year starts. At the moment all the students are on holidays and will return on January 28 to start their school year.

Last week, after three months of soaring temperatures, we got a good downpour, and the ground is starting to get green once again.

With that I wish you a Happy Christmas and Happy New Year.

December 16, 2019 I hope you are keeping well after another year has gone by. The year 2019 has been one of the best for me, though we had a few sad moments too. The Carmelite Sisters decided to leave last April as they had no replacements, and the few that were there needed home care. They were here in Bomana since 1973 and they were always available to give spiritual direction to our priests, sisters, and students. We SVD priests celebrated Mass in their convent on a regular basis, and on April 24 we were invited to their farewell party. Now the Monfort Fathers have taken over the convent.

On September 11, one of our younger priests, Alias Tapi, died from cancer. I knew Fr. Alias well as he came from Amboin, an out-station in Timbunke. I used to visit his village when he was a young boy back in the eighties. You could say I had a hand in cultivating him to be a priest. I used to stay in his parents' house before Br Jack's workmen built a permanent priest's house in Amboin back in 1983.

Two of our senior missionaries, Bishop Henk Maarssen and Br. Anthony Hollenstein, have returned to their homeland to retire after giving over a hundred years' service between them to the mission in PNG. Both men were a shining example to all of us younger missionaries.

There was one incident that I think is worth telling. A Chinese businessman was robbed of all his takings when traveling to Wewak after Christmas. He was taking the money stored inside a plastic bag and stacked inside a slaughtered pig after the internal organs were removed. The armed gang went straight to the slaughtered pig and removed the money, leaving the Chinese man with his dead pig. There was a strong suspicious it was an inside job. This story was in the *National* newspaper of January 18, 2019.

During the year two companies came to the college to drill for water.

The first company came with a landcruiser and a half dozen men to drill, using manpower. Two men turned the drill and one man sat on top of the cross bar to keep pressure on the drill bit. After two attempts to find water they were unsuccessful, and the whole exercise was a failure.

The second company were more professional. They arrived with all the modern equipment on a big lorry, wearing yellow vests and helmets to match. After two days they reached the depth of twenty-seven metres. At that depth they were satisfied a good supply of water was found. In the meantime, Mr Zhang from China built a two-metre-high water stand for a 3,000-gallon tank and a cement base for another water tank the same size. We have to thank our donors from Indonesia, Poland, and Ireland for financing this water project. On October 25 our Provincial, Fr. Joe Maciolek, blessed our new water supply. We have enough water now to water our vegetable gardens during the dry season, and when the main water supply is cut off due to broken pipes or land disputes, we have a stand-by supply.

We started our new school year 2019 with twenty-one seminarians. Each student was given the responsibility to make a contribution to the community and help out wherever needed during the school year. I was appointed garden supervisor. I was the one to provide the seeds and garden tools to the students when the need arose. I must admit the garden did provide a lot vegetables and bananas this year. Next year (2020) we are expecting twenty-eight students and we realise now we need extra cups and plates, bedsheets and pillows, chairs and tables to cater for this growing number. Fr. Alias Aiyako, a local priest, is doing an excellent job as vocation director, and this is the result of his hard work.

As regards myself, I gave six preached retreats to religious and lay people plus two director retreats and one thirty-day retreat, which is in progress at this time. The total number was 105 retreatants. I was available for spiritual direction for our students and sisters on request. Overall, it was a very grace-filled year, and I also made myself available for prison ministry every Sunday for Mass, until ten prisoners made a dash for freedom on September 16.

Every year, PNG holds a big display of culture on September 16 to celebrate their independence from Australia. This year was no different.

The inmates and their families were allowed to dress up in traditional dress, paint their faces, and dance to the beat of the wooden drum. Everything went well until departure time came, and ten of the inmates walked out with the crowd undetected. This meant no church services were allowed until things settled down again inside the compound. I went to the main gate a few times to enquire how things were, and the gate warder asked me for my phone number and said he would contact me when services were allowed again. All is back to normal at this time. Cardinal John Ribat will celebrate open-air Mass on the playing field on December 19. It's always well attended, as the Sisters give the inmates a little plastic bag with soap and toiletries as well as a packed lunch.

Bertie Ahern, Ireland's former prime minister, has made several trips to PNG. He was appointed chairman and mediator to bring peace to the troubled island of Bougainville. At first, they were calling him Mr Hern. Someone must have corrected them because now they have got his name right. The Bougainville inhabitants, among whom the Catholic Church has a strong influence, were a peace-loving people until a dispute erupted over the rights of the rich deposits of copper and gold. Civil war broke out and lasted over ten years. During that time over 20,000 people lost their lives in the conflict. Now the people of Bougainville want independence from PNG, and we are waiting to see the results of the referendum. The locals have spoken very highly of Mr Ahern for being courageous enough to act as peacemaker to a people whose culture and tradition is so different from his own.

With that, I wish you all a Happy Christmas and peace, joy and good health for 2020, and again thank you for your prayers and donations. I will also keep you in my thoughts and prayers. God Bless and take care.

December 21, 2020 Greetings from PNG and Happy Christmas to all of you. I hope you are keeping well after a difficult year for most people; it was not just Covid-19 but bush fires, floods, and cyclone in many parts of the world. Hopefully we can get back to normal in 2021. The following are some of the activities that took place during 2020.

On March 4, over 700 inmates of the Bomana Corrective Institute assembled, when we informed them of the Church's activities for 2020.

For the first hour we were entertained with gospel music, and some of the inmates stood up and danced as if we were holding a charismatic rally. After that, the more serious matters began. One commander, in an address to the inmates, said, "You hold the key, but I hold the lock. You behave well and show us you have reformed. You will be released sooner by your good behaviour and corporation." One elderly inmate from the Sepik told me he was being released the following week. "I am worried about how I will cope back in the village," he said. "I had three meals a day in here for the last ten years and now I will have to adjust to a new life when released."

Little did we know then that our year planner would come to a sudden death due to Covid-19. And major adjustments were in store for everyone, all over the world. We are back again for Sunday services but this time at a low key.

It was a lovely morning on March 13 when I drove in Fr. Philip Gibbs's little Mini car to bless the unveiling of the new University of Business Studies here in Port Moresby. On seeing all the government cars and every one dressed to perfection, I realised it was something bigger than I expected. The prime minister, James Marape, the minister of education, the Chinese ambassador, and many other dignitaries were all sitting in front of me as I was asked to start the celebrations with an opening prayer and bless the new buildings. I came prepared with my book and Holy Water and reminded all present that we must be aware of how the unseen hand of God is present in all we do, and we ask Lord to bless this multi-million building and all who use it. After that I blessed the building and concluded with a closing prayer. That was followed by several speeches.

Before we made a grand tour of the buildings, the prime minister unveiled a marble slab to declare it was now a university and no longer an Institution. Light refreshments were served while some students entertained us with live drama. It was an enjoyable day and I was happy to be part of it, even though I was only standing in for Fr. Joseph Vunuk who had other commitments the same day,

On Monday, June 1, I was asked to bless the first commercial drone to arrive in Papua New Guinea. Cardinal John Rabat was asked to do the blessing but he had a meeting with his priests and wasn't available. Eventually the job fell to me. We waited the most of one hour before the big box arrived and there was great excitement getting it opened. Several newsmen and business people came for the launching. I blessed it and gave it the name "Tourkade" after the mission boat that Fr. Jellic, SVD, used to serve the Sepik River and the islands parishes around Wewak. James Murry, who is in charge of this enterprise, is from Kairiru Island and he thought this name would be suitable. The drone will be used to map out the country and places that have not been surveyed.

Light refreshments were served to all present, and one journalist, Jason Kaut, told me he studied at Divine Word University. For me my mission was complete but for the Drone it was just beginning. It was encouraging to see all these business people putting their trust in God, even though they may never see with the human eye how the Lord interacts in their everyday lives.

On September 12 I celebrated my fortieth year in the priesthood, and Fr. Zenon Szablowinski, SVD, celebrated his sliver Jubilee. Our lay partners and a few SVD friends also attended. Fr. Zenon was the main celebrant and thanked the lord for the graces and blessing he received over the years. I was asked to give the homily and I gave a run-down on my forty years as a priesthood and the various ministries I held during that time. I told all present it was the people's appreciation and welcoming of my pastoral visits got me hooked me on the Sepik after six months. It was hard to leave my boats behind, but I promised the Lord and the Society I will go where ever I am sent. I am also grateful to the Lord for his goodness to me over those forty years. The students decorated the church and prepared the liturgy, while other students decorated the dining room. Sever others helped in the kitchen with Margaret, our main cook. They prepared a great variety of food for the menu and every one enjoyed the Jubilee cake which was Fr. Zenon and I cut.

During the year I gave seven retreats, one to Cardinal John Rabat and his twenty-nine priests in the Archdiocese of Port Moresby. The other retreats were for sisters from different congregations and retreats for the seminarians here at the college. I also had over forty students and junior sisters for spiritual direction before the Coronavirus disrupted our year planner. I also did prison ministry every Sunday except for the Sundays I wasn't left in due to Covid-19. Overall, it was a good year, but our normal schedule had to be altered to follow the government relegations. With that I wish you Happy Christmas and God Blessing for 2021. God bless you.

January 10, 2021 Here at the Divine Word College we got off to a good star to the year 2021. We invited our neighbours, the John Bosco Community to join us for dinner which was prepared by our staff and students. Today I am winding down and taking a look back at the past year 2020.

Our new rector, Fr. Yosep Messa, has made his mark since he arrived at the beginning of the school year. One of the first things he did was to plant over one hundred pawpaw trees. Now after twelve months these trees are bearing fruit. He has also planted other fruit trees, and there is still some unused ground to cultivate. The Mercy Sisters had a motto, "How to make money grow". Well, planting pawpaw is one way.

Another project Fr. Yosep was to achieve was the erection of two headstones to Fr. Patrick Murphy, SVD, and Fr. James Franks, SVD. For some years we were praying at the wrong grave until Br. Radge and Sr. Emelia pointed it out to us: one headstone was at the wrong grave. The headstone was removed and at last the two graves are clearly marked. Both are buried at the Nine Mile cemetery outside Port Moresby where Carmelite sisters and hundreds of PNG people are laid to rest. Our two confrères are in good company. May they rest in peace.

This year the Divine Word Missionaries will be 125 years in PNG. The celebrations of the jubilee year began in Madang province last August, and hopefully it will end there on August 15, 2021. All depends on the control of Covid-19. For the celebrations we are planning to ordain our four newly ordained deacons, Jerry Kuria, Herman Kunow, Jeremiah Kaumbai, and Joseph Sen, who is unfortunately stranded in Ghana due to the pandemic. The ordinations are a result of the seeds of faith sown by the Divine Word Missionaries over 125 years.

We also have another Jubilee coming up on March 20, when Fr. Norman Davitt will hopefully celebrate his hundredth birthday. Fr. Norman worked in PNG for many years and retired to Ireland at the turn of the century. He is fondly remembered by the people he ministered to, and long after his departure he continued to support parents with school fees to educate their children. He always stood out from the crowd because of his six foot plus in height and his long white beard.

Last year I celebrated forty years of my priesthood and this year I will be forty years in PNG. How life unfolds from here I don't know. However, when the Lord calls me again to go somewhere, I know there will always be a part of me in Papua New Guinea. God bless for now.